Football

at Historically Black Colleges and Universities in Texas

ROB FINK

Texas A&M University Press
College Station

This paper meets the requirements
of ANSI/NISO Z39.48-1992 (Permanence of Paper).
Binding materials have been chosen for durability.
Manufactured in the United States of America

Library of Congress Cataloging-in-Publication Data

Names: Fink, Rob (Robert), author.
Title: Football at historically black colleges and universities in Texas / Rob Fink.
Description: First edition. | College Station: Texas A&M University Press,
   [2019] | Includes bibliographical references and index. |
Identifiers: LCCN 2019001713 (print) | LCCN 2019004878 (ebook) |
   ISBN 9781623498009 (ebook) | ISBN 9781623497996 |
   ISBN 9781623497996 (cloth: alk. paper)
Subjects: LCSH: Football—Texas—History. | College sports—Texas—History. |
   African American universities and colleges—Texas—History. | African
   American football players—Texas—History.
Classification: LCC GV959.52.T4 (ebook) | LCC GV959.52.T4 F56 2019 (print) |
   DDC 796.332/63—dc23
LC record available at https://lccn.loc.gov/2019001713

Front cover: Members of the 1947 Texas State College football team. Courtesy Texas
   Southern University Archives.
Back cover (top): Texas College versus Hardin Simmons University in Abilene 2017.
   Photograph by author.
Back cover (bottom): Texas Southern University versus Texas A&I University in 1972.
   Courtesy Texas Southern University Archives.

For Tiffany, Andrew & Dylan
with love

Football at Historically Black Colleges and Universities in Texas

SWAIM-PAUP SPORTS SERIES

Sponsored by James C. '74 & Debra Parchman Swaim
and T. Edgar '74 & Nancy Paup

Contents

Acknowledgments

Several years ago, I sat in the archives of the Southwest Collection at Texas Tech University working on another project. As I went through the pages of the *Houston Informer* and *Dallas Express*, as well as other African American newspapers, I continually read articles detailing the dynamic history of football at schools like Wiley College and Prairie View A&M. Being a sports fan, this dynamic history captivated my attention and inspired me. The sport played such a prominent role in the history of Texas, as well as in the cultural identity of the state's African American population, yet almost no record existed of the teams and players. As a result, I decided to tell this long-neglected story.

During the writing of this book, I have accumulated a large list of people to whom I owe enumerable amounts of thanks. First, I would like to thank Thom Lemmons and Texas A&M University Press for all their assistance in seeing this project reach its final stage. I also want to thank Jorge Iber for his guidance and support. He played an invaluable role in revising and editing portions of the book.

Numerous other people and groups deserve recognition. Alwyn Barr and Paul Carlson are both mentors of mine whose instruction, guidance, and friendship influenced this work. They, along with people like Randy McBee and Julie Willet, helped me hone my craft as a writer and historian. Other friends who deserve similar thanks for encouraging and supporting my research in the fields of African American and sports history are Cary Wintz and Bernadette Pruitt.

For the fact-finding stage of the book, the Southwest Collection at Texas Tech University, the Dallas Public Library, the Houston Public Library, and the archives at both Prairie View A&M University and Texas Southern University provided invaluable resources and treasure troves of information. I want to thank Michael Hurd for connecting me with several former college football athletes who shared their experiences with me. Tommy Dean deserves special recognition and thanks for his assistance in the collection of photographs for the book. Furthermore, I cannot express enough my gratitude for Joyce Thomas of the Texas Southern University Archives, for all the assistance she gave in the accumulation and sharing of photographs from her university's archives for use in the book.

Finally, I want to thank my family. Dinah and Curby Ligon opened their home to me and my family while I conducted research. My parents, Bob and Trina Fink, have provided love and support to me throughout all the years of my life. They raised me to love words and history, as well as to embrace learning, show kindness, and treat all people with respect. To my brother and sister-in-law, Jon and Julie Fink, as well as their girls Sibley and Margaret, you fill me with love and laughter.

To my sons, Andrew and Dylan, thank you for your gracious and encouraging spirts. You exemplify courage and strength of character and inspire me. I love you so much and am proud of you.

Finally, to my wife Tiffany, "thank you" cannot sum up everything that you mean to me. You are my lifelong love, my research and teaching partner, my proofreader and editor, and my best friend. You bring me joy and happiness. This book is as much yours as it is mine. I love you.

Football at Historically
Black Colleges and
Universities in Texas

Introduction

In 1950, an unnamed writer for the *Houston Informer* expressed concern that African Americans focused too much attention on older and more publicized sports. The writer acknowledged the level of success achieved by African Americans in such sports as boxing, baseball, and track, but he was concerned about the lack of involvement in sports without mass audience appeal. The author encouraged African Americans to participate in golf, tennis, and swimming. He also challenged black communities to build the facilities needed for such sports.[1] His plea went mostly unnoticed in Texas, though, where football remained the most popular sport among African Americans. In Texas, black college football played a major role as a source of racial pride and cultural expression throughout the twentieth century.

Despite the importance of black college football in the history of the African American community in Texas, historians have virtually ignored the subject. The studies that exist on Texas black colleges focus on the histories of the schools themselves, not their sports teams. Historians have written about the formation of these schools, significant college presidents and leaders, and important political events. Cultural events and sports have been neglected in these histories of higher education. Furthermore, in broad historical studies of African Americans in Texas, black colleges and their football teams receive only minimal recognition.

Historians in recent years have started to write about African Americans and sports. Most of these works cover national events, prominent athletes, and specific teams. Other publications serve as reference books, presenting a broad survey of sports history. But a few books do look specifically at black college football in the United States. In *Black College Football*, Michael Hurd offers an overview of the history of football at black colleges, as well as profiles of the schools' famous coaches, teams, and players.[2] The lack of additional historical studies about black college football offers an opportunity to explore other aspects of the sport.

Football at Historically Black Colleges and Universities in Texas looks to fill the void in the historiography by focusing on a group of schools that for decades played each other within an organized conference. The experiences of these Texas colleges provide an example of how football developed at African American schools across the nation through several stages and time periods. This study considers the important teams, coaches, and athletes, and the reasons for their success, but also explores the cultural role of black college football in the African American community in Texas, as well as ways that role changed over time.

The history of black college football in Texas falls into eight distinct stages defined by decades. The first stage began in the period following reconstruction and lasted until 1920. This period marked the beginning of both African American colleges and college football. Black colleges in Texas sought to provide an education for a population recently removed from slavery. Once the schools were established, football teams soon appeared on campus. Following the formation of the teams, regularly scheduled games and organized play developed. As fan bases grew, so did the cultural importance of the sport.

The second stage expanded the importance of the sport. With the formation of the Southwestern Athletic Conference (SWAC), black college football in Texas achieved equal status with the top African American athletic conferences in the country. The popularity of the sport increased, and as a result, the cultural importance attributed to the games also grew. With the creation of special events, such as the State Fair Classic in conjunction with Negro Day at the Texas State Fair and the Prairie View Bowl on New Year's Day, black college football in Texas served as a public outlet for racial pride among black Texans. The role of the sport in developing racial pride placed it in the "New Negro" movement, which celebrated the unique black culture in America.

The Great Depression and cultural power dominated the third stage of black college football in Texas. In the 1930s, the economic crisis created by the Great Depression weighed heavily on the minds of all Americans. Black college football offered African Americans in Texas an escape from the pressures of daily life. As a result, the popularity and cultural importance of the sport increased. Since black college football existed entirely within the control of the African American community, the sport allowed for the expression of desires and the celebration of community. The uniqueness of the sport also encouraged a push for social change within the system of segregation that existed in the South. The game brought cultural power to the Texas black community, allowing black Texans a symbol of their difference from whites that included positive attributes like physical prowess, while also presenting to the state music, education, and other cultural elements that existed entirely within the African American sphere. Through the success, popularity, and distinctiveness of black college football, as well as all that the sport encompassed, the game increased the cultural power within the community.

The 1940s brought the fourth stage, and with it changes in the cultural importance of black college football. With the onset of World War II, African Americans became involved in the war effort in large numbers. The loss of fans and students to the war effort caused black college football to experience a decline in attendance, but not a loss in popularity and community importance. When the war came to an end, the attendance figures and popularity of the sport surpassed the levels experienced before the conflict.

The high level of popularity of black college football in Texas at the end of the 1940s carried over to the fifth stage. In the early 1950s, thousands of fans attended African American college games in Texas each week. Contests such as the State Fair Classic regained their place as major cultural events, with the activities that accompanied the games receiving more attention from the black community than the games themselves. But by the end of the decade, things had changed. With the onset of the civil rights movement, football at the segregated colleges in Texas lost community support. Black Texans began focusing their attention on the struggle for equal rights, ignoring segregated institutions, an experience mirrored in other segregated sports and cultural institutions, like the Negro Leagues.

The decline in the importance and popularity of black college football dominated the 1960s. During this sixth stage, the civil rights movement became the primary focus of the black community in Texas. The desegregation of public places, like Fair Park in Dallas, became the main concern of many African Americans. At the same time, the white colleges in Texas integrated their football teams. The integrated colleges, along with the arrival of professional football in Texas, attracted the attention of the black community. This change, which played out in sports and leagues throughout the United States, saw the players on the integrated teams become the new heroes, as well as sources of identity and cultural expression, for black Texans. By the end of the decade, the loss of support and cultural importance caused five of the eight black colleges in Texas to drop their football programs.

Black college football found itself in a diminished state during the seventh stage of its history. During the 1970s, the loss of popularity and cultural identity stunted African American college teams in Texas. Crowd sizes dropped, as only students and alumni placed much interest in the efforts of the teams. Integrated college and professional football attracted the best athletes, and as a result received most of the attention from the African American community. The popularity of integrated college football became solidified in 1977 when Earl Campbell, a black running back at the University of Texas, won the Heisman Trophy as the best college football player in the country. At the same time, the remaining black college teams in Texas received the new Division I-AA classification of the NCAA, a distinction that would later be changed to "Football Bowl Subdivision." By joining the predominately white governing body, the black college football teams in Texas gave up their independence and accepted secondary status in college football.

With the end of independence for current African American teams, the Texas black college teams entered the eighth stage of their history. During the last two decades of the twentieth century and the early twenty-first century, black college football in Texas focused all its efforts on surviving. Unable to attract the best athletes in the state, the Texas black teams found competition difficult. The African American college teams no longer possessed the same level of cultural importance. Prairie View A&M illustrated the diminished status of black college football in Texas when the Panthers, who won five national championships in the 1950s and early 1960s, set an NCCA record when they lost eighty straight games between 1989 and 1998. The black colleges adapted to their new situation. By focusing on balanced athletic budgets and fiscal responsibility instead of competing with white colleges, football survived, but only at the public African American colleges in Texas.

By closely examining these eight stages of black college football in Texas, we gain insight into the cultural and historical importance of the game in the black community and Texas as a whole, extending even beyond state lines. These themes are not unique to Texas football; they are played out in multiple ways throughout the world. In his article "Cricket and Politics in Colonial India" from *Past and Present*, Ramachandra Guha expressed this when he argued that sports offer a microcosm of society at large that we can study.[3] In Texas, football is king, so it provides a prominent window into Texas culture. Furthermore, by studying black college football in Texas, we gain a better understanding of the history of the African American community in Texas, along with the themes of civil rights, identity, racial pride, and cultural power.

1

The Early Years

As the United States emerged from the Civil War, African Americans sought to establish their social, economic, and political rights. African American leaders throughout the United States worked diligently in efforts to promote racial pride and elevate their peers physically, morally, and intellectually. At the same time, college football began around the country, and black colleges opened to offer African Americans an opportunity at higher education. During the period from 1865 to 1920, institutions of African American higher education and college football grew and intertwined. The Emancipation Proclamation and Reconstruction raised hopes, but these dreams soon crumbled under the reality of racism and segregation. African Americans found their rights as citizens denied in Texas and the South. In response, blacks relied on their own communities, since in the dominant white society of America, the color of one's skin, not accomplishments, brought acceptance. By 1920, a well-established African American culture in Texas, including black colleges and black college football, offered black Texans a level of control over their own lives and provided a countermovement against racial segregation.[1]

On June 19, 1865, slavery officially ended in Texas when federal troops landed at Galveston Island. African Americans in Texas, along with former slaves from throughout the South, felt excited and optimistic—it was the end of their servitude. With emancipation, former slaves began creating a new and unique culture, one that reflected their new free status. The joy brought by their freedom decreased, though, once they realized that abolition offered only limited protection of their social, political, and economic rights.[2]

Four years after emancipation, college football began in the United States. The first intercollegiate football game took place on November 6, 1869, between Rutgers University and Princeton University in New Brunswick, New Jersey. Rutgers won the game by a score of six to four.

The contest occurred under soccer rules, with twenty-five players to a side.[3] Over the next fifty years, college football grew into a major cultural influence for both blacks and whites.

At the same time, higher education for African Americans was established throughout the South. The hope existed among the black community and sympathetic whites that with education, the four million freed slaves in the United States could assert themselves economically and politically, while at the same time not falling prey to manipulation by outside forces. What form African American education would take proved a topic of many opinions and much debate, though. Some people believed black education ought to follow the same classical pattern and curriculum as white education. Others, particularly white southerners, wanted African Americans to receive only the most basic form of vocational training, thus preparing them for manual labor. During the period from 1865 to the end of World War I, African American education progressed through a mixed pattern, with the majority of black colleges graduating teachers and ministers, while also including agricultural and technical courses.[4]

The job of founding the first formal education for African Americans in the South fell to the Freedmen's Bureau, aided by northern missionary societies.[5] The level of education provided existed mainly at an elementary level of improving basic academic skills, such as reading and writing. In Texas, the first Freedmen's Bureau school appeared in Galveston in 1865. Within a year, more than one hundred bureau schools existed in the state.[6]

After the Freedmen's Bureau shut down in 1872, the administration of African American schools fell to the towns and states in which the schools existed. With local white-led governments in charge, black schools across the South received unequal funding and treatment compared to white schools.

In the 1876 Texas constitution, the state legislature officially imposed segregation upon the school system. As a way to compensate for segregation, the 1876 constitution stated that Texas would provide impartial funding to both white and black schools. Furthermore, the constitution provided for the creation of an African American college or branch university.[7] In reality, the State of Texas delayed building a public college for African Americans and never provided equal funding for black schools in the state as compared to white schools.

In response to this situation, African Americans founded their own private colleges. The first African American college in Texas, Paul Quinn College, appeared in Austin in 1872. Founded by preachers of the African Methodist Episcopal Church, the college existed as an African American–run institution of higher education. Paul Quinn, which moved to Waco in 1877, offered freed slaves a chance to elevate themselves out of "desperate conditions" through education.[8]

Soon other private black colleges appeared across the state. One year after Paul Quinn opened, members of the Freedmen's Aid Society of the Methodist Episcopal Church founded Wiley College in the town of Marshall. The Methodist Episcopal Church, a white, primarily northern denomination, began the Freedmen's Aid Society in 1866 in an effort to provide "relief and education" to freed slaves.[9] At Wiley College, the Freeman's Aid Society sought to uphold its mission statement by promoting education and providing African American teachers and preachers with the basic skills to go out and educate Texas' black population. Wiley marked just one of twenty black colleges the society founded across eleven states by 1878.[10]

In 1881, Marshall, Texas, experienced the opening of a second black college within its city limits. The new institution, Bishop College, received its charter from the American Baptist Home Mission Society. The school served as the first Baptist college for African Americans in the Southwest.[11]

More private black colleges appeared in the state. Texas College, which began on 101 acres of land north of Tyler, received a charter under the Colored Methodist Episcopal Church. In 1900, the Freedmen's Aid Society founded Samuel Huston College, the society's second black college in Texas. When the school opened, its classes met in a five-room basement in East Austin.[12]

Several smaller, private African American colleges also arose in Texas. The founding of Tillotson College in 1877 gave black Texans in Austin another choice for higher education. Black Baptists founded Guadalupe College in Seguin in 1884, while the white Protestant Episcopal Church created St. Philip's College in San Antonio in 1898. One school, Mary Allen College of Crockett, served as the only all-women college for African Americans in Texas.[13]

The last private black college in Texas, Jarvis Christian College, opened its doors in 1912 at Hawkins, Texas. The college was founded by a white benevolence society, the Christian Women's Board of Missions of the Disciples of Christ. Jarvis Christian received a gift of 456 acres of land near Hawkins from Major and Mrs. J. J. Jarvis of Fort Worth, for whom the school was named. The college eventually developed a relationship with Texas Christian University, the white Disciples of Christ college in Texas.[14]

From their inception, the private black colleges in Texas faced financial problems and lacked adequate facilities. Samuel Huston College opened in 1900 but took sixteen years to complete construction on its first building. Texas College began with three students in 1895. Jarvis Christian College saw its first seven students and one professor meet in an old logging camp for classes in 1912.[15]

The first public college for African Americans in Texas, Prairie View A&M College, finally opened its doors to eight students on March 11, 1878.[16] The first Morrill Land Grant Act, passed by the US Congress in 1862, created Texas A&M University, and also included provisions for a black land grant college. Since Prairie View's charter came as a part of the Morrill Act, the college operated under the control of Texas A&M, yet most of the federal money went to the white school.[17] When the State of Texas received funds from the federal government under the second Morrill Act in 1891, the state legislature set aside a portion of the funds for Prairie View.[18]

During the period when black colleges opened their doors in Texas, college football as a whole also grew and matured. White colleges and universities along the East Coast of the United States established football teams. These teams originally operated as sports clubs, organized and coached by students. As the popularity of the sport spread, though, an effort began to unify rules and organize play.[19]

College football spread rapidly throughout the country and became a part of American culture because many Americans believed the sport promoted character and a spirit of camaraderie. An image of virility soon surrounded football. College students and administrators supported this image because it went against the traditional view of college life and education as effeminate.[20]

For Americans, sports came to embody the criteria for masculinity and socially acceptable male conduct. Participation in sports allowed men in sedentary industrial and business jobs to improve their health while also reaffirming values of hard work, morality, and character. Proponents of the benefits of sports proclaimed athletes found their character tested, and thus became strong, disciplined, moral men who worked as team members at their jobs and stood as living embodiments of the masculinity and vitality of American men.[21] Football, with its natural violence, fit perfectly with the concept that sports both built character and affirmed masculinity.

In the South, many coaches went even further, espousing how their sport reinforced Christian values learned at home and church. For some, though, college football presented a threat to their way of life, since the game came from the North and potentially could bring other "dangerous ideals" from the disliked region.[22] Ultimately, the view of college football as a measure of courage, manliness, and honor won out in the South. In the era of industrialization, southern college football came to be seen as an expression of the difference—and to white southerners the dominance— of southern culture in relation to their northern brethren. A prominent element of the southern culture, though, was racial segregation.[23]

The idea of white superiority faced a challenge if African Americans excelled at football. As a result, southern whites tirelessly worked to maintain segregation in all aspects of life and society. In 1882, the Texas State Medical Association released a statement that African Americans' lungs were "lighter and smaller in cubic size than whites." The conclusion followed that the physical difference made African Americans less successful at strenuous or physical activities.[24]

"Scientific racism" such as that presented by the TSMA allowed for racist claims of African American physical inferiority, and thus justification for exclusion in sports. Furthermore, most southern football programs employed older African American men as janitors, trainers, equipment managers, or water boys. These roles delegated blacks to subservient, nonthreatening roles in connection with white college football.[25]

While whites in Texas and the South denied blacks the opportunity to participate in football, a few African Americans suited up for northern, mostly white, colleges. The first African American to play in an intercollegiate football game remains unknown. Two of the earliest black players were William Tecumseh Sherman Jackson and William Lewis, who competed for Amherst College. The two men made their college football debut in 1889, three years before the first intercollegiate football game played by an African American college.[26]

While Lewis and Jackson played at Amherst, other African Americans joined previously white college football teams around the country. In 1890, George Jewett punted, kicked field goals, and played halfback for the University of Michigan. The same year, William Arthur appeared at halfback for the Massachusetts Institute of Technology. At the University of Nebraska, George Flippin served as the team's star halfback from 1892 to 1894.[27]

A small stream of African Americans played football for some colleges in the North during the late 1800s. Charles C. Cook played for Cornell University, before becoming the coach at Howard University. Howard J. Lee competed for Harvard in 1896 and 1897. Charles Winterwood, a member of the Beloit College football team, went on to serve as the first nonstudent coach at the Tuskegee Institute. Also in the late 1800s, William Johnson played for Nebraska, while James Phillips competed for Northwestern.[28]

Throughout the 1890s, college football grew in popularity. As a result, predominantly white colleges organized themselves into conferences with governing bodies in an effort to standardize play, as well as to capitalize on the increased attendance and revenue associated with the game. Several white colleges in the South created the Southern Intercollegiate Association (SIA) in 1894. The SIA mission involved regulating all collegiate athletics for its members, as well as scheduling football games.[29] In 1895, a second regulating organization appeared in the United States, The Intercollegiate Conference of Faculty Representatives, later renamed the Big Ten, sought to govern athletics at schools in the Midwest.[30]

By the late 1800s, college football ranked as the second most popular sport in the United States, coming in just behind baseball. At schools such as Yale, Harvard, and Princeton, football games drew large crowds, created alumni support, and helped establish an identity for the schools, which in turn attracted new students. Students and alumni scoured the country looking for talented youths whose play on the football field might bring added success to the college. These prize recruits usually came from eastern prep schools where students received considerable coaching on the fundamentals of the game. For boys who showed athletic prowess but came from poor mining families in Pennsylvania or industrial families in the Northeast, the schools made arrangements to secure these prized athletes' services. Usually college alumni provided tuition to preparatory schools, where the youths then honed their talent, with the agreement that the grateful recipients would attend their benefactors' alma maters.[31]

African American colleges lagged behind white colleges in the growth of college football. Before 1890, all sports at black colleges existed only as intramurals. Black colleges in the United States possessed poorer facilities and few coaches. No leagues or conferences existed to assist the teams. Few school administrators wanted to spend money on fun and games when the schools needed to purchase books, build classrooms, and pay teachers.[32]

The cultural importance of sports was not totally ignored at these schools. Many reformers supported W. E. B. Dubois' idea of a "Talented Tenth," where the accomplishments of elite African Americans would bring acceptance and equality to the race. Some proponents of this idea looked to sports as a means of developing a national image of black morals, intellect, and physical equality.[33]

African American colleges throughout the country, including the schools in Texas, adopted this view of sports. Fisk University in Nashville, Tennessee, provides an example representative of the attitudes held by black colleges in Texas: The school's administration promoted sports, and particularly football, in an effort to establish physical fitness among the students. The advocates believed that the development of strong, athletically fit bodies in turn led to the development of strong, mentally fit minds, thus preparing black student bodies for the difficult life in a modern world.[34]

As a result, intercollegiate football emerged at African American colleges, despite the financial limitations. The first football game involving two black colleges occurred on December 27, 1892, when Biddle College faced Livingston College. The two North Carolina schools met at the Livingston campus in Salisbury.[35] On December 3, the *Indianapolis Freeman* printed a dispatch from a representative at Biddle, stating, "Our football eleven has received a challenge from one Livingston College to play a match game of ball . . . [T]he challenge will most likely be accepted, and the boys are now kicking the leather bag over the field."[36]

The game proved an exciting event for both schools. On its way to the game, the Biddle football team and supporters occupied half of the African American car on the train. The college's students also decorated the train in the Biddle school colors.[37] Unfortunately, attendance at the game proved low, as a snowstorm covered the Carolinas the night before and the day of the game.[38]

Evidence of the unequal funding received by black colleges as compared to white colleges existed in the Biddle-Livingston game. Since both schools possessed little money to support their teams, players competed in jerseys sewn by their school home-economics departments. The teams did use a regulation football, purchased from the Spalding Company, and paid for with donations collected by the Livingston players. A white law student from the University of North Carolina named Murphy agreed to serve as the referee.[39]

The same fall as the Biddle and Livingston game, another African American college, Howard University in Washington, DC, began holding football games between the different classes on campus. These intra-class games soon grew into an intercollegiate football team. Howard even hired a coach, Charles Cook, who previously competed at Cornell. Cook assembled a powerful squad in 1893, a season that saw Howard defeat the local black YMCA team, forty to six. Howard also defeated several athletic clubs, including one from Annapolis.[40]

In 1893, college football also spread to Texas when the University of Texas played its first game. Other white colleges in the state soon fielded football teams. The University of Texas and Texas A&M faced each other for the first time in 1894, beginning their rivalry. In 1896, Texas Christian University opened its football career with an eight to six victory over Toby's Business College in Waco. Three years later, Baylor University fielded its first team, losing to Texas A&M, thirty-three to zero.[41]

As college football grew, rivalries between schools developed. The annual contests between white schools like the University of Texas and Texas A&M became intense. African American colleges developed their own rivalries. On November 29, 1894, Howard University faced Lincoln University of Pennsylvania for the first time. The game, played in Washington, DC, between the two schools became an annual contest. By the twentieth century, the Howard-Lincoln game served as one of the most anticipated and fiercely competitive rivalries of black college football.[42]

Even as the sport grew, black college football teams faced several problems not experienced by white schools. One problem faced by black teams involved the lack of training African American students received in high school. Most black football players possessed rudimentary skills and training before attending college. Edwin B. Henderson discussed the training problem in his book *The Negro in Sports*: "The reason we can't use the Notre Dame system in many of our colleges is because the boys from our own high schools haven't sufficient knowledge of fundamentals and of 'inside' football to fit into an intricate system. Thus we must adapt a less intricate system to conform to the players."[43]

Northern colleges did not face these problems. Instead, they saw the profits from football skyrocket in the late 1890s. For the Harvard-Yale game in 1894, each school made almost eleven thousand dollars from the gate receipts. The profitability of college football also spread to auxiliary businesses. The railroad companies that brought people to the 1894 Harvard-Yale game made seventy-five thousand dollars.[44]

Football continued and prospered into the twentieth century, partially because of the perceived function of the sport as a facilitator of manly qualities and virility. Theodore Roosevelt continued to express these sentiments when he stated his fears that urbanization and the abandonment of a tough, frontier mind-set created a loss of manliness and virility for Americans. He praised college football for returning these characteristics to American youths.[45] His ideas rang true with the sons of middle class and socially elite families that made up the group of college men at the time. For college students in the early twentieth century, football offered proof of a new urban manhood.[46]

As the number of fans attending games increased, so did the number of African Americans participating in the sport. On November 30, 1899, Thanksgiving Day, almost a thousand fans came to the Howard University campus to watch Howard face Morgan College. Howard won the game, seventy-one to zero.[47] More and more African American colleges fielded football teams as the popularity of the sport grew. Atlanta Baptist College, later renamed Morehouse College, fielded its first team in 1900. Atlanta Baptist failed to record its first victory until 1904, when it defeated the Atlanta YMCA. Following this first win, though, Atlanta Baptist went on to win consecutive conference championships in 1905, 1906, 1907, and 1908.[48]

With black players more visible in the sport, especially at some predominantly white, northern colleges, racial incidents began to occur at games. Samuel Simon Gordon played for Wabash College in 1903. As Gordon's team prepared for a game against DePauw University in Chicago, the DePauw manager and players refused to compete against Wabash. They stated that they refused to play against an African American. The game eventually took place, but only after General Lew Wallace of the US Army interceded on Wabash's behalf and convinced DePauw to play.[49]

Black college football faced even more problems in the early twentieth century. One problem involved a lack of competent officiating and governing bodies among the African American colleges. In November of 1900, four hundred people watched Virginia Union College face Virginia Normal and Collegiate Institute in Petersburg, Virginia. With Virginia Normal up eleven to zero, Virginia Union left the field in protest. When the referee ruled Virginia Normal made a first down, a call Virginia Union protested, arguing that they had stopped the ball carrier. When the referee overruled the Virginia Union challenge, the teams went home.[50] Virginia Union never faced any repercussions for its actions.

African American colleges also had difficulty finding opponents. Since black colleges possessed few funds for travel, and white schools refused to compete against black colleges, African American colleges played few games in their seasons. In 1902, Atlanta Baptist College played two games, while Hampton Institute played its first ever football game—its only one for the season. Tuskegee played three games that year. Howard University only played one game in 1902, defeating Morgan College twenty-three to zero. The victory gave Howard a thirteen-game winning streak without giving up a single point, a streak that covered five seasons.[51]

The funds for football received little attention at Texas black colleges in the early twentieth century. Instead, the schools worried about the educational level of their students, as most of the black colleges in Texas consisted of a high school and a college. The focus on both secondary and higher education created an overlap in the material taught. Some smaller schools, such as Houston Baptist College, focused all of their attention on non-college-level classes. Yet the older established colleges, for example Bishop College and Paul Quinn College, refused to place their main emphasis on the high school level classes at the colleges.[52]

A major factor in the growth of football among African Americans came from the black elite in the United States. For the most part, the black elite who sent their children to African American colleges liked football.[53] Then, when Walter Camp selected William Lewis to the All-American team in 1892 and 1893, the interest among African Americans skyrocketed. Football suddenly became an endeavor at which African Americans might achieve success.[54] Also, with the masculine image surrounding football, black success in the sport continued to challenge ideas of white superiority.

Another factor that allowed college football to grow at the beginning of the 1900s involved the physical space and equipment required at the schools. All a college needed to hold a game was a chalked off field, a goal post at each end, and a ball. Despite budget constraints, African American colleges found it possible to meet these basic requirements.[55]

Without conferences to govern actions and organize play, black college football experienced many irregularities in the early 1900s. Since each school made its own schedule, the number of games fluctuated from school to school, with most black colleges playing between three and six games a year. Colleges used ineligible players who did not attend classes. Also, some football players competed for more than four years. One factor in the long tenures of some African American players on school football teams came from the fact that many black colleges offered preparatory, collegiate, and professional classes. A gifted football player who received his elementary, secondary, and higher education from the same college found himself able to compete on the football team for more than twelve years.[56]

Black colleges during this period also dealt with players jumping teams. In the Meharry Medical College and Fisk University game on Thanksgiving Day in 1907, Meharry featured a player named Floyd Wellman "Terrible" Terry. A running back, Terry previously played on the Talladega College team in 1903. Meharry was not the last black college for whom Terry played. He continued to play college football and switch teams, finally ending his career in 1911 with Howard University.[57]

The success of college football led representatives from thirteen white or predominantly white colleges to create the Intercollegiate Athletic Association (IAA) in 1905. In 1910, the IAA changed its name to the National Collegiate Athletic Association (NCAA) and became the supreme authority for college sports in the United States. The NCAA established standards of conduct for colleges and conferences. It also created a rules committee for college sports.[58] But the NCAA failed to admit African American colleges.

Faced by increased limitations on their rights as citizens, African Americans relied more and more on their own culture and community as a defense system. In 1912, African Americans in Houston organized the original Texas chapter of the National Association for the Advancement of Colored People (NAACP).[59] At the national level, the black press in the United States copied Walter Camp and named its own All-American team in 1911, consisting entirely of football players at black colleges.[60]

Within the system of expanding segregation within southern society, black colleges in Texas came to play a major role in the development of an independent African American community. The schools offered social and cultural events, as well as educational opportunities. Eventually, the social and cultural events, such as intercollegiate football, attracted a wide array of African Americans not associated in any way with the colleges' academic programs.

The movement toward organizations and activities exclusively for African Americans also occurred at white and black colleges around the country. In 1906, seven students at Cornell University founded Alpha Phi Alpha, the first college fraternity for African American males. Then, in 1908, Alpha Kappa Alpha, the first sorority for African American females, began at Howard University.[61] The first black fraternity in Texas, Phi Beta Sigma, formed at Wiley College in 1916.[62]

In the early 1900s, the Prairie View A&M administration took an approach of total control concerning student life. The school instituted a uniform system of dress, a plain, wholesome diet, and promoted physical health through hygiene and exercise.[63] At the private colleges in Texas, a strict religious atmosphere existed. Colleges such as Wiley and Paul Quinn possessed strong expectations for student participation in campus religious activities like chapel and prayer meetings. In the 1906 Wiley catalog, the school listed three mandatory church services every Sunday.[64]

The African American students at the schools, though, wanted more freedom and a social life. In December of 1905, six students at Prairie View led an uprising for two days because the faculty refused to allow a "sociable." Five of the ring leaders received monthlong suspensions, while the school kicked the sixth student out permanently.[65] The students at Prairie View A&M continued to push for extracurricular and social activities. They followed the basic model of recreation exhibited by students at white colleges at the time. The students at the African American colleges in Texas found ways to turn light classical music, essay presentations, and orations into social gatherings and functions.[66]

At the same time, intercollegiate football began at the Texas black colleges. In 1901, Wiley College became the first to field a team, declaring: "The athletic sports are not only allowed, but encouraged. It is thought that the best education is that which develops a strong, robust body as well as other parts of the human makeup. Football, as it is played at Yale and other Eastern colleges was introduced this year . . . Roughness and rowdyism, which have brought these games into disrepute in many places, are not allowed at Wiley."[67]

Quickly, the other African American colleges in Texas created football teams. Over the next fifty years, almost every black college in Texas fielded a team for at least a short period of time. The private colleges, Wiley, Bishop, Paul Quinn, Texas College, Samuel Huston, and Jarvis Christian, faced each other on a regular basis, establishing strong support within the community in the state.[68]

In 1904, the desire for athletics among the students at Prairie View A&M manifested itself in the creation of an athletic club. W. C. Rollins served as the club's first manager, and A. J. Sykes became the first president. The purpose of the athletic club centered on planning athletic programs, financing these contests, and training the student athletes.[69] The athletic contest that most stirred the students was football. Student pep squads supported the Prairie View team with yells and songs during games. While the athletic club and the football team proved very popular among the students, Prairie View A&M possessed no funds to support athletics. As a result, players and coaches paid their own way for off-campus games. One out-of-town game cost Prairie View coach W. P. Terrell fifty-one dollars—a hefty sum in the early 1900s.[70]

Then, in 1912, black college football took a major step forward with the creation of the first athletic conference for African American colleges. Several colleges on the East Coast, including Howard, Hampton, Shaw, and Lincoln, came together and formed the Colored Intercollegiate Athletic Association (CIAA).[71] A year later, representatives from ten colleges met on the Morehouse College campus in Atlanta and created a second black athletic conference, the Southeastern Intercollegiate Athletic Conference (SIAC).[72]

The CIAA and SIAC marked a second era in black college football. The new athletic conferences provided an organizational structure. The creation of the athletic conferences also resulted in the proliferation and popularization of the idea of college football as a representation of black community. Yet problems still existed. The CIAA, SIAC, and black college football in general lacked the financial infrastructure necessary to carry out organized college sports on a large scale. The second Morrill Act of 1890 worked to alleviate the problem by providing more state assistance for land grant colleges. Unfortunately, African American land grant colleges never received their promised share of state and federal funds.[73]

Without state funds, private black colleges turned to philanthropic organizations for assistance in order to meet their annual budgets. In 1902, John D. Rockefeller founded the General Education Board (GEB) to provide funds for higher education in America. The GEB served as one of the major sources of funding for private African American colleges in Texas. From 1924 to 1929, Texas' black colleges received a cumulative total of $596,700 from the GEB.[74]

To join the conference organization trend in 1914, L. Theo Bellmont, the athletic director at the University of Texas, mailed questionnaires to the larger white colleges in the Southwest, asking if they wanted to create an athletic conference. In May, representatives of nine colleges from Arkansas, Louisiana, Oklahoma, and Texas met at the Orient Hotel in Dallas and formed the Southwest Conference (SWC). The Southwest Conference served as the governing body for football at the largest white colleges in Texas for the next eighty years. At the same time, the SWC members imposed racial segregation on the top level of intercollegiate football in the state.[75]

Outside the South and Southwest, the African American struggle for equality, both in society and in football, saw two champions appear in 1915 when Paul Robeson and Frederick "Fritz" Pollard entered college. Robeson and Pollard both dominated the sport of football at largely white northern colleges. In the end, they changed the way the public, both black and white, viewed African Americans' role in college football.[76]

The star fullback on his high school football team, Robeson enrolled at Rutgers University on an academic scholarship. Rutgers featured talented athletic teams, and as a result, few freshmen made the varsity team. However, Robeson was too gifted an athlete and played in half of the team's games in 1915.[77]

In 1917, Robeson, who now played defensive end and offensive tackle, led Rutgers to a record of seven wins, one loss, and one tie. By his senior year in 1918, Robeson presented an easy selection for first team All-American. Camp even called Robeson "the finest end that ever played the game."[78] Despite his success, the Rutgers coaches benched Robeson when they faced Washington and Lee University from Virginia so as not to offend the southern team.

Frederick "Fritz" Pollard was the other outstanding African American football player in the first part of the twentieth century. Pollard played football for Brown University at the same time that Robeson played for Rutgers. Standing five feet, seven inches tall and weighing 165 pounds, Pollard presented a very different physical appearance than Robeson. As the most elusive running back seen in college football to that date, Pollard changed the role and status of black players in the game. He showed that African American athletes possessed skill, grace, and speed, not just brute strength, as some whites argued.[79]

During the 1915 and 1916 seasons, Pollard dominated college football. On New Year's Day, 1916, he became the first African American to compete in the Rose Bowl when Brown lost to Washington State, fourteen to zero. The following season he was the first African American running back named to Walter Camp's All-American Team. [80] Furthermore, after leaving college, Pollard received a contract in 1919 with the new American Professional Football Association, making him one of the racial pioneers of the league.[81]

When the United States entered World War I, many African Americans hoped their participation might bring about social changes at home. Thus thousands of African Americans sought to prove their worth and loyalty to the United States by enlisting in the armed forces. Tens of thousands of other African Americans moved to cities to take advantage of the many opportunities, especially industrial jobs in the North, made available by the loss of white workers to the military.[82] For those who entered the military, black soldiers faced segregation and tougher treatment than whites, with fewer exemptions in the draft and less social interaction in military camps.[83]

Most African Americans in Texas contributed to the US war effort. They joined programs to conserve food, aided the Red Cross, and also bought War Bonds. W. L. Davis, a community leader from Houston, even received a Federal Food Administration appointment as the Secretary for its Negro Division.[84] African Americans also made up about one-fourth of the soldiers drafted in Texas, a total of thirty-one thousand men.[85]

The First World War affected college football programs throughout the country as both black and white young men answered the call to service. The colleges in the United States worked to help the war effort. Student Army Training Corps (SATC) personnel filled both black and white college football teams in an effort to improve their physical conditioning. As a result, the SATC teams for Howard and Hampton faced each other, in place of the colleges' regular football teams.[86]

During the war, Texas became a focus of the racial struggle in the United States on August 23, 1917, when 150 members of the all-black 24th Infantry attacked the neighborhood around their Houston camp. The violence occurred as a direct response to the abuse of an African American enlisted man and an African American woman by a Houston policeman. The riot left seventeen people dead and thousands of dollars in damage. A military tribunal gave thirteen black soldiers the death penalty for their actions during the riot, while forty-one others received life imprisonment.[87]

Higher education and college football developed into prominent social institutions in the United States during this time. College football grew from sports clubs organized that were managed by students into a big business with professional coaches, athletic conferences, and unified rules. African Americans' access to northern colleges and football teams was limited.

As the United States entered the 1920s, African Americans found themselves excluded from white society, denied their political rights in much of the country, and forced to attend segregated schools. World War I brought hope for improvement. Black Texans who moved to the state's large cities in hopes of capitalizing on the war industries settled in large, segregated neighborhoods. These neighborhoods allowed for the expression of a unique culture. As a result, in the 1920s, African Americans increased efforts at self-help. By 1919, black Texans had formed thirty-one NAACP chapters.[88] Black colleges in Texas became involved in the movement as they focused more on liberal arts education over vocational training. Black college football in Texas also came to play a prominent role as African Americans focused their attention on developing black culture and community outside the control of whites.

The "New Negro" and Community Pride

In the 1920s, black college football joined with other social institutions and events to create an expanded African American culture. Black college football also served as a means of cultural expression. Through the games, as well as accompanying events and school marching bands, African Americans found themselves able to celebrate their heritage, express joys and hopes, and feel pride as a race. Most importantly, during the 1920s, the cultural importance of black college football took place entirely within the African American community, away from the control of whites.

After World War I, college enrollments boomed as returning veterans pursued college degrees. The prosperity of the 1920s gave more students the financial ability to pay for college. At the same time, the job market included more positions for college graduates, creating motivation for students to pursue a higher education degree.[1]

As schools' enrollments grew, so did the focus on football. Colleges built large stadiums to showcase their football teams to tens of thousands of alumni and fans. By the end of the decade, ten million people annually attended white college football games.[2] As a result, college football became a central feature of American culture, and racial prejudice increased in the game.

Scientific racism was one way in which racial prejudice manifested itself. Scientific racism allowed whites to disguise their racist views under the heading of legitimate science. Whites looked at things such as differences in the skull sizes of Africans and Europeans to argue in favor of racial characteristics such as intelligence. As a result, this false science offered added strength to ideas of white supremacy.[3] The use of the "scientific" explanations to exclude African Americans from participation in sports, as well as in cases where black athletes competed, served to discount and degrade any accomplishments made by African American athletes.[4]

In the 1910s, the Ku Klux Klan also revived. The organization rose to prominence again in the United States as it played off the antifor-eign sentiments in the country. The KKK pitched itself as "100 percent American" and stated that it fought a perceived threat posed by African Americans and immigrants.[5]

Faced with these problems, African Americans fought back in a number of ways. During the 1920s, the NAACP increased its member-ship and developed more influence around the country. The NAACP chose to fight for civil rights through legal actions, such as pressuring Congress to pass the Dyer Anti-Lynching Law in 1921.[6]

Another challenge to segregation and racial prejudice in the South was through black college football. Football at these colleges served as a source of pride, because the games and teams belonged entirely to the black community. The college football games became "must see" events.[7] By 1922, Howard University had built its own stadium on the college's campus. The rivalry between Howard and Lincoln University of Pennsylvania was so popular that in order to compensate for the large fan turnout, the two teams played their annual Thanksgiving Day game in Griffith Stadium, the home of the Washington Senators, a Major League baseball team.[8]

The focus on black college football and all of its accompanying pag-eantry and events as unique aspects of African American culture followed a larger trend in the country at the time. In the United States during the 1920s, African Americans experienced a new cultural focus and spiritu-ality, finding the black community further removed from white society. This movement received the title "New Negro."[9]

The New Negro movement sought to express African American desires, issues, and culture outside the control of white society. The movement included features of black pride and black exclusiveness. This cultural independence manifested itself in art, literature, and music. Albert C. Barnes explained the movement's importance in his article, "Negro Art and America": "The contributions of the American Negro to art are representative because they come from the hearts of the masses of a people held together by the like yearnings and stirred by the same causes."[10]

For African Americans, the New Negro movement offered a sense of pride and self-help, as well as a safe way to respond to the racial prejudice in the United States. Jazz proved one of the widest reach-ing forms of emotional and cultural expression during the 1920s. J. A.

Rogers explains why jazz became so important to the African American community: "Jazz is a joyous revolt from convention, custom, authority, boredom, even sorrow—from everything that would confine the soul of man and hinder its riding free on the air . . . It is a revolt of the emotions against repression . . . Jazz is a release of all the suppressed emotions at once."[11]

The ideas of self-help, racial pride, and solidarity that were expressed through art and music extended to other aspects of African American life. Often African American community leaders supported these ideas as a way to oppose economic racism. African Americans faced limits on housing and jobs. As a result, blacks pursued options within the African American community and neighborhoods that existed beyond the control of whites. Black-owned barbershops, funeral parlors, clothing shops, and dance halls all served entirely African American clients in cities across the country.[12]

In Houston, African Americans found themselves able to establish social and political organizations, as well as business enterprises, for the black community. The reason for this growth came from the fact that the black community totaled between 20 and 30 percent of the city's population during the early twentieth century. As a result, businesses like the HT Taxi Company thrived as Jim Crow laws gave them a virtual monopoly in the African American community.[13] Black businessmen became the social and political leaders within the African American community.

The focus on culture in the "New Negro" movement also manifested itself through sports where the games became expressions of creativity. Sports and all of the accompanying events served as a point of commonality for the community. Black college football in Texas, like other segregated teams and sports throughout the country, provided a social function for self-esteem and identity, where athletes and fans could experience feelings of self-competence, and revel in athletic ability despite racial and economic hardships.[14]

But the role of sports in the migration experience of African Americans to the larger US cities differed from the experiences of other immigrant groups. For European immigrants, sports offered an inroad for acceptance and acculturation into American culture.[15] For other groups who faced stricter prejudice, such as Chinese immigrants, sports allowed for acculturation but also allowed community members to transmit traditional cultural values, as teams mainly played sports within their own neighbor-hoods but also occasionally played against white teams.[16]

The opportunity, or lack thereof, to compete against white teams marked a significant difference between the experiences of African American athletes in Texas and those from other ethnic groups. In the 1920s, the Haskell Institute Indian School football team competed against col-lege powerhouse programs, such as the University of Texas, the Univer-sity of Nebraska, the University of Oklahoma, and Texas A&M University. For the young men on the Haskell team, these games helped build strong racial pride, not school pride, as the players believed they were playing for all Native Americans.[17] For African Americans teams in Texas, no such opportunity existed. As a result, black sports operated in the same cultural environment of the "New Negro" movement as business, music, and art.

Following the model set by the state's white schools and the Southwest Conference, as well as fitting the themes of the "New Negro" movement, the black colleges in Texas formed their own conference in 1920, the Southwestern Athletic Conference (SWAC). The charter members con-sisted of Bishop, Wiley, Paul Quinn, Samuel Huston, Prairie View, and Texas College.[18] The move marked a major turning point for black college football in Texas. A committee consisting of each member college's head football coach and president performed the administrative duties of the conference. The majority opinion approach to administration allowed the SWAC to best serve as a governing body to regulate competition and rules among the members. Also, the formation of the conference raised the level of play in Texas to that of the best black colleges in the country.

In the 1920s, these football games in Texas took on an even greater atmosphere of excitement and celebration. The positive atmosphere that surrounded black college football came from the fact that several games annually occurred in conjunction with other African American events. In 1921, the Paul Quinn–Wiley game took place on Thanks-giving in Dallas during the Teachers State Association meeting.[19] L. C. Anderson, the founder and first president of the TSA, sought to unite African American teachers with black businessmen, fraternal orders, and religious groups. The TSA annual meeting brought all of these groups together. By holding their football game in conjunction with the meeting, Paul Quinn and Wiley looked to attract a good-sized crowd.[20]

Not every African American college in Texas joined the SWAC. Jarvis Christian originally stayed out of the conference. As a result, its team played fewer games and found itself unable to compete equally with the other colleges in the state. For example, the Wiley Wildcats began their season in 1921 by beating Jarvis Christian forty-four to six.[21] The Wildcats finished the 1921 season with a record of seven wins, no losses, and one tie, which tied them with Talladega College in Alabama for the black college national championship.[22]

Black college football in Texas achieved such a level of popularity in the early 1920s that the African American newspapers in the state sought to capitalize on the excitement. The role of these Texas papers, as well as national newspapers like the *Chicago Defender*, in covering African American sports and teams created a national black sporting culture similar to the white sporting culture in the United States. Over the ensuing decades, the role of the national and local black press in promoting and protecting African American culture increased.[23]

By 1921, both the *Dallas Express* and the *Houston Informer* created separate sports pages that published articles on local and national sporting events. The two newspapers hoped that the special sections covering only African American sports would attract readers, especially since the white newspapers in Texas failed to report on segregated sports.[24]

On October 28, Prairie View University met Texas College of Tyler in the first Southwestern Athletic Conference football game of the 1922 season. The season schedule for the Prairie View Panthers in 1922 consisted of four games against the Texas College Steers, the Samuel Huston Dragons, the Wiley Wildcats, and the Paul Quinn Tigers.[25] Prairie View's management also expressed hopes of adding two or three postseason games. The school wanted to play one game against Tuskegee University and one game against a "strong Texas team" in conjunction with the annual Colored Teachers' Association meeting on Thanksgiving Day in Fort Worth.[26] Prairie View also hoped to add a third game to take place in Houston in order to capitalize on the many fans of the college in the city.[27]

While Prairie View outlined its plans for the 1922 season, the Panthers watched their game against Samuel Huston College end in a tie. The last-place team in the conference, Texas College, held Prairie View to a score of zero to zero, an event that the *Houston Informer* called an "unexplainable mystery."[28] The game illustrated some of the problems faced by black college football during the early 1900s as the sport matured. Only one timekeeper worked the game, and in this instance, he accidentally cut the first quarter short by a couple of minutes. The mistake assisted Samuel Huston by stopping a Prairie View drive that threatened to score a touchdown. At the end of the game, a penalty by Samuel Huston on the Prairie View five-yard line called back a potential winning touchdown.[29] Overall, though, the game proved a success, with the final attendance reaching five hundred spectators.[30]

Despite the problems, a quote from the *Houston Informer* following the game expressed the positive role black college football played in the Texas African American community. In these early games, the play of the teams as a whole received the most recognition. The paper declared, "The sport of the thing is as much to be enjoyed as the victory, if the true spirit moves those engaging therein. All that can be wished for is fair play."[31]

On December 23, 1922, the front page of the *Houston Informer* announced a New Year's Day game between the Bishop College Tigers and the Paul Quinn College Tigers. Both schools completed the football season undefeated. Paul Quinn finished with a record of three wins and no losses after defeating Prairie View, Wiley, and Samuel Huston. Bishop compiled a record of five wins and no losses by defeating Southern University, Jarvis Christian, East Texas Academy, Arkansas Baptist College, and Texas College.[32]

The positive impact of black college football was reflected in the accounts of the 1922 Bishop–Paul Quinn New Year's Day game. In the *Houston Informer*, the headline proclaiming "Bishop–Paul Quinn Game a Draw" appeared above another headline stating that Texas led the country in lynching deaths in 1922.[33] The newspaper, without giving specifics on the crowd size, went on to declare that the two schools "thrilled and electrified a huge mass of humanity as they battled for the titular honor of 1922."[34]

For Texas' black colleges, the football season remained dependent on the academic schedule. Practice began after the school term started. For example, in 1923 Bishop started classes on September 10. Once classes began, coaches learned which players from the previous year had returned to school and who planned to play football. Only then could coaches assign positions and work on plays.[35]

Occasionally, questions concerning which football team members returned to school extended beyond players to also include coaches.

Bishop College, following a successful 1922 campaign, opened the 1923 season with a new head coach, L. P. Collins. No mention existed in the black press as to why the previous coach at Bishop, Talcott, failed to return. The *Houston Informer* only told of Collins's accomplishments as a halfback and end on the University of Iowa football team.[36]

When the black press in Texas reported accounts of football games played, usually team effort received more recognition than the accomplishments of individual players. In a victory for Prairie View over Samuel Huston on November 3, 1923, the press focused its attention on the strong play of both schools' offensive and defensive lines. Prairie View's left tailback, a man who the *Informer* only referred to by his last name of Thompson, received the only individual recognition of the game.[37] In an account of Wiley's twenty to six victory over Texas College, which also occurred on November 3, the *Dallas Express* discussed the "line plunging of the husky warriors," instead of individuals' accomplishments.[38]

As black college football became more and more popular among the Texas African American community, the activities surrounding the games developed a celebratory atmosphere. Prairie View defeated Texas College fifteen to zero in November of 1923. The game took place on Armistice Day, and the festivities honoring the end of World War I received as much recognition as the game itself. The performance by the two schools' bands, speeches by prominent black Texans, along with the fact that the national government made the day a federal holiday, received as much attention as the football game.[39]

Another factor that helped black college football become so popular involved the development of rivalries between different colleges. For schools such as Wiley and Bishop, both of which were located in Marshall, a heated competition existed. These rivalries allowed fans to debate which college possessed a better team, and who were the best black athletes in the state. The debates proved important because they existed outside the control of the white establishment in Texas. On November 25, 1923, Wiley defeated its "ancient rival," Bishop, by a score of seven to six.[40] More than three thousand fans watched "one of the greatest games ever played in Texas."[41] The *Houston Informer* described the game as "the cleanest and hardest fought games ever played between Bishop and Wiley."[42] The paper went on to recognize several players on each team for their outstanding play, such as Jeremy and King of Bishop, and Orange and Donnell of Wiley. Along with the individual recognition, the paper made sure to point out that "every man who went on the field played hard and fought to the last whistle."[43]

The fact that black colleges in Texas offered competitive football teams also increased the popularity of the sport among the African American community. In 1923, Wiley won the Southwestern Athletic Conference championship. Of the six schools in the conference, four schools finished the season in contention for the title.[44]

The Bishop Tigers and the Paul Quinn Tigers finished out the 1923 football season with a Christmas Day game in Waco. Taking advantage of the reduced holiday rates offered by Texas railroads, three thousand fans witnessed the Paul Quinn victory. Led by "Hub" Tinsley, Paul Quinn played with "machine-like grace" as they "outclassed" Bishop.[45]

While the popularity of black college football in Texas grew during the 1920s, enrollment at the colleges in Texas also increased. During the 1924–25 academic year, the enrollment at Prairie View increased to 1,087 students. The school found itself forced to deny admittance to between two hundred and five hundred applicants because of a lack of dormitory space. At the 1925 Prairie View commencement ceremony, Professor Monroc Work of Tuskegee University recognized the increased role of sports at black colleges when he stressed the importance of both education and cultural activities in the establishment of political and social rights for African Americans.[46]

During the second half of the 1920s, changes occurred in both the play of black college football games and the coverage of the games by the black press. These changes coincided with black college football reaching a place of prominence in the African American community in Texas. At this point, not only did the sport capture the attention of thousands of fans; the athletes achieved a level of celebrity in the community.[47]

In 1924, Wiley won its second national championship, sharing the title with Tuskegee.[48] Using a simple T-formation offense, Wiley, led by the "dashing" Bennie Cavil and the "galloping" Captain McMillan, ran over their competition.[49] Cavil came to occupy a place of prominence in Texas black college football as the star of the Wiley football team and one of the first statewide African American football stars.

With the rise of star players on the Texas teams, the actual games played reached a new level of excitement and event status. One example occurred when Wiley prepared to play Langston University of Oklahoma on Monday, October 19, 1925. The game took place in Dallas in conjunction with Negro Day at the State Fair of Texas. A special train consisting of twelve cars ran from Marshall to Dallas in honor of the event and carried approximately four hundred Wiley students, faculty, and fans.[50] Before the game, the Wiley band paraded down Central Avenue in Dallas in an effort to attract even more fans to the football game. In the end, more than two thousand spectators watched Wiley and Langston battle to a zero to zero tie.[51]

The State Fair Classic and the use of special trains illustrated the racial prejudice in Texas society during the 1920s. Black Texans only received admittance to the fairgrounds twice a year—on Juneteenth and Negro Day, the second Monday in October. While Negro Day attracted large crowds, it was the only opportunity that African Americans had to view the State Fair.[52]

The special trains used by the railroad companies to carry fans to the Wiley-Langston game also represented the dual standard toward African Americans in Texas society. While the train companies added special cars to accommodate the extra passengers, the railroads remained segregated. Instead of allowing black passengers into all cars on the trains, the railroads added special trains to maintain segregation.

Other games also reached event status. The 1925 contest between the Prairie View Panthers and the Wiley Wildcats took place in Houston. The black press played a role in the spectacle of the African American games. A large advertisement ran in the Houston paper, proclaiming the game as the only chance for African Americans in the Houston area to watch the two strong football teams together. Also, both schools vowed to win the contest, while each head coach promised a "mighty fine show."[53] Prairie View won the game twelve to six.[54]

Another important advancement for black college football in Texas took place during the 1925 season. Beginning in November, advertisements for the "season's football classic" between New Orleans University and Prairie View College appeared in the *Houston Informer*.[55] The game, slated for December 4 at West End Park in Houston, served as the first major intercollegiate football game to take place in Houston involving an African American college from outside Texas. In anticipation of the large crowds, the H&TC railroad operated a special train from Prairie View to Houston to allow faculty, students, and fans a chance to witness the game. The *Houston Informer* stated, "the game will be the biggest social event preceding the Christmas period, and everybody will meet everybody at West End Park on this occasion."[56] For the next four weeks, advertisements for the Prairie View and New Orleans University game ran in the press. In the meantime, all the black colleges in Texas continued to compete.

The 1925 edition of the contest between Wiley and Bishop received a high level of support. "Big Ben" Cavil of Wiley was too much for Bishop in the annual Thanksgiving Day game. The nineteen to zero Wiley victory upset a perfect season for Bishop, which already had posted wins over Prairie View, Paul Quinn, Texas College, and Samuel Huston. Bishop still won the 1925 Southwestern Athletic Conference championship, but the loss caused the "Bishop rooters to lose their speaking or cheering facilities."[57]

The Wiley-Bishop game witnessed other important events. The game marked the first time a white official worked a black college football game in Texas. Also, fans from all over Texas, Arkansas, and Louisiana attended the game.[58]

When the game between Prairie View and New Orleans University finally took place on December 4, Prairie View defeated New Orleans fifty-one to six. The victory, according to the *Informer*, "upheld the reputation of the Lone Star State."[59] The end of the 1925 season saw Paul Quinn further the reputation of black college football in Texas when the school from Waco beat Straight University of New Orleans in a New Year's Day game in Beaumont.[60] The victories of the two Texas schools allowed their supporters to declare superiority over their neighboring state.

As the decade progressed, the importance placed on black college football increased. When Prairie View held its opening ceremonies for the 1926 school year, nine hundred students attended the exercises.[61] This school spirit carried over to the football team, with sixty-five young men trying out for the squad. Coach J. H. Law expressed optimism for the upcoming season. Prairie View's principal W. R. Banks, a former football player himself, stated that he believed in developing the athletics of an institution as well as other activities.[62]

This excitement carried over to other African American colleges in Texas. Wiley College featured a number of new players in 1926. Two of these new players, offensive linemen Issacs and Campbell, received coverage in the Houston black press because of their recent graduation from Samuel Houston High School. Players like Issacs and Campbell added name recognition to their college football team. As a result, even more fans followed the college teams.[63]

Preparations took place for the October 18 game between Langston College and Wiley College at the State Fair in Dallas. The annual game served as the beginning of the college football season. Because of the zero to zero tie the previous year, excitement over the game ran high as four thousand fans attended, the largest crowd ever to witness an African American football game in the South.[64] To accommodate the large fan turnout, the Texas and Pacific Railroad and the Beaumont, Houston, and Galveston Railroad chartered special trains to carry fans to the game.[65] The Southern Pacific Lines and the Santa Fe Lines offered round-trip tickets of seven dollars and fifteen cents and eleven dollars and forty-five cents to Dallas for Black Heritage Day at the State Fair and the Wiley-Langston game.[66] The Texas and Pacific also sent a special train from Marshall, carrying 350 Wiley students and supporters, as well as the school's twelve-piece orchestra. The orchestra then provided the half-time entertainment at the game. Langston won the contest thirteen to zero.[67]

In 1926, Prairie View officially declared November 11, Armistice Day, its homecoming. Principal W. R. Banks invited all graduates, former students, and friends of the school to attend the festivities. The homecoming activities centered around the Prairie View football game against the Bishop College Bears. Because the day of the game also served as a national holiday, Prairie View expected a large number of fans to attend the events.[68]

At the same time, Samuel Huston College continued its march toward the Southwestern Athletic Conference championship when the Dragons defeated Wiley on October 29 by a score of three to zero. The victory marked Samuel Huston's first ever win over Wiley in Marshall. The Dragons scored the only points of the game on a forty-two-yard field goal. The closest Wiley came to scoring took place in the fourth quarter when Samuel Huston quarterback Russ fumbled inside his team's ten-yard line. Wiley gained three yards on its first play from scrimmage, but lost yards on the next two plays when the Wildcats' attempts at trick plays failed to work. Wiley lost the ball on downs and never returned to a scoring position during the game.[69]

On November 13, the front page of the *Houston Informer* declared, "With the University of Texas playing away on November 18, all of Austin is agog over the coming Samuel Huston-Bishop homecoming game at

Culberson Field."[70] The game promised to be a highly popular one. Bishop, the Southwestern Athletic Conference champion the previous year, fielded a veteran team. Samuel Huston, on the other hand, boasted the strongest team in the Austin school's history. Since Bishop overwhelmingly defeated Samuel Huston the previous year, the Dragons vowed to win in 1926.[71] The fact that Bishop beat Texas College forty-three to zero the week before only added to the excitement surrounding the game against Samuel Huston.[72] When the two schools eventually played, Samuel Huston won.

The next week, Samuel Huston steamrolled Texas College by a score of seventy-four to zero before eight hundred spectators in Austin. Star quarterback and defensive back Russ again led the way for Samuel Huston. In the game, Russ put on a spectacular individual performance. He threw for two touchdowns, rushed for three more touchdowns, returned an interception ninety-five yards for a sixth touchdown, and also kicked all of his team's extra points.[73] The victory gave Samuel Huston a five and zero record, placing them with Howard University and Tuskegee University as the only undefeated teams in black college football. The lopsided victory in the game against Texas College allowed Samuel Huston to total three hundred points in their first five games.[74]

As a result of the successes of Samuel Huston and the other Texas schools, black college football in Texas achieved an increased level of recognition nationally, as well as at home. Amos Alonzo Stagg, coach of the University of Chicago, declared "Silver Toe" Russ of Samuel Huston the best football player in Texas, black or white. Stagg also named Russ to the All-American Team for 1926. The *Houston Informer* went further in its praise, declaring Russ a better open field runner than Red Grange, the University of Illinois' All-American running back. Russ's Samuel Huston Dragons proved to be so popular that one of their games in Austin generated a higher attendance than a football game between the University of Texas and Southwestern University that took place in Austin on the same day.[75]

As the 1926 season came to a close, Wiley and Bishop prepared to face each other in their annual Thanksgiving Day game. No opponent had crossed the Wildcat's goal line during the season. Despite only giving up six points all season, Wiley found itself with two losses and out of the conference title picture. The game served as some consolation for the Wiley players who defeated their crosstown rivals, thirty-three to zero, the worst loss in Bishop school history. The rivalry proved so popular that the teams agreed to move future games to the East Texas Fair Grounds in Marshall, to accommodate the large numbers of spectators.[76]

Samuel Huston College finished the season undefeated. The accomplishment marked 1926 as the most outstanding football season in school history. As a result, Samuel Huston reigned victorious as the champion of the Southwestern Athletic Conference.[77]

Prairie View and Bishop concluded the season by competing in a New Year's Day game at Beaumont. The game, which Prairie View won by a score of nine to zero, marked another advancement for black college football in Texas. The New Year's Day game allowed black Texans a chance to celebrate their schools and culture on the holiday the same way white colleges celebrated New Year's Day games. According to the black press, the "hard fought and well played contest" brought "thrill after thrill" to the three thousand fans in attendance.[78] Ideal weather prevailed, and the game marked the social event of the season for the local black community.[79]

As the 1927 football season began, the *Houston Informer* declared, "Extracurricular activities which are becoming more and more a vital part of the higher education program everywhere promise to lend life and spirit to things academic around Wiley College this year."[80] Football topped the list of nonclassroom interests. The focus on football at Texas' black colleges also saw Samuel Huston sign a preseason contract to face Langston at the Oklahoma State Fair on October 7.[81]

The Wiley versus Langston contest in Dallas again kicked off the season. For the 1927 contest, Wiley stated that its team entered the game "unhampered by a list of crippled veterans as the season before."[82] Langston, meanwhile, promised to put up the fight of its life in order to maintain dominance over Wiley.

Coach Anderson of Langston promoted a special train to carry fans from Oklahoma to Dallas. Special trains again carried fans from Wiley and East and South Texas to the game. Further adding to the excitement and ceremony, the Wiley alumni organized a reunion to correspond with the weekend events. As a result of all the festivities, attendance at the game and the State Fair's Negro Day was even higher and more exciting than in previous years.[83]

The use of special trains to bring fans to football games was common in both white and black college football. In 1923, when the University of Illinois faced the University of Pennsylvania, hundreds of fans from

Illinois, along with the school's band, traveled on a special charter train from Urbana to Philadelphia. The attraction to make the trip, in this case, was the opportunity to cheer on Illinois' star running back, "Red" Grange.[84]

The rest of the Southwestern Athletic Conference's members experienced an increase in fan support and excitement during the late 1920s. The Texas black press covered the preparations of every school for the upcoming season, while also listing each school's schedule. The college coaches also expressed their optimism for the 1927 season. The race for the conference championship appeared to be between Samuel Huston, Prairie View, and Wiley. The early season prediction went to Prairie View, which hosted the other two schools on its campus.[85]

The colleges also saw their enrollments continue to increase. Samuel Huston College entered the 1927 season ranked twentieth in the nation in size, based on student enrollment. The Samuel Huston football team brought back all but two of its 1926 championship team. Coach Bill Taylor also added twenty-six new members to his squad. The Samuel Huston Dragons boasted a roster of players from all over the country, including states such as Alabama, Illinois, Kentucky, New Jersey, Ohio, Oklahoma, and Pennsylvania, as well as Texas.[86]

Prairie View possessed the brightest prospects of all of the Southwestern Athletic Conference schools. It maintained the second largest student population in the country, surpassed only by Howard University. This large student enrollment carried over to the Prairie View football team, which consisted of more than one hundred athletes. Prairie View coach Jimmie Law brought back every letterman and member of his 1926 squad for the 1927 season.[87] Returning players also increased the team's recognition among the fans.

In Marshall, the third school expected to compete for the conference title, Wiley College, returned all but one varsity athlete from the previous year's squad. Injuries to key players, such as fullback Ben Cavil, kept Wiley from winning the SWAC in 1926.[88] The Wildcats, though, came out united in 1927, with the goal of capturing the conference title. Led by All-American candidate Leroy Taylor, "one of the greatest backs developed in the South," Wiley's goal appeared obtainable.[89]

Paul Quinn selected former football player Ray Sheppard as its head coach, following the distinct pattern for coaching hires in black college football. When enlisting new coaches, Texas' black colleges mainly sought experienced former players; this was their main prerequisite. Also, since African American colleges possessed less funds than their white counterparts, football coaches also doubled as professors in the physical education department.[90]

On October 8, 1927, the headline of the *Houston Informer* declared the Wiley-Langston game a "big affair."[91] The annual game between the two schools now served as the star attraction of Negro Day at the Texas State Fair in Dallas. M. W. Jordan, a Houston citizen and a Wiley fan, organized a special train through the Southern Pacific Lines to carry fans from South Texas to the game. H. J. Mason, the executive secretary of Wiley College, urged fans to attend. He stated that Wiley possessed the "strongest team of its career."[92] Led by "Big Ben Cavil, the galloping fullback," Wiley was primed for the game, as was Langston University, who Mason referred to as "being fed gun-powder for Wiley."[93]

In the end, six thousand fans turned out to watch the contest. Langston won twenty-seven to zero, but the thing that most concerned the black fans was the institution of Jim Crow segregation at the stadium. African Americans found themselves denied access to the main gate and were forced to enter the stadium by the back entrance.[94]

At Prairie View, optimism ran high concerning star quarterback "Jap" Turner. Every school that met Prairie View on the gridiron during the 1927 season found themselves forced to deal with the triple threat athlete. According to the *Houston Informer*, the Panther's star from Beaumont made the most of the 1927 season by "plunging, dashing, sidestepping, tossing, kicking and literally running wild."[95]

Turner received assistance from other outstanding Prairie View players like "Jeru" Mark, the team's fullback and captain. Mark received praise as a player "good for a five-yard plunge anytime."[96] Coach Law declared, "You can tell the Prairie View fans I am ready for Langston and Wiley anytime the whistle blows."[97]

Bishop prepared for its first game of the 1927 season against Paul Quinn on October 21. Bishop expressed determination to avenge its loss from the previous year. Unfortunately for Bishop, the headlines of the *Houston Informer* the next week declared, "Paul Quinn eats bear meat."[98] In the game, Paul Quinn scored a touchdown just three minutes into the first quarter. The Bishop halfback fumbled a punt, and Gentry for Paul Quinn recovered in the end zone. Paul Quinn scored a second touchdown in the first quarter.[99]

Bishop outplayed Paul Quinn the remaining three quarters of the game. Paul Quinn found itself unable to stop Bishop halfback "Corkscrew" Henderson for a loss. The only Bishop touchdown came in the fourth quarter of the game when "Thunderbolt" Mitchell made a leaping catch before racing to the end zone. Unfortunately, the touchdown came too late to change the outcome of the game. Despite the loss, Bishop coach Mumford expressed optimism for his players as they prepared to face their next opponent, the Samuel Huston Dragons.[100]

The other favorite for the conference title, Texas College, defeated Jarvis Christian in Dallas by a score of seven to six. Forward passes served as the theme of the game when Texas College scored on a long pass from Garrett to Harris. Another pass accounted for the extra point. Texas College attempted to score another touchdown via a pass, but Cass of Jarvis Christian intercepted and returned it sixty yards for a touchdown for his school's only points. Jarvis Christian unfortunately missed the extra point, which was the difference in the game. The use of the forward pass, a play rarely seen in white college football at the time, gave African Americans one more thing to express as unique about their brand of football.[101]

As black college football grew in prominence and popularity, the fans expected good quality play from the athletes. When the contest offered less than stellar efforts, the fans expressed their disappointment. In a game declared "listless" by the black press, Wiley defeated Prairie View before three thousand fans in Prairie View on October 28. Wiley running back "Big Ben" Cavil dominated the game but failed on the goal line. At the same time, Prairie View quarterback "Jap" Turner failed to exhibit talent equal to his reputation.[102]

In Austin, 1,500 hundred fans witnessed the defeat of Samuel Huston by Wiley at the new Lovinggood Stadium. The *Houston Informer* described the game as the "toughest in Southwestern Athletic Conference history."[103] Samuel Huston led two to zero at the end of the first half. "But in spite of the apparent gloom; the little band of seven Wiley rooters, with spartan-like courage, kept up a battery of yells and cheers for their warriors who were far from discouraged and beaten."[104]

In the second half of the game, Wiley exhibited "indomitable courage, fighting tradition, and unyielding strength."[105] Wiley dominated the second half. One touchdown came when, according to the *Houston Informer*, Wiley running back Scott carried the ball, along with three Samuel Huston players, fifty yards and across the goal line.[106]

Wiley undertook elaborate preparations for its annual Thanksgiving Day game against Bishop. Wiley decided to make the 1927 game its homecoming, and as a result, gave former students and visitors an exciting time that extended beyond just football. Wiley hosted a special turkey dinner after the game in the school cafeteria for all fans and students who wished to attend. Several social functions also entertained alumni and visitors. The excitement over the events ran high enough for the *Houston Informer* to declare the homecoming activities "the greatest occasion of its kind in the history of the institution."[107]

President Mathew Dogan of Wiley stated that he believed the school had failed to manifest the proper interest in its students in the past. As a result, he hoped the homecoming festivities would establish a new relationship between the school and its alumni and students.[108] The homecoming ceremonies marked a change in black college football in Texas. The actual Wiley-Bishop game in 1927 received little attention because of Bishop's poor record for the season. Instead, the social activities surrounding the game gave the African American community other reasons to express their pride.[109]

The 1927 Southwestern Athletic Conference season ended with Bishop shocking Wiley, holding the highly favored Wildcats to a zero to zero tie. Texas College also tied Prairie View. The results of the games allowed Wiley to finish first in the conference and Prairie View to finish second.[110]

In the *Houston Informer*, sports editor Dean Mohr offered an end-of-season wrap-up. He stated that the Southwestern Athletic Conference championship never stayed at a school for more than one year. This fact allowed fans around the state to feel optimistic every year that their school might prove victorious. The conference also focused on running offenses, and postseason honors all went to running backs like Scott of Wiley, Owens of Samuel Huston, and Posey of Bishop.[111]

With the regular season over, for the second year in a row Wiley and Prairie View agreed to play a Christmas Day game in Beaumont. Having finished first and second, respectively, in the conference, the game promised a highly competitive contest between the two schools. Prairie View expressed their desire to avenge their earlier season loss to Wiley.[112] Yet Wiley won the game.

In recognition of the accomplishment of its football team, Wiley held a formal banquet on January 27, 1928. At the banquet, Wiley received the championship trophy for the 1927 season. Also, sixteen athletes received varsity sweaters and gold footballs in recognition of their accomplishments. Wiley's President Dogan presented the awards; the school orchestra provided entertainment; and C. F. Richardson, editor of the *Houston Informer*, and J. W. Rice, editor of the *Dallas Express*, attended as honored guests.[113]

While black college football offered African Americans an escape from the segregation in Texas and the South, racial problems still occurred. On June 20, 1928, the city of Houston recorded its only documented lynching. Robert Wood, the victim, killed a white police officer in a shootout. A white mob took Wood from Jefferson Davis Hospital, where he was undergoing treatment for wounds received in the fight. The mob then hung Wood from a bridge on Post Oak Road, west of the city.[114] The lynching proved extremely embarrassing for the city of Houston, as it occurred while the city was hosting the Democratic National Convention.[115]

As a new football season began for the SWAC in 1928, all conference schools felt optimistic about their chances at victory. A. W. Mumford, the Bishop College head coach, expressed high hopes based on the showing by his team in two weeks of hard practices he referred to as "survival of the fittest."[116] Other schools looked at the play of their teams in preseason scrimmages as evidence of their overall excellence. Once such football team, Wiley College, defeated Arkansas Baptist College in a scrimmage held in conjunction with the Central East Texas Fair. Wiley dominated the entire game. Its team scored touchdowns on the first two plays of the game, on their way to a forty-seven to zero victory.[117]

Other colleges also expressed optimism about the upcoming season. Paul Quinn coach Ray Sheppard announced that nearly twenty men reported for the team's first practice. While the number of football players at private Paul Quinn fell dramatically short of the one hundred players on state-supported Prairie View's 1927 team, the twenty athletes at Paul Quinn marked an increase over the previous year. As a result, coach Sheppard stated that things looked more promising for his team in 1928 than they did in 1927.[118]

The Wiley Wildcats faced Langston College for the fourth consecutive year as the featured sports attraction of Negro Day at the Dallas State Fair. Wiley entered the contest following a forty-seven to zero victory over Arkansas Baptist. With confidence running high, Coach Long expressed faith in his team.[119]

The Negro Day football game had become a major event in the African American community. A special train provided by the Texas and Pacific Railroad again brought the Wiley student body to the game. Also, a group calling themselves the Dallas Wiley Rooters organized a squad to cheer on their team.[120]

More than eight thousand fans attended the game and watched the two schools play to a seven to seven tie.[121] The *Houston Informer* sought to capture the excitement and emotion of the game: "As the shades of autumn were enveloping the Fair Park Stadium, where the thrilling and hectic contest had been bitterly waged, as the irresistible force and immoveable object clashed on the gridiron, the Wiley supporters . . . rent the air with a shout of joy and exultation; for the fact that Wiley had held to a tie her traditional enigma was sufficient reasoning for shouting and rejoicing on the part of the purple and white adherents."[122]

The halftime show received just as much attention as the football game. The featured attraction was the bathing suit revue. "Beautifully clad bathing models" paraded before the stands, with awards going to the winning contestants.[123]

The other Texas black college football teams also experienced positive outcomes the same weekend as the Wiley-Langston game. The Bishop Bears defeated New Orleans University by a score of forty-seven to zero. In the game, Joe Wilson, Bishop's fullback, collected twenty-four first downs. Also, the Bears' defensive line held New Orleans to exactly two positive rushing plays for a total of five yards.[124] On the same day, Paul Quinn defeated Houston Junior College, six to zero, and Prairie View A&M beat the Beaumont YMCA.[125]

On October 27, Wiley easily defeated the Samuel Huston Dragons by a score of twenty-six to zero. For many of the fans, the fact that their team lost proved to be of little consequence. In the Wiley-Samuel Huston game, the halftime performance of the Samuel Huston "Dragonettes" marked the highlight of the game. The drill team gave an exhibition, "the like of which has never been equaled by any college prep squad in the state."[126] The Dragonettes' performance culminated in the women forming the letters S. H. C. on the field in perfect unison.[127]

The Prairie View homecoming in 1928 offered a lively time for students, alumni, and fans. In the game, the Panthers outplayed Langston in every aspect of the game, dominating on both offense and defense. Unfortunately for the Prairie View faithful, Langston scored on a forward pass in the last minute of play to cause the game to end in a nineteen to nineteen tie.[128]

The Wiley-Bishop game on Thanksgiving Day in 1928 became a battle between two undefeated teams for the conference championship. Fans came from all over the state to witness the contest. In Marshall, ten thousand spectators, the largest crowd to ever watch the annual contest between the two colleges, sat through the wind and the rain and saw Wiley defeat Bishop, twelve to zero.[129] Wiley's ability to run the football provided the difference in the game on the muddy field. As a result, Wiley marched away with the 1928 conference champion.[130]

The Wiley-Bishop game created such excitement among Texas' African American community that several groups scheduled events in conjunction with the contest. The Colored Teachers' Association held its annual meeting in Marshall to coincide with the football game. Bishop College provided an alumni banquet the night before the game, complete with a student orchestra and a performance by the pep squad. After the game, Bishop held a social.[131]

The undefeated season by Wiley earned the team the black college national championship. Given out by the *Pittsburgh Courier*, Wiley shared the title with Bluefield State College of West Virginia. The award marked the third national championship for Wiley during the 1920s.[132]

As the 1928 season drew to a close, Prairie View coach James Law announced that his team planned to face Atlanta University at West End Park in Houston on New Year's Day. Prairie View commissioned a special train to carry fans from the college to the game. At the same time, the Southern Pacific Lines offered a special fare for the contest. Seventy-five percent of a normal one-way ticket purchased a round trip ticket to the game.[133]

The postseason bowl game between Prairie View A&M and Atlanta University attracted a large amount of interest. On December 29, the *Houston Informer* ran banners at both the top and bottom of the page announcing the New Year's Day game. The Prairie View squad even saw the paper publish a full team picture.[134]

Special trains came from Shreveport, Galveston, Dallas, Austin, San Antonio, and Fort Worth to carry fans to the game. Five to six hundred spectators alone rode the Galveston train. The San Antonio train also attracted large groups of people as the train company used five to six coaches for fans.[135]

The game eventually took place before more than six thousand spectators. The game offered a defensive battle that Atlanta University won, seven to zero. Reserve defensive end "Red" Jones for Atlanta intercepted a pass in the last minute of play and ran sixty-five yards for the winning touchdown.[136]

Following the excitement of the Prairie View bowl game, African Americans in Texas saw nine players from black colleges in Texas make the All-American team. Picked by Frank Young, sports editor for the *Chicago Defender*, four players—Roberts, a Bishop tackle; Harding, Wiley's quarterback; Marks, Prairie View's halfback; and Livingston, a Wiley end—all made first team All-American.[137]

When the 1929 SWAC season began, H. J. Mason, the Wiley business manager, announced that his college chose to face Prairie View A&M at the Dallas State Fair on October 21, instead of Langston College. The move ended a four-year rivalry between Wiley and Langston. Despite the change, the State Fair game still served as the kickoff to the black college football season in Texas.[138]

The switch also received support from several prominent African Americans in the state. O. P. DeWalt, owner of the Lincoln Theater in Houston, stated that with the growing importance of the state fair game, it made sense that the contest would feature the top two black colleges in Texas.[139] James D. Ryan wrote a letter to the *Dallas Express* extolling the business possibilities of a Prairie View–Wiley game.[140]

When the change took place, Mason refused to tell the black press the reasons behind the switch, but speculation followed Ryan's ideas and focused on the greater economic opportunities a Wiley versus Prairie View game offered. Of the five thousand fans who regularly attended the Wiley versus Langston game, all but a couple hundred supported Wiley. By replacing Langston with Prairie View, the attendance projected to double or triple.[141]

The State Fair game between the two Texas black colleges created more than economic opportunities. The game also provided a unifying point for the African American population around the state. The game, known as the State Fair Classic, promoted African American identity and cultural unity. The State Fair Classic followed a similar model as the Prep Bowl in Chicago that pitted the city's public-school champion against the top team from the Parochial Catholic League. The annual contest allowed Chicago Catholics to use sports to promote their identity, in a similar way the State Fair Classic worked for African Americans in Texas. Furthermore, football served as a means for Chicago Catholics to challenge the Protestant cultural hierarchy in the city.[142] The cultural importance placed by white Texans on the University of Texas' annual game against the University of Oklahoma, also at the Texas Stair Fair, reinforces the role of the Wiley and Prairie View contest for black Texans.

Wiley still planned to play Langston later in the season, just not in the State Fair game. But Langston refused to face Wiley in 1929, giving no reason for its decision to cancel its game against Wiley. The black press in Texas speculated the change occurred because of bitterness on the part of the Oklahoma college over being removed from the State Fair Classic.[143]

Excitement grew around the Wiley–Prairie View game at the State Fair in Dallas. The game's promoters believed the contest would attract the largest crowd to witness an African American football game in the South.[144] The *Houston Informer* declared, "Dallas has gone football crazy."[145] Thousands of fans poured into Dallas for the game, filling up hotels. Most of the early arrivals took part in the pregame festivities, "that seem to have almost as important a part to the success of the occasion as the game itself."[146] The Texas and Pacific Railway ran special trains for the game, while the Prairie View team and supporters arrived on a special fourteen-car train provided by the Southern Pacific Line.[147]

As far as the actual game preparations went, Wiley was the favorite. Led by quarterback "Runt" Johnson and fullback "Big Ben" Cavil, Wiley entered the game on a hot streak. The previous week they defeated Straight College of New Orleans, eighty-one to zero.[148]

A total of 8,500 fans attended the Wiley–Prairie View game, which ended in a zero to zero tie. The number marked an attendance record for African American day at the State Fair. The black press also reported that a number of white fans attended the game.[149]

The entertainment events added to the excitement and pageantry of the game. At halftime, the Wiley pep squad, led by Ruby Bedford, spelled out WILEY on the field, while accompanied by their college band. The Prairie View pep squad also spelled out their school's name on the field, making a giant P. V. Led by Rosetta Molett and Hermine Tabb, the Prairie View pep squad performed a step routine, accompanied by their school band.[150] According to the *Houston Informer*, the game marked "a new era in gridiron history in Texas."[151]

The State Fair Classic featuring Wiley and Prairie View was such a success that white college football sought to imitate the game. In 1929, the University of Texas and the University of Oklahoma resumed competition after a hiatus of more than five years. The two colleges chose to compete at Fair Park Stadium in Dallas in conjunction with the State Fair of Texas. Taking place two days before the Wiley–Prairie View contest, the University of Texas–University of Oklahoma game recorded an attendance of more than eighteen thousand fans.[152]

The week after the State Fair Classic, Wiley defeated Texas College, twenty-one to zero. Ben Cavil, the star fullback for Wiley, proved the difference maker in the game. Injured in the Wildcats game against Prairie View and not expected to play against Texas College, Cavil entered the game and immediately rushed for almost fifty yards. He also returned a punt seventy-eight yards for a touchdown.[153]

For the African American community in Texas, the football games that received the most attention occurred during holidays when a large number of fans were off work. In a rain-soaked game on Armistice Day, Bishop defeated Prairie View fourteen to six before several hundred fans.[154] Also, on Thanksgiving Day, three thousand fans journeyed to Marshall to watch Wiley edge past Bishop ten to eight. The only touchdown of the game came at the start of the second half when Wiley fullback Ben Cavil returned the kickoff ninety-nine yards for a touchdown.[155]

The 1929 black college football season came to a close when Prairie View faced Fisk University on New Year's Day. The second annual contest followed the pattern of postseason bowl games occurring in white college football. The game also offered African Americans a chance to celebrate their community outside the control of whites.[156]

The 1920s served as a period of substantial cultural growth for black Texans. Enrollment at the African American colleges in the state increased with the rise of the black middle class. As student populations went up, black colleges in Texas found themselves more financially stable. The increased revenues allowed Wiley and Prairie View, for example, to add classes and programs, thus improving the educational opportunities of African Americans in Texas.

One program that benefited from the increased finances was football. Black college football in Texas entered the 1920s as a popular but loosely structured sport. With the establishment of the Southwestern Athletic Conference in 1920, the college teams in Texas became an organized athletic conference with uniform schedules and a yearly champion. Administered by a committee consisting of the coaches and presidents from the member colleges, the SWAC set rules and regulations for play that brought black college football in Texas to an equal status with the best African American college teams in the country.

Black college football in Texas experienced other advancements during the 1920s. The colleges all employed professional coaches instead of having a professor to perform the job as a volunteer beyond his regular teaching responsibilities. Coaches like Fred Long of Wiley were former college football players, sometimes hailing from the college at which they coached. Unlike their counterparts at Texas white colleges, African American football coaches supervised more than one sport, and served as members of the faculty. In order for Wiley to afford a full-time football coach, Fred Long taught physical education classes in addition to coaching basketball, baseball, and track, but his primary position was football coach.

On the field, success caused black college football in Texas to become a source of community pride. Wiley College's three national championships during the decade, along with the creation of the State Fair Classic and the Prairie View Bowl, gave black Texans opportunities to celebrate their community and express their pride as a race. This community pride also caused attendance numbers for black college football to dramatically increase during the 1920s. Attendance for the State Fair Classic went from two thousand spectators in 1925 to more than six thousand in 1927. In 1928, the Wiley-Bishop contest on Thanksgiving Day attracted a record ten thousand fans to Marshall.

At the same time, individual players at Texas' black colleges achieved success and became heroes in the black community. During the 1920s, more than fifteen Texans earned All-American honors from the *Pittsburgh Courier*. One of the All-Americans, Samuel Huston quarterback "Silver Toe" Russ, received accolades from Alonzo Stagg, head coach at the University of Chicago.

For the African American population in Texas, another reason black college football became a dominant form of social expression was the style of play exhibited by the teams. For the most part, black college football teams in Texas followed successful predominantly white northern colleges like Notre Dame and used a running-based offense. The basic college offense at the time involved a variation of the T-formation, which used two halfbacks, a fullback, and a quarterback to carry the ball. However, black college football teams in Texas distinguished themselves by incorporating the forward pass more extensively. The use of the pass proved more exciting for the fans, in addition to making the African American version of college football unique.

As the country entered the 1930s, black college football in Texas began to experience a shift in focus. Throughout the 1920s, the colleges grew and thrived in Texas. The African American community focused on developing its own institutions and culture outside the control of whites. Black college football played a central role in the development of the community, since football games offered African Americans opportunities to celebrate their achievements in both physical and artistic endeavors. With the onset of the Great Depression, new issues and challenges dominated life. The general population primarily focused on acquiring or maintaining jobs, buying food, and paying rent. As a result, black college football in Texas changed to meet the new challenges that lay ahead.

3

The Great Depression
and Cultural Power

Beginning with the stock market crash of 1929, the Great Depression was one of the most catastrophic events in US history. The national income fell from eighty-one billion dollars in 1929 to forty billion dollars by 1932.[1] Millions of Americans watched as their life savings disappeared as a result of bank closings and foreclosures.

College football felt the economic crisis existing in the country caused by the loss of jobs and disposable income. In the 1920s, college football attendance skyrocketed. With the onset of the Great Depression, attendance figures dropped by 25 percent. During the boom period of the 1920s, many white universities amassed large debts in order to build new, bigger stadiums. Now these institutions found it hard to pay the interest on their loans. Schools that previously publicly promoted the greatness of their athletic revenues found themselves in debt. At universities like Ohio State and the University of Iowa, the administration cut minor sports in order to balance the athletic budget. At other colleges, members of the coaching staff found themselves among the unemployed as schools sought to ease debts by freeing up coaches' salaries.[2]

African Americans throughout the country felt the impact of the economic crisis. The majority of blacks still lived in the rural South. For these mostly agricultural workers, the Great Depression caused a drop in the demand for cotton and other staple crops. At the same time as the decrease in demand, farmers grew more crops, increased the supply, and caused the price of staple crops to fall dramatically. As a result, black sharecroppers found themselves unable to pay their rent and were thus evicted from their land.[3]

The Depression hurt African Americans in Texas severely. Black unemployment almost doubled from more than 4 percent in 1930 to more than 8 percent by 1933. An increase in the use of technology in farming, along with falling crop prices and less availability of credit, drove fifty thousand black Texans out of agriculture and forced thousands more to give up independent farming and become hired workers.[4] In towns, wages decreased, while many people lost jobs.[5]

In the 1930s, black culture became a source of strength against both the economic hardships of the time and racial prejudice. Building off the "New Negro" movement of the 1920s, African Americans found that through segregated institutions, they could express their opposition to the social injustices that were highly prevalent in American society. All-black institutions, such as colleges and college football, created positions of relative power and prominence for African Americans. From these positions of prominence, segregated institutions served as a form of resistance against aspects of white society.[6] Cultural power grew out of this resistance that allowed African Americans to express their feelings and emotions, as well as comment on social and political problems in the United States without white control.[7] Writers like Ralph Ellison, sports teams like the Kansas City Monarchs, and colleges such as Prairie View A&M created cultural power by presenting an image of the black community as strong, intelligent human beings who deserved equal rights.

At the same time, the new African American culture received some attention from white audiences. Black performers and sports stars became popular among white audiences, giving the black community access to new mediums and a stronger cultural voice. Duke Ellington performed in clubs that refused black patrons. Jesse Owens and Joe Louis both became world champion athletes whose accomplishments made them national heroes to both blacks and whites. While these two men found themselves limited in their social and professional opportunities because of racism, stars like Joe Louis served as a symbol and source of strength for African Americans in the struggle against economic and racial oppression.[8]

The interaction of African American culture and sports with white society, though, was limited. For the most part, African Americans participated in activities within their own communities. In Texas, black college football and other elements of society were isolated within the African American community and, similar to the experiences of Nisei Japanese in California, served as a cultural sanctuary away from outside influences. For both the Nisei and black Texans, this isolation included almost total avoidance of coverage by the white press.[9]

Black colleges struggled against the Depression. Schools such as Prairie View, with its state funds, and Wiley College, which possessed the most private funds of the schools in Texas, found themselves able to field well equipped, superior football teams. Prairie View, for example, enrolled more than one thousand students in 1930.[10] At the same time, schools with less financial flexibility, like Jarvis Christian College, felt pressure from students, alumni, and fans to field a football team, yet these teams rarely possessed a chance for success.[11] One Texas school, Paul Quinn, won two SWAC titles in the 1920s, but left the conference in 1929 because of the financial hardships brought on by the Great Depression.[12]

The SWAC held its annual meeting in Houston on December 20 and 21, 1929. The meeting marked the end of the 1920s version of black college football and ushered in a new, more organized style of play. The college representatives agreed to completely revise the conference constitution and bylaws, establishing stricter eligibility requirements and limiting the number of years a player could compete. The changes were prompted by the use of two ineligible players by Samuel Huston, as well as the fact that Ben Cavil of Wiley had just finished his fifth straight season on the Wildcat football team.[13]

As a result of the conference changes, Samuel Huston forfeited every game it won or tied in 1929. Wiley found itself allowed to keep its victories from the season, but the SWAC instituted a strict four-year eligibility rule. Also, Paul Quinn College, which left the conference before 1929, received readmittance, but only after paying a fifty-dollar fine, repaying conference dues, and maintaining a baseball season for the coming season.[14]

Supporting the new idea of cultural power, the *Houston Informer* ran an article extolling the virtues and importance of higher education for African Americans. The article praised the black colleges in Texas for "raising the standard of citizenship" and challenged every black parent to make sure their children attended some form of school.[15] Without an education, the paper warned, African Americans found themselves "left at the mercy of the cold, cold world."[16]

Sports played an important role in this push for higher education, in that sports like college football served as significant publicity for the schools' fielding teams. Future students' first exposure to a particular college might come from following a sports team. At the same time, once at the college, sports like football served as an impetus to stay enrolled in school for many current students.

The Texas colleges expressed hope for the 1930 season. Samuel Huston believed that it would have the best year in its history, as the school experienced its highest enrollment since 1927.[17] Meanwhile, Bishop College announced its new football coach, Thomas Harvey. Hailing from Washburn College in Topeka, Kansas, Harvey sought to "get every last ounce of energy and fight out of his men by gentle yet forceful persuasion."[18] Bishop also decided to change its mascot from the bear back to the tiger, which the school used until the mid-1920s.

The success of Negro Day at the State Fair of Texas saw other fairs copy the practice. The Central East Texas Fair in Marshall held its own Negro Day. Most Marshall businesses that employed African Americans gave their workers the day off, and the black schools in the city closed, allowing people to attend. Twenty-five black agricultural exhibits were displayed. Wiley College's twelve to zero victory over Houston Junior College in the fair's football game, followed by Gordon's gigantic fireworks, served as the centerpiece of the day's excitement.[19]

More than nine thousand spectators attended the annual Wiley–Prairie View State Fair game the next week. The game, which took place at new Fair Park Stadium in Dallas, was not decided until the closing minutes. Prairie View held a thirteen to ten lead with three minutes to play, but Wiley quarterback Johnson completed an eighty-yard pass to right halfback Evans for a touchdown and a seventeen to thirteen victory.[20] Fan excitement proved so high for the game that the *Houston Informer* devoted almost its entire sports page to coverage. The *Informer*'s article recounted every offensive possession for both teams, also including the starting rosters and a list of officials.[21]

The same weekend as the Wiley–Prairie View game, Bishop College won its first game of the season. Bishop defeated Samuel Huston by a score of two to zero. The only points in the game occurred when Samuel Huston safety Chandler attempted to return a punt from his own end zone. E. Calvert Flournoy, the Bishop captain, tackled Chandler for a safety and the two points.[22]

As the Depression worsened, the economic disparity between the African American colleges in Texas became more apparent. Schools with fewer resources, such as Texas College, saw their football teams lose continually. Other economically challenged colleges, such as Paul Quinn and Jarvis Christian, dropped their football programs altogether by the early 1930s as a result of the economic crisis. An example of the disparity occurred on November 1. That day saw Prairie View defeat Texas College, sixty-nine to zero, and Wiley beat Philander Smith of Arkansas, sixty-six to six.[23]

For the fans, though, the difference in the quality of play at the black colleges in Texas proved of little importance. Football games on national holidays continued to attract fans. Several thousand paid a one-dollar admission and sat through the rain to watch Prairie View defeat Bishop twenty to zero on Armistice Day. The game, which served as Prairie View's homecoming, featured the bands, cheerleaders, and female pep squads of the two colleges. Another attraction was the "brother act" that occurred. Prairie View featured running backs W. A. Nellum and A. Hardee, while Bishop employed running backs J. N. Nellum and L. F. Hardee.[24]

Another major holiday game, the annual Wiley-Bishop contest, took place on Thanksgiving Day. Before a couple thousand fans that traveled to Marshall, Wiley triumphed sixteen to zero. The victory gave Wiley the conference championship and a four-year winning streak over its crosstown rival.[25] The celebratory atmosphere surrounding the football games was most important. These celebrations fostered both cultural power and a way to combat the psychological impact of the Depression.

The 1930 season ended with two cultural events. First, the *Houston Informer* and Wiley coach Fred Long named the first all-southwest football team. Following the model established by Walter Camp in naming his white All-American team, Long and the *Houston Informer* featured players from African American colleges from throughout the Southwest, not just the SWAC. Players from schools such as Langston, Philander Smith, Southern, and Xavier received recognition, along with players from Bishop, Wiley, and Prairie View.[26]

The annual Prairie View Bowl on New Year's Day was the second cultural event to round out the season. For the first big game of 1931, Prairie View faced Tuskegee at Buffalo Stadium in Houston. Before the bowl, though, Prairie View played Texas College in a charity game to raise money to help African Americans fight the hardships of the Depression. Prairie View handled the money, and in turn distributed it to local families in need of assistance with bills or food. The charity game took place in Austin at Texas Memorial Stadium, the home of the University of Texas.[27]

When the New Year's Day game finally took place, Tuskegee

defeated Prairie View by a score of nineteen to seven. Fifteen thousand fans paid an admission fee of one dollar to watch the game, which featured performances by the school bands and pep squads. The game provided economic assistance to Houston's black community, while also furthering the idea of cultural power by accentuating the unique and more lively styles of performance by the colleges' bands and pep squads. The victory gave Tuskegee the black college national championship.[28]

The Prairie View Bowl was the second oldest bowl game in the United States behind the Rose Bowl. The profitability of these postseason games presented such an enticement during the Depression that several cities in the South and Southwest created postseason bowl games of their own for white college football. Places like Dallas, Miami, and New Orleans soon established the Cotton, Orange, and Sugar Bowls annually on New Year's Day as means to promote their cities and attract white fans by featuring the top white college football teams in the country. By copying the Rose Bowl, the host cities sought to use the revenue brought in by the games to improve their economic situation.[29]

The economy worsened going into the next academic year. Bishop attempted to lower its cost of living for students by creating a housekeeping department. Female students who agreed to participate in the program lived in dormitories for free, and in exchange performed light housekeeping work for the college.[30]

The 1931 football season started with a couple of coaching moves. George Collins began a second stint as the head coach of Bishop. Collins previously served as Bishop's coach in 1924 and 1925. He led the Tigers to their first conference championship in 1925. A. W. Mumford became the other black college coach to change jobs, taking over duties at Texas College. Mumford previously coached at Jarvis Christian in 1925 and Bishop from 1927 to 1929. The higher salaries Collins and Mumford received at their new schools prompted these coaching moves.[31]

But how much funding a college received was of little importance to the black community in the state, as long as the football team won. Prairie View opened its season by defeating the Houston Negro Junior College, thirty-two to zero. The larger roster of Prairie View allowed the coach to continually send in fresh players, thus overwhelming its smaller opponent.[32] Prairie View's greater economic standing allowed it to attract superior athletes, and fans grew more excited with each win.

The other Texas college with some financial resources, Wiley, also won its first game of the season, defeating Xavier College forty-nine to zero. Wiley dominated from the beginning, with freshman running back "Packing House" Adams scoring a touchdown three minutes into the game.[33] The game was a bit unusual in that it took place at night, under lights at Beidenharn Park in Shreveport. The night game allowed more fans to attend, while also offering a novelty not seen much in black college football at the time.[34]

The Wiley–Prairie View game at the State Fair of Texas still served as the dominant football game for Texas' African American community. The game's promoters expected the "biggest crowd to witness any race football game in the country this fall."[35] The *Houston Informer* added to the publicity and excitement surrounding the game when the paper called the previous year's contest "the best staged game in the Texas State Fair Stadium last fall."[36] The statement ranked the Wiley–Prairie View game over every white college game that also took place in the stadium.

Thousands of fans journeyed to Dallas to watch Prairie View defeat Wiley, twenty to zero. The *Houston Informer* gave a play-by-play account of how Prairie View "swept the ends, . . . ripped the lines into jagged holes, and . . . passed and kicked expertly."[37] The paper also offered a list of the many visitors and friends who added "class and fineness" to the affair, which "befitted the Southwest premier football classic."[38] The spectators consisted of local middle class and black elite whose names the readers would have recognized.

The few games that Bishop and Paul Quinn played in 1931 tended to go poorly for the two schools. Before a couple hundred fans in Little Rock, Bishop lost to Arkansas State College, twelve to seven.[39] The same day, the Houston Negro Junior College blanked Paul Quinn, twenty-four to zero.[40]

Holiday games drew significant fan attendance, and several Thanksgiving Day games took place around the state in 1931. In their annual game in Marshall, Wiley defeated Bishop twenty-six to zero. It marked only the third game of the season for Bishop, compared to seven for Wiley.[41]

Also on Thanksgiving Day, the Samuel Huston Dragons played the Don Juan Pirates, an all-star team from Galveston. Led by several players from black college teams, including Tweezer Williams from Wilberforce who returned a kickoff ninety yards, the Pirates defeated Samuel Huston by a score of seven to six. Several thousand spectators turned out in Austin to watch the game.[42]

As the 1931 season came to an end, Prairie View met Alabama State in the Panthers' annual New Year's Day game. Prairie View entered the game confident in its ability. This pride centered on the fact that no conference opponent had yet scored on the Panthers. In addition to showing the dominance of Prairie View, this record also illustrated the disparity between state-supported Prairie View and the private black colleges in Texas.[43]

Prairie View's optimism was well founded, as the Panthers defeated Alabama State twenty-seven to two. Between four and five thousand fans attended the game. The *Houston Informer* again published a play-by-play account, as well as a large picture showing the "sections of throngs who attended the football game."[44]

The economic problems brought on by the Great Depression continued into the 1932 season. The colleges still faced financial hardships brought on by the fact that the students possessed few resources to pay tuition. As a result, schools trimmed budgets and cut programs. Football teams felt the budget crunch. Wiley saw only twenty students report for the team's first practice. Unable to pay tuition, several players failed to return to school, including star running back "Packing House" Adams.[45] Also, the Wiley coaches cancelled a game against Fisk University in Nashville because of the travel expense.[46]

The 1932 season saw Paul Quinn College and Jarvis Christian College attempt to revive football after sitting out a couple of years. No longer members of the Southwestern Athletic Conference, Paul Quinn and Jarvis Christian found it hard to schedule opponents and to compete. As a result, both schools played a reduced number of games. Paul Quinn, for example, opened its season against Jackson High School from Corsicana. Jarvis Christian lost its opener to Texas College, thirty-three to zero. The game marked the first ever night game to take place in Tyler.[47]

The SWAC made efforts to survive the Depression, allowing new schools to join the conference. The Langston Lions began conference play in 1932, making them the first non-Texas college in the SWAC. Langston opened its SWAC affiliation by defeating Samuel Huston by a score of thirteen to zero.[48]

As the annual Wiley–Prairie View State Fair Classic approached, excitement grew among the African American population in Texas. Wiley entered the game on a winning streak, after defeating the Houston Negro Junior College thirty-six to zero before five thousand fans at the Central East Texas Fair in Marshall.[49] At the same time, the Texas press included a small mention that Houston bet makers favored Prairie View to win.[50]

The inclusion of the reference to gambling by the *Houston Informer* is interesting. Betting on sporting events has been a constant throughout history. Bookies taking odds on games and fans placing bets occurred weekly in college sports. The acknowledgement of such activities, while commonplace in the late twentieth and earl twenty-first centuries, rarely occurred in the black press during the first half of the century. The fact that the *Houston Informer* mentioned the odds makers for the contest serves as further proof of the high level of interest in the football game, and the significance of the contest for the black community.

Fans and companies clamored to be part of the event. The Southern Pacific Railroad offered a round trip ticket to the game for eleven dollars and forty-five cents. The Katy Lines offered a cheaper round trip fare of three dollars, but also advertised as part of the day's festivities a meeting of the "Colored Ferguson-for-Governor Club of Texas," a political organization that sought to garner black votes for Miriam Ferguson's 1932 campaign, with the hope that she in turn would support African American issues.[51] The special train fares and political rally increased the excitement surrounding Negro Day, causing the *Houston Informer* to declare, "Dallas is all agog over the outcome. Already, great plans are laid by the alumni of both schools to entertain the thousands that trek annually here to witness these premier football teams of the Southwest."[52]

The *Houston Informer* was correct in its prediction, as eight thousand spectators watched Wiley upset Prairie View thirteen to zero. Wiley dominated Prairie View from the start of the contest. One play that brought the fans to their feet occurred when the "fleet-footed, hip-shaking Pat Patterson" returned a punt seventy-five yards for a Wiley touchdown.[53] The large fan turnout made the Negro Day game at the State Fair the highest attended black college football game in the Southwest.

Meanwhile, Langston took the conference lead, after defeating Texas College, six to zero. Despite only scoring six points, Langston ran over the Steers, amassing twenty-six first downs. At the same time, fan attention grew for the Wiley-Langston game scheduled for Armistice Day, since it would determine the conference champion.[54] Wiley added to the excitement over the Armistice Day game by declaring the contest its homecoming. The school made preparations to entertain its returning graduates. For the fans, the accompanying dances, parades, and other festivities added to the celebration and importance of the holiday.[55]

When Armistice Day arrived, Wiley finally faced Langston. The *Houston Informer* declared the game "one of the fiercest gridiron contests in the history of the Southwestern Conference . . ."[56] In the end, Wiley emerged victorious, winning thirteen to eight.[57] The victory allowed black Texans to proclaim the athletic superiority of their state over neighboring Oklahoma.

Other Texas black colleges also sought to capitalize on the fan excitement surrounding the Armistice Day games. The Samuel Huston Dragons defeated the Texas College Steers by a score of eighteen to six, and Prairie View beat Bishop twenty-three to zero. In honor of Armistice Day, the Prairie View student body and college cadets marched from the stadium to the chapel for scripture readings, the singalongs, a performance by the cadet band, and a guest speaker. After the festivities, approximately one thousand fans attended the football game.[58]

For the conclusion of the 1932 season, Prairie View again hosted Tuskegee in the annual Prairie View Bowl on New Year's Day. Two thousand fans filled Buffalo Stadium in Houston to watch Prairie View defeat Tuskegee. Led by triple-threat running back Howard Love, who scored two touchdowns, the Panthers won the game by a score of fourteen to zero.[59] "Snake" Williams, sportswriter for the *Houston Informer*, stated that the Prairie View victory over Tuskegee proved the superiority of black college football in Texas.[60]

With the 1932 football season, black Texans received another reason to express pride in their community. On account of its record of nine wins and zero losses, Wiley College won the black college national championship. The title marked the fourth for the school, and the third for head coach Fred Long.[61]

The possibility of economic recovery for the United States appeared in 1932. In November, Americans elected Franklin Delano Roosevelt president. FDR's New Deal created a wide array of government agencies and programs to combat the Depression.[62] Programs like the Civilian Conservation Corps (CCC) provided jobs for youths in an effort to stimulate the economy. Discrimination did exist within the programs, though. For example, the CCC built segregated camps and saw local officials administer the program unfairly. In its first year, only 5 percent of CCC spots went to black youths. While the percentage of African Americans aided by the CCC and other New Deal agencies remained smaller than the white population percentage, the government programs served as the only protection for thousands of black families from starvation.[63]

In Texas, a group of African American leaders, including C. F. Richardson, editor of the *Houston Informer*, met with Governor Miriam Ferguson and proposed ideas to aid black Texans in combating the Great Depression. The leaders also asked for the creation of a committee to prepare legislation to help African Americans. This committee planned to stay in Austin during the legislative session to pressure the state government for new efforts.[64]

The optimism surrounding the New Deal and the potential of an improved economy carried over to black college football. Schools saw their enrollments increase and attendance numbers grow. One school, Texas College, felt its prospects looked brighter since the majority of the previous year's team returned to campus.[65] The *Houston Informer* also got caught up in the excitement. In an effort to show appreciation to the fans of the SWAC for their support of college football during such hard times, the paper created a silver plated thirteen-inch loving cup to go to the conference champion.[66]

Texas College's optimistic view of its future included more than just success on the football field. In 1932, Texas College received senior college accreditation.[67] The accreditation raised Texas College academically to an equal level with the other black colleges in the state and nation.

For African Americans in Texas, the SWAC championship had come to mark a major source of pride. If a college competed for or won the title, its financial resources grew because the victory brought increased enrollment, higher game attendance, and more alumni and fan support. Wiley felt its chances for the championship trophy appeared slim after the Wildcats' first game. It defeated an inferior Jarvis Christian team by a score of only eighteen to zero. Despite the poor play, a large crowd attending the Central East Texas Fair watched Wiley struggle to win the game. One bright spot for Wiley came in the return of running back "Packing House" Adams. Adams failed to return to school on the first day of class as he attempted to find a job. After not finding work, he returned to Wiley.[68]

The success and popularity of football at the Texas black colleges created an increase in interest in other extracurricular activities. Wiley's debate team established itself as one of the best in the United States during the 1930s. The team, coached by poet and Wiley professor Melvin

Tolson, faced Oklahoma City University in 1929 in the first interracial debate in the country, defeated national champion University of Southern California in 1934, and at one point had a ten-year winning streak.[69] Sports like tennis, track and field, and basketball also grew during the 1930s as students became excited about competing for their college after watching the success of their respective schools' football teams.[70]

Despite increased student interest in athletics, interracial competition still did not occur (beyond the realm of the Wiley debate team). In Texas and the South, competition between white and black colleges simply did not occur. In other parts of the country, interracial sports contests slowly increased, however. In San Francisco, for example, basketball contests between people of diverse racial and ethnic backgrounds took place at levels ranging from community park gatherings to semiprofessional team play.[71]

The excitement that surrounded the Wiley–Prairie View State Fair game remained as the two schools met in 1933. Wiley entered the game after beating Samuel Huston forty-five to zero, while Prairie View beat Paul Quinn the week before forty to zero. Fans were energized by the annual contest between the two elite teams. With the accompanying events, such as a half-time performance by Prairie View's forty-piece band, the game also took on a celebratory atmosphere, which appealed to fans as an expression of their culture, as well as an escape from the problems of the Great Depression.[72]

Seven thousand spectators watched Wiley defeat Prairie View six to zero. Prairie View fumbled on the opening possession, and Wiley converted the turnover into a touchdown for the only points of the game. An example of the prominent cultural role played by the game occurred on the front page of the *Houston Informer*, where the paper ran an article listing the black social elite who attended. The spectator list consisted of just names with no mention of their employment or background, assuming the newspaper readers knew the occupation and social position held by the spectators. The *Informer* left the details of the actual game itself to a small article on the sports page.[73]

The African American community in Texas followed Wiley closely as the 1933 season came to an end, when it appeared that the Wildcats might win back-to-back national championships. The excitement really grew when Wiley beat undefeated Kentucky State, thirteen to twelve. Before five thousand fans in Louisville, Kentucky, Wiley running back

"Packing House" Adams scored the winning touchdown on a twenty-two-yard run in the closing minutes.[74]

The possibility of a national championship existed as a more exciting topic for Wiley and its supporters than economic fears concerning the Depression. As a result, Wiley paid for its football team to travel to Louisville to face Kentucky State, and then the next week to travel to Atlanta to face Morris Brown University. Unfortunately for the Wildcats, their hopes of a national championship came to an end in Atlanta. Morris Brown won twelve to seven, giving Wiley their first loss since October 26, 1931.[75]

The dominant element of life in the 1930s, though, remained the Great Depression. With the election of Franklin Delano Roosevelt in 1932, the federal government played a more direct role in helping people find work and shoring up the national economy. The assistance given to African Americans in the "New Deal" was less than the aid received by white Americans. Furthermore, when administered, the relief programs were not uniformly enforced throughout the country. Southern farmers, for example, sought to keep African Americans from joining relief programs that might encourage black laborers to leave their positions as inexpensive farm hands for better paying city jobs. Compared to other southern states, though, Texas established a better record on African American involvement in government programs.[76]

In 1933, African Americans in Texas received more assistance from the New Deal. In November, the Civil Works Administration hired one hundred black men. These men received a steady government paycheck to clean drainage ditches of wood and trash.[77] For the men who had been unemployed, the work was a godsend, both monetarily and psychologically.

Meanwhile, Wiley and Prairie View, whose economic situations were slightly better than their fellow black colleges, focused on a different theme for the football season. Wiley prepared for its homecoming game against Tuskegee. The Wildcats scheduled a breakfast dance before the game, a special homecoming chapel program, and a postgame party hosted by Eula Williams, "Miss Wiley."[78] As far as the actual football game, four thousand spectators watched Wiley win thirteen to zero. The *Houston Informer* built up the importance of the win and its support among the community. The paper stated, "Sweeping down from their lair with the fury of an angry sea that carries all in its path to oblivion, the Wiley Wildcats smothered the mighty Tuskegee Tigers."[79]

The 1933 season came to an end in interesting fashion, one that offered black Texans much to debate. Prairie View defeated Langston University in the Panther's annual New Year's Day game. The victory left Prairie View, Langston, and Wiley all one loss in conference, thus creating a three-way tie for first place. As a result, no team received the new loving cup trophy the *Houston Informer* had commissioned and planned to give to the conference champion.[80] Fans argued among themselves over which school was superior. The *Houston Informer* furthered the excitement before the game by holding a drawing in which the paper gave away tickets to the New Year's Day game. The hope of winning the free tickets added to the fans' excitement, which in turn carried over after the contest in the debate over which school's football team was superior.[81]

Prairie View chose to celebrate its successful season by holding a banquet for the fifty-member football team. Since the Depression limited the amount of money the school could spend, the juniors and seniors of Prairie View's home economics department prepared a turkey dinner. The next night, the college held a "Varsity Football Hop," at which "fair ladies informally yet gloriously attired in the season's latest creations, and stately knights of gridiron fame" danced to the music of Jacquet and his Merry Makers from eight until midnight curfew.[82]

Black colleges in Texas also found academic accomplishments to celebrate. Wiley College received an A rating from the Southern Association of Colleges and Secondary Schools in 1933. The award made Wiley the first black college in Texas to earn the ranking. Samuel Huston received an A rating the next year,[83] as did Prairie View.[84]

The difference in the caliber of play at Texas' African American colleges didn't go unnoticed by the black press in 1934. After Prairie View beat Paul Quinn by a score of thirty-three to zero, the *Houston Informer* described the Tigers as "lighter."[85] Most of the paper's attention went to the upcoming Wiley–Prairie View game. The numerous articles on the State Fair game gave team rosters, descriptions of star players such as Wiley's quarterback Pat Patterson, and predictions of the contest's outcome.[86]

The black press in 1934 covered a new star player, poised to possibly take away attention from the college football teams in Texas. The player was Ossie Simmons of the University of Iowa. Simmons, who hailed from Gainesville, became one of the first black players from Texas to play for a white university. As a sophomore, the Texas native became an instant success for the Hawkeyes. In his first play from scrimmage, the "streak of ebony lightning" rushed fifty-one yards for a touchdown.[87]

Cracks now began to appear in the system of segregation in college football. A long-standing tradition existed where integrated northern colleges agreed to bench their African American athletes when facing southern schools. By the 1930s, this practice began to change. For example, when the University of North Carolina faced New York University at the Polo Grounds in New York City in 1936, Ed Williams, the African American running back for NYU, competed in the contest. A decade before, his college would have held him out of the action.[88]

Still, the racial situation in football faced a long, difficult climb. In 1933, Ray Kemp and Joe Lillard, two African American professional football players, were cut by their National Football League teams. With the release of the two men, no black athletes suited up for any professional football teams in America until 1946.[89]

Simmons's accomplishments received praise from the bulk of Texas' African American community, but his popularity still came in second to the Wiley–Prairie View game. Special trains again ran from Houston and Marshall to carry fans to the game. Also, Dallas citizens planned parties and dances to accompany the game, lasting from Friday evening to Tuesday morning. The *Dallas Express* even told of one Wiley supporter who placed a two hundred dollar bet on his team, an enormous sum considering the economic times.[90] The paper then summed up the excitement, saying, "Dallas is one big happy family waiting for its flock of visitors from all parts of the Southwest to enjoy real Southern hospitality."[91]

Unfortunately for the Wiley bettor, Prairie View won the game thirteen to ten. Nine thousand spectators filled the State Fair Park and took part in the accompanying parties, open houses, dances, and other social events sponsored by alumni and fans of Wiley and Prairie View. The baby parade and contest, won by three-year-old Betty June Hornsby, attracted the largest audience of all the social activities.[92]

The 1934 season followed the same pattern as the previous years, with Wiley and Prairie View dominating the state, and Bishop and Paul Quinn occupying the bottom positions. The only surprise on the season came from the Texas College Steers, whose team challenged for the conference title. Evidence of the Steers' powerful new team came when they tied Wiley, seven to seven. In the closing minutes of the game, Texas College running back Myles Anderson threw a halfback option pass to Ed Turner for a tie.[93]

Texas College followed its solid effort against Wiley by thoroughly trouncing Mary Allen College, 102 to 0. The Steers scored thirty-eight points in the first eight minutes of play. Texas College coach Mumford then sent in his second and third teams in an effort to slow the scoring, but to no avail. In the end, every player on the Texas College team saw action.[94] The victory for Texas College was lessened by the fact that Mary Allen previously served as an African American women's college until 1933, when the school became a coeducational junior college.[95]

Texas College's success attracted more fan attention to black college football. The Steers appeared the favorites to win the conference title after defeating Prairie View at the Panthers' homecoming. Texas College then beat Southern University fifty-four to seven before eight hundred spectators in Tyler.[96]

The 1934 season came to an end with Texas College's thirteen to two victory over undefeated Langston College. Led by coach A. W. Mumford, the Steers finished the season with a record of nine wins, zero losses, and one tie. As a result, Texas College won its first ever Southwestern Athletic Conference championship.[97]

Texas College continued its winning ways in the 1935 season. Despite losing six veterans off the previous year's team, coach Mumford reported that many of the black high school stars from Texas applied for admittance to the college. Texas College even announced that several students from the Midwest and New England sent applications in the hope of playing football for the Tyler college.[98]

Other changes took place in 1935. Wiley announced that it had erected lights at its Marshall field, and as a result planned to play five night games. The night games allowed more spectators to attend, thus improving the team's popularity.[99]

Some relief from the Depression came to Bishop College by way of the Federal government. The National Youth Administration, a government agency created to help students pay for college, gave scholarships to 150 students. The awards ranged in amount from fifty dollars to two hundred fifty dollars. Without these awards, the recipients had no possibility of attending the college.[100]

Bishop's optimism for a successful season increased after winning its first two games. In one, the Tigers defeated Jarvis Christian twenty-eight to twelve. Bishop then turned its attention to Wiley, which beat Paul Quinn by a score of forty-seven to seven to open the season.[101]

Texas College, though, remained the dominant team in the conference. The Steers opened their season by beating Arkansas State sixty-five to six. Texas College scored its first touchdown two minutes into the game on a fifty-six-yard run by star running back Anderson.[102]

With support for black college football running high, the Wiley–Prairie View game became the most attended African American game in Texas. With the 1935 game, though, the black press advertised the social events accompanying the game as much as the press covered the actual contest itself. For the proceeding weeks, articles appeared that told of the upcoming house parties, dances, stags, and smokers scheduled for the State Fair weekend. One article promoted the upcoming performance of the Original Wiley Collegians, a band made up of Wiley students, at the North Dallas Club, and compared the excitement surrounding the State Fair game to the excitement associated with Juneteenth celebrations.[103] The accompanying events illustrated the segregation at the Fair and in Dallas since all of the dances, parties, and concerts took place in African American citizens' homes or in black clubs, like the Original Wiley Collegians' concert at the North Dallas Club, and not at Fair Park or City of Dallas public facilities.

The game ended in a zero to zero tie before six thousand fans in Dallas.[104] The black press covered the game but focused more attention on the social events. The *Informer*'s women section devoted its entire page to the attire of the spectators, declaring, "Costumes at football classic portray height of fashion."[105]

While Texas College ran away with the conference, the other colleges also fielded quality teams. Bishop's team won several games on the season, a vast improvement over the previous few years. Wiley kept its title hopes alive by beating Samuel Huston seventy-one to zero.[106]

For African Americans in Texas, the highlight of the 1935 football season occurred on Thanksgiving Day when Wiley and Texas College faced each other for the conference championship. Texas College entered the game undefeated, while Wiley sported only the tie with Prairie View. Three thousand fans came to Marshall to watch the contest. Texas College found itself shorthanded when All-American fullback Myles Anderson missed the game after sustaining injuries in an automobile accident. As a result, the game ended in a zero to zero tie, but Texas College still won the conference title.[107]

The 1935 football season came to an end with two postseason bowl games. Prairie View faced Wiley in the Panther's annual New Year's Day game. The Prairie View Bowl, which usually occupied a prominent place in the African American community of Texas, found itself second behind the "Chocolate Bowl" in Tyler.[108] The Tyler game saw Texas College face Alabama State, champion of the Southern Intercollegiate Athletic Association, for the black college national championship. In the end, one thousand fans sat through wind and freezing rain to watch Texas College defeat Alabama State, nine to zero, to become champions.[109]

Before the 1936 season, black college football in Texas underwent some changes. First, Arkansas State University and Southern University joined the SWAC. The addition of these schools and their annual dues increased the monetary reserves of the conference. Second, the Texas College coach for the 1935 national championship team, A. W. Mumford, left the Steers for Southern University of Louisiana and a larger paycheck.[110]

That fall, another major event took place. In 1936, the state of Texas planned a Centennial Exposition to take place at the Texas State Fair in Dallas. The Centennial Expo organizers sought for the event to be one of the largest and most prominent in recent history in the country. As exhibits came in from all over the state and country, the US federal government provided one hundred thousand dollars for the collection, transportation, and housing of African American exhibits as a part of the Expo. Even though the federal funding guaranteed the inclusion of African American exhibits, the Centennial Expo further illustrated the nature of segregated life in Texas. The state government and the city of Dallas both refused to provide any assistance for the black artists who participated. African Americans faced segregated facilities and a lack of help from building contractors, which made it exponentially more difficult for black participants to show their work, compared to their white counterparts. Even with the difficulties, seventy thousand people turned out on the designated African American days to view the exhibits and see performers such as Cab Calloway and Duke Ellington.[111]

With the publicity surrounding the 1936 Centennial, fans in Texas became enthusiastic about the football season as soon as the school year began. The black press wrote articles on the upcoming Wiley–Prairie View

State Fair game over a month before the contest. These articles stressed the celebratory atmosphere of the day. Early hype around the game focused on achievements in African American education. Several black fraternities and sororities operated booths at the fair, while also entering floats in the annual parade.[112] Since the 1936 State Fair also served as the Texas Centennial celebration, Texas Governor Allred declared October 19 the day of the Wiley–Prairie View football game, a holiday for all African American school children, in the hopes of attracting more fans.[113]

The 1936 Centennial State Fair Classic between Wiley and Prairie View lived up to expectations as the social event of the year for Texas' black community. An estimated seventy thousand people flocked to Dallas. Every black restaurant, hotel, and café in Dallas, along with the black YMCA, rented all available rooms. Thousands of visitors found themselves forced to sleep in their cars.[114]

Of the many visitors to the State Fair, eighteen thousand fans attended the football game at the Fair Park stadium. Wiley emerged victorious in the contest, seven to zero. The game was so popular that several celebrities from around the country attended, including musician Duke Ellington.[115] Further illustrating the community interest in the State Fair game, the *Houston Informer* limited coverage of defending national champion Texas College's victory over Jarvis Christian to a paragraph in the bottom corner of the sports page.[116]

The promoters of the state Centennial were so impressed by the turnout for the Wiley–Prairie View game, they wanted to book a second black college football game for the Cotton Bowl in Fair Park. They sought to schedule the game for Thanksgiving Day, hoping that the holiday, along with the Texas State Teacher's Association's meeting in Dallas on the same day, would attract a record-setting crowd. The promoters targeted the Wiley–Texas College game, previously scheduled for Thanksgiving Day in Tyler.[117]

At the same time, the *Houston Informer* began a weekly serial entitled "Big Time Football." The story took place at Samuel Huston College, and discussed the excitement and life brought to the college campus by football.[118] This piece of fiction, which ran in the gossip section, illustrated the prominent role college football held in the African American cultural identity at the time. By serving as the subject of a popular literary work, college football was a topic that most readers understood and in which they expressed interest; otherwise the serial would not have been successful.

Black college football in Texas rode the wave of enthusiasm created by the State Fair game. Prairie View planned the "greatest homecoming program in the history of the institute."[119] Along with the Panthers' game against Xavier, Prairie View held a parade led by the school's fifty-piece marching band, a fireworks show, several dances, banquets, and the crowning of the "Alumni Sweetheart."[120]

The celebratory atmosphere of homecoming games next spread to Texas College. A total of 1,500 spectators attended the Steers' three to zero victory over Southern. Along with the football game, Texas College also held a pigskin review, a bonfire, and a parade. The parade featured the school's orchestra, several student and alumni floats, and the crowning of Rhoelia Cook as "Miss Texas College." The parade was especially popular, with five thousand spectators lining the parade route.[121]

While the Texas Centennial celebration hoped to move the Wiley–Texas College game to Dallas, the plan never came to fruition. Instead, three thousand spectators traveled to Tyler to watch Texas College triumph by a score of eight to zero. The victory gave the Steers their third straight Southwestern Athletic Conference title.[122]

Texas College's win represented the school's first ever victory over Wiley. The Steers' fans became so excited that they "swarmed over the restraining fence" and stood around the field.[123] Not everyone in the state expressed excitement over the victory. The *Houston Informer* declared that the Texas College supporters "exercised very poor taste" by storming the field and by criticizing the officials' calls during the game.[124]

Prairie View finished off the season by competing in two postseason bowl games. First, the Panthers defeated the Florida A&M Rattlers six to zero in the Orange Blossom Classic. Held in Jacksonville, Florida, the Orange Blossom Classic brought in fans from all over the country. The contest offered African Americans another national bowl game through which they could celebrate their culture.[125]

Prairie View also competed in the Panther's own New Year's Day Prairie View Bowl. Four thousand fans filled Buffalo Stadium in Houston to watch Prairie View beat Tuskegee six to zero. Prairie View's victory in the two bowl games allowed black Texans to express a great deal of pride. Since the next to last team in the SWAC defeated two of the top black college programs in the country, fans in Texas could brag about the superior quality of the state's athletes.[126]

The cultural power African Americans derived from success in athletics proved substantial by the late 1930s. In Texas, college football played a prominent role, but nationally no sporting event received more coverage by the black press than the 1936 Berlin Olympics. Because of the successes by Jessie Owens and other African American athletes at the games, the Olympics broadened the perspective of some whites in regard to black Americans. For other whites, Owens's defeat of Nazi racial ideology remained completely separate from racial attitudes in America, where new arguments about African American athletic superiority became based around physical strength and "unthinking" competitions. At the same time, the black press in the United States believed that the triumphs of the athletes in Berlin served as an incentive for African Americans at home to push for advancement in other fields, to avoid stereotypes of blacks as only athletes.[127]

As the 1937 football season began, Roy E. Dixon, sports editor for the *Houston Informer*, expressed black Texans' optimistic view of the future. Dixon wrote, "Pre-season interest on the part of football fans, a decided change in business and employment conditions and the substantial improvements and innovations made in various athletic plants are all indicative that football is on the threshold of its most promising and profitable era."[128]

The most important game for establishing the fan interest continued to be the State Fair Classic. In the 1937 edition of the contest, promoters anticipated around sixty thousand spectators for Negro Day at the fair. These fans attended the game, but also participated in the "gala round of bon vivant festivities that parallel the acme of sport promotions in this area."[129]

The *Dallas Express* ran several front-page articles promoting the contest between Wiley and Prairie View. The articles again focused on the events accompanying the game. Prairie View's swing band performed for a dance in the Agricultural Building at the Fair Grounds. The Dallas Black Chamber of Commerce also obtained a permit to hold a citywide parade. The participation of Dallas's African American policemen marked the highlight of the parade.[130]

When the football game occurred, more than twelve thousand spectators converged on the Cotton Bowl. Prairie View exacted revenge for its defeat the previous year by beating Wiley thirteen to zero. The *Houston Informer* declared the game the "most colorful and best played game in the history of the Annual Dallas Classic."[131]

Jarvis Christian, Bishop, and Texas College all experienced positive outcomes in their games that weekend. Jarvis Christian defeated Butler College, twenty-seven to zero. At the same time, Bishop pulled off an upset by holding Xavier to a zero to zero tie. Two frontrunners in the quest for the conference championship, Arkansas State and Texas College, also played to a six to six tie.[132]

By the end of October, though, Texas' colleges brought up the bottom three places in the SWAC. Langston and Arkansas State tied for first place with two conference wins and zero losses. At the same time, Prairie View's record stood at one win and two losses, and neither Wiley nor Bishop had yet won a conference game. Still fan support ran high.[133]

When Texas College faced Langston in Tyler on October 30, a large and enthusiastic crowd gathered for the Steers' homecoming. Fans from North and East Texas attended the festivities, including the "pigskin review" that featured coeds and students, a bonfire, and a parade. Doris Ragsdale, who the Texas College student elected "Miss Homecoming," led the parade on a float shaped like a giant football. The entire student body took part in the parade, which attracted thousands of spectators.[134]

Of the many people who attended the homecoming festivities, three thousand "rabid, thrill-tinged football fans" watched Texas College triumph over Langston twenty to thirteen.[135] Quarterback Izzy Girdy led the Steers in the "wide open devil-may-care offensive thriller."[136] With the victory, Texas College took the lead in the conference standings.

For Texas' African American population, the interest in the football season wound down with a pair of football games on Thanksgiving Day. In one game, Prairie View came out victorious over Southern by a score of thirteen to seven. The victory gave Prairie a winning record on the season.[137]

The other Thanksgiving game took place between Texas College and Wiley. The two teams entered the contest ranked first and second in the conference, respectively, and as a result, the victor would be SWAC champion. Four thousand fans packed Marshall's East Texas Fair Park Stadium to watch Texas College win its fourth consecutive championship.[138]

The 1937 season wrapped up with the annual Prairie View Bowl game on New Year's Day. Prairie View faced Florida A&M. At the same time, black Texans celebrated the selection of Texas College quarterback Izzy Girdy to the black All-American first team.[139]

Bishop started the 1938 season by defeating crosstown rival Wiley by a score of twelve to zero. Five thousand "amazed" fans converged in Marshall for the East Texas State Fair game. For Bishop, the win was extra special since the victory marked the first time in fourteen years that the Tigers beat the Wildcats.[140]

For the African American community, Bishop's victory created a great deal of new excitement around black college football. The success of the once hapless Tigers energized fans who had become complacent with the winning streaks of Prairie View, Wiley, and Texas College. Also, with Prairie View's victory over Texas College, and Wiley's defeat of Arkansas State, it appeared that the Texas schools would dominate the conference in 1938.[141]

The enthusiasm over football grew with the coming of the annual Wiley–Prairie View matchup. Both schools came into the contest following victories the previous week. As a result, eight thousand spectators attended the game, which ended in a six to six tie.[142]

Texas College, though, managed to take a lot of the attention away from the State Fair Classic. Playing on the same day as Wiley and Prairie View, Texas College defeated Kentucky State thirty-three to six. Texas College's victory over the defending national champions also occurred in the Cotton Bowl, following the Wiley and Prairie View game.[143] As a result of the two games in Dallas, black college football in Texas received national attention.

Texas African Americans turned out in droves for the college football games. Five thousand people attended Prairie View's homecoming game against Arkansas State.[144] A total of 3,500 fans traveled to Shreveport to watch Wiley beat the Southern Jaguars in the Louisiana State Fair Classic.[145] Even Jarvis Christian saw several thousand spectators attend the Bulldogs' seven to zero homecoming victory over Samuel Huston.[146]

Langston College won the SWAC in 1938, but Black Texans found an opportunity in the Prairie View Bowl to erase the disappointment that occurred during the regular season. Widespread interest for the game existed among fans that looked to Prairie View and Tuskegee as a means to celebrate a new year. As a result, a record crowd attended the game, which ended in a thirty-four to zero victory for the Panthers.[147]

By the end of the 1930s, college football thrived. The weekly game offered fans an escape from the problems of everyday life.[148] For Texas' black colleges, the late 1930s also marked an increase in enrollment figures. Bishop, for example, enrolled six hundred students in 1939, a record for the school.[149] Bishop saw forty students come out for football on the first day of classes. Forty-two young men answered the call for players at Prairie View. Only twenty-nine players came out for Wiley's team, however. The absence of the Wildcats' veterans proved a mystery.[150]

Wiley scheduled ten football games for the upcoming season, including a game against national powerhouse Kentucky State. Samuel Huston hoped to end its losing ways by hiring a new coach, Jesse Chase, a graduate of Boston University.[151] The *Houston Informer* even ran a headline declaring "Football Is Vogue in Southwest."[152]

In Texas, black college football remained a main source of cultural power. For example, Bishop College opened its season with Leland College, while Texas College prepared to face Kentucky State. These games received a great deal of coverage by the black press, but the game that continued to receive the most attention from black Texans was the State Fair Classic. Coverage of the October 16 game began a month before the two schools faced each other at the Cotton Bowl.[153]

The popularity of the Wylie–Prairie View matchup, along with the improved financial situation in the country, saw the promoters of the football game raise ticket prices from seventy-five cents to one dollar and ten cents. Special trains and buses again offered discounted fares to spectators traveling to Dallas for the State Fair's Negro Day. [154]

When Negro Day took place at the State Fair, the black community's turnout exceeded expectations. Eighty thousand African Americans attended the fair. They participated in the attractions, including the opening parade through North Dallas, a baby derby, and a bathing beauty contest. The day was so popular that the Dallas Negro Chamber of Commerce created a permanent organization to promote the day every year.[155]

Twelve thousand of the State Fair's visitors attended the Wiley–Prairie View football game at the Cotton Bowl. According to the *Houston Informer*, the fans made up "one of the gayest crowds in the classic's history." They witnessed an exciting, offensive-oriented game, which ended in a thirteen to six victory for Wiley.[156]

The increased popularity continued throughout the season. When Wiley faced Xavier at a neutral site in Waco on November 17, an estimated ten thousand spectators attended the game.[157] Three thousand fans sat through freezing rain to cheer on the Panthers as they tied SWAC champions Langston on November 25. The same day, four thousand fans watched Wiley beat Texas College by a score of twenty to six.[158]

The 1939 black college football season came to a close in Texas with Wiley receiving an invitation to face Florida A&M in the Orange Blossom Classic, which moved to Tallahassee, on December 9.[159] Also, Prairie View chose Xavier University as its opponent for the annual Prairie View Bowl on New Year's Day. The two games each drew more than five thousand spectators.[160]

The 1930s marked a period of major highs and lows for the African American community in Texas. The Great Depression represented the worst economic disaster in US history. Black college football, though, experienced some growth and success during the Depression. The SWAC amended its constitution to impose stricter rules for player eligibility, making black college football in Texas more regulated and organized. Two of the colleges won the national championship during the 1930s, Wiley in 1932 and Texas College in 1935. Seven players from African American college football teams in Texas also made the *Pittsburgh Courier* All-American team during the 1930s.[161]

These events increased the popularity of black college football. Special games like the Prairie View Bowl on New Year's Day and the State Fair Classic in October annually attracted larger crowds. The events that accompanied the special games, like the baby parade or swimsuit competition at the State Fair Classic, became major celebrations and points of pride in the African American community.

African American culture changed in the 1940s as the world's problems came to dominate the thoughts and affairs of black Texans. African Americans continued to push for more social and economic equality in the United States. Ultimately, World War II became the significant feature of life during the next decade, bringing with it significant changes.

4
War and Peace

During the 1940s, American society changed, and black college football shifted its role and existence in response. Black college football decreased in popularity during World War II as African Americans joined the war effort. The sport returned to prominence in the postwar period as a force for social change, as well as a defining feature of the black community.

Early in the 1940s, interest in black college football took a back seat to the war in Europe. Throughout the late 1930s, African Americans intensely followed Italy's takeover in Ethiopia and Hitler's expansion in Europe. A. Philip Randolph, president of the Brotherhood of Sleeping Car Porters, sent a letter to the black press in 1940 in which he called the Battle of Britain a battle of "ideas, philosophies, and ways of life."[1] He went on to declare that the German threat against Britain presented a "matter of life and death to democracy and freedom as we know it."[2] Therefore, Randolph argued that it was in African Americans' best interest that the United States give such goods to Britain as guns, battleships, planes, and food.[3]

Other black leaders in the United States went further than Randolph and called for the United States to join the fight against Hitler. C. C. Spaulding, president of the North Carolina Mutual Life Insurance Company, foresaw the United States' entry into the war. When the United States eventually joined the fight against Hitler, Spaulding argued, "The American Negro in all possibility will share the common lot of all Americans."[4] He went on to say that African Americans, therefore, deserved equal treatment as citizens, specifically in their roles as soldiers.[5]

In Texas, citizens addressed their position in a segregated society. In 1920, a group of black educators met with representatives from Prairie View A&M and formed the Texas Interscholastic League of Colored Schools (TILCS). The TILCS, which later changed its name to the Prairie View Interscholastic League, served as the governing body for interschool competitions between black public high schools in Texas. After dividing the schools up into four different divisions based on enrollments, the league allowed the schools to compete for state championships. The classification and competition format followed the model of the white University Interscholastic League.[6]

At the same time, African Americans in Texas followed integrated northern teams with more interest. The accomplishments of the black players on these teams illustrated the hypocrisy of segregation at the state's white colleges. The *Dallas Express* summed up the new attitude among African Americans toward college football in the 1940s in an article entitled, "The Plight of the Negro Athlete, What?"[7] The article looked at the cases of Kenny Washington of UCLA and Lou Montgomery of Boston College. Washington, the Bruins' All-American running back found himself excluded from the annual East-West All-Star game because the contest's promoters worried about upsetting southern players and fans. Boston College left Montgomery and his 9.7 yards per carry average at home when the Eagles played in the 1940 Cotton Bowl. According to the paper, the events proved "awfully embarrassing" to the coaches and players, and at the same time revealed the plight of black athletes in the United States as a "bit sad." The article concluded by calling for more African American players on football teams as a way to push integration throughout the country.[8]

Nationally, challenges to the system of Jim Crow in sports increased during the 1940s. One such incident occurred in October of 1940 when students at New York University protested the planned exclusion of their team's starting fullback, Leonard Bates, from an upcoming game against the University of Missouri when the administration at Missouri objected to their white athletes competing against an African American. The NYU students' outrage stemmed not from their southern opponent's bigotry, but from the fact that the NYU administration agreed to the demand to leave Bates at home. In response, two thousand students and sympathizers picketed the NYU administration building. Over the next week and a half, the protests continued, attracting the attention of the national media. New York University leaders refused to change their prohibition to play Bates, and ultimately Missouri won the game thirty-three to zero. After the loss, the issue did not go away, as in past decades when similar issues arose. Instead, the lopsided defeat for NYU only caused protests to increase on the northern university's campus.[9]

In Texas, black college football came out of the Depression with a high level of fan support and success. Winning teams found their economic situations equal to their popularity among the black community. Accomplishments on the field during the previous decade bought Texas College a new stadium in Tyler. The Steers christened their stadium by defeating Jarvis Christian twenty to zero.[10]

Wiley, another successful team, also began its season by beating Jarvis Christian. The game, which ended in a thirty to zero Wildcat victory, attracted five thousand fans to Marshall. Jay Don Davis, a sports reporter for the *Houston Informer*, praised the turnout: "Wiley is a small school and Jarvis packs no circus-like appeal, but you see where 5000 cheering fans saw Wiley smother the Bulldogs."[11]

The African American community in Texas waited anxiously for the Wiley–Prairie View game at the State Fair of Texas. The game's popularity reached such a level by 1940 that the remainder of Texas' black colleges scheduled a day off for the weekend of October 11–14 so as not to lose spectators to the fair.[12]

Seven major events accompanied the football game at Negro Day. The activities included a parade through greater Dallas with fifty dollars going to the best float, musical events, agricultural exhibits, Boy Scout activities, and the crowning of the "All-State Queen," who also received a fifty-dollar prize.[13] The activities, along with the game, were a huge success as Negro Day attracted more than eighty thousand people, despite rain and cold throughout the day.[14]

Prairie View came out victorious in the contest, beating its opponent eighteen to zero. The game took place in a slight rain, which kept the crowd numbers down to about two thousand, but overall, the event achieved its usual success. According to the *Houston Informer*, "Not only was it a perfect day for the football team, but Prairie View in general stole the whole show."[15] The Panther band attracted more attention. The "girls outstepped the Wiley girls, and the boys outplayed the Wiley boys. The drum major, too, got the better of the duo."[16]

At the same time, the war in Europe grew as a point of interest for African Americans. In October 1940, the *Houston Informer* proclaimed in a banner on its front page, "Houston Negroes Break Record Entering U. S. Army."[17] Two weeks later, the paper declared, "20,000 Negroes Answer Uncle Sam's Call."[18]

For black college football teams in Texas, the location and date of their games existed as vital pieces of importance for attracting the most spectators. An example of the necessity for good planning took place with Bishop's schedule in 1940. The Tigers played two games in a span of five days. First, Bishop faced Prairie View for the Tigers' annual homecoming game on November 11, Armistice Day. The scheduling of the game on the national holiday continued to be of significant importance to attract fans to Marshall. Four days later, Bishop played Texas College at the Cotton Bowl in Dallas. Dallas possessed a black population greater than both Marshall and Tyler, thus creating the possibility of a bigger crowd. In its article promoting Bishop's homecoming, the *Houston Informer* summed up the importance of strategically located and holiday games (in terms of attendance), stating that the world now focused its attention on the war in Europe instead of football.[19]

The Texas College victory over Langston also received a good amount of press coverage. Since the Steers had two conference wins on the season, they appeared to be contenders for the SWAC championship. As a result, the *Houston Informer* published a good amount of publicity for Texas College's November 9 homecoming game against Southern on the Steers' new field. The festivities, which the school expected to attract five thousand alumni and fans, included a parade, pigskin revue, crowning of the homecoming queen, and numerous social activities.[20]

Following the pattern of scheduling games for major holidays, Wiley and Bishop prepared to meet each other on Thanksgiving weekend. Both teams entered the contest following losses that left them out of the conference title hunt. Still, the crosstown rivalry, coupled with the holiday atmosphere, made the game a top draw for the season.[21] Prairie View also chose to play on Thanksgiving Day, facing Southern University. The Louisianans defeated Prairie View seven to two. The loss knocked the Panthers out of a chance for the SWAC championship.[22]

Since the season records of both Wiley and Bishop offered nothing to get excited about, the social events surrounding Wiley's homecoming continued to receive a good amount of fan interest. Fraternities and sororities at the school headed up the activities that began with a Friday night bonfire and ended with "Miss Wiley's Homecoming Prom" after the game on Saturday.[23] Unfortunately, the social activities provided the only positive experience for the fans and alumni because the Wildcats lost to Bishop six to three.[24]

The 1941 football season began with the same predictions as always for Texas' black colleges. J. Don Davis, sports editor for the *Houston*

Informer, picked Texas College to finish near the top in the SWAC, mainly because of the Steers' twenty-two returning lettermen. At the same time, Davis predicted Bishop would field a fairly talented team, but eventually finish behind its fellow Texans because of the Tigers' small roster and lack of reserves.[25]

A total of 1,500 fans attended the first game of the black college football season in Texas, which involved Jarvis Christian and Texas College. Texas College defeated the Bulldogs fourteen to zero. Showing how much of a disparity there was between the SWAC schools and the other, smaller black college teams in Texas, Texas College amassed 233 yards in the game, while Jarvis Christian only accumulated 84 yards.[26]

The black press reserved most of its sports pages for the upcoming State Fair game. Along with the annual energy that surrounded Negro Day at the State Fair in Dallas, the 1941 Wiley–Prairie View football game featured "two of the best fullbacks in sepia football."[27] The fullbacks, "Hippo" Hopkins of Prairie View and "Black Beauty" Ingram of Wiley, both made their last appearances in the Cotton Bowl contest.[28]

The *Houston Informer* ran two advertisements promoting Negro Day at the fair. One ad gave the details for the Wiley–Prairie View football game, including admission prices of seventy-five cents for presale and one dollar ten cents at the gate. The other advertisement promoted Negro Day itself. The ad listed the day's events, including the parade, a street band contest, a baby parade, a spelling contest, and the "tap dancing contest and queen's ball."[29]

The publicity worked, as ninety thousand people—a record number—attended.[30] The *Houston Informer* dedicated its "Amusement Page" to the "Sidelights of Negro Day at the State Fair." The paper praised the winners of all the different contests, as well as the Prairie View Band for its halftime performance. In the performance, the band spelled out "V-I-C-T-O-R-Y" on the field, a first for any black college, according to the paper. The article placed emphasis on the fact that the majority of whites stayed away from the State Fair on Negro Day, making the crowd of ninety thousand about 96 percent African American.[31]

Of the large number of spectators at the fair, twelve thousand attended the football game. Prairie View came out the victor, demolishing its opponent thirty-two to seven. The game offered many highlights for the fans as Prairie View scored twice on passes, as well as a lateral following an interception.[32]

Texas College, Jarvis Christian, Paul Quinn, and Bishop all took off that week because of the State Fair game. The next week, though, Texas' black colleges returned to action. Texas College rebounded from a season opening tie against Prairie View to achieve a thirty-six to seven victory over Arkansas State. Prairie View continued its winning ways, coming from behind to beat Xavier twenty-one to six.[33]

Texas' black colleges dominated the SWAC in 1941. Going into November, Texas College and Prairie View were tied for the conference lead.[34] Texas' non-SWAC colleges also fared well. Samuel Huston easily defeated Butler College by a score of thirty-two to zero. The Dragons then prepared to face Jarvis Christian in a night game at Austin's Anderson Field. The black press built enthusiasm among supporters of the two schools by praising the ability of Jarvis Christian's quarterback, "Runt" Smith. According to the *Houston Informer*, Smith's effort in the opening game for Jarvis Christian against Texas College accounted for the Bull-dogs' only losing fourteen to zero.[35]

Meanwhile, the effort to mobilize for war and the struggle against racial prejudice converged in Texas in 1941. On November 1, a riot broke out in Brownwood involving a few black soldiers from Camp Bowie who became angry over the physical treatment they received from the city's white policemen. The riot began when a policeman used violence to make several African American soldiers stop rough housing. When the fighting stopped, two hundred black soldiers were arrested.[36]

The energy and excitement among the fans over the football contests were felt by the players. At Samuel Huston's homecoming game against Philander Smith, the players' spirits got so worked up that a fight broke out. The incident took place with a minute left to play and Samuel Huston up twenty-four to seven. A Philander Smith player jumped off-sides and kneed a Samuel Huston lineman. The lineman took offense and responded by punching the Philander Smith athlete. Once the fight ended, Philander Smith left the field in protest and forfeited the game.[37]

Prairie View went into the month of December as the leader in the SWAC. Jarvis Christian became the champion of the Bi-State confer-ence, a new conference created by the smallest of Texas' black colleges, including Jarvis, Paul Quinn, Samuel Huston, and Tillotson, along with Louisiana Normal.[38] While the Bi-State conference never equaled the caliber of the SWAC, it allowed its members a chance to compete, a factor that maintained fan support and kept the college teams going.

Prairie View won the SWAC outright when the Panthers defeated Southern University. The victory made Prairie View one of only a handful of undefeated black colleges in the United States. As a result, when they prepared to face Kentucky State, champions of the Midwestern Athletic Association Conference, in the annual Prairie View Bowl, the game carried national championship potential.[39]

All of the excitement surrounding the bowl game disappeared in an instant when the Japanese bombed Pearl Harbor on December 7, 1941. When the attack occurred, the football season had just come to an end for most colleges, but the postseason bowl games remained to be played. The very strong fear of a Japanese invasion of the Pacific coast led the Rose Bowl committee to choose to move the game to Durham, North Carolina.[40] The fear of a Japanese attack also affected Texas. The excitement and interest surrounding the Prairie View Bowl disappeared on December 7, 1941. Where the black press had actively publicized the upcoming bowl game, after the war began, the front page of the *Houston Informer* now proclaimed, "Negroes Promise Unity in War Against Axis."[41]

At the same time, student unrest occurred at Prairie View that further diverted attention from the bowl game. In December of 1941, students issued a petition to the administration asking for several changes, including the freedom to sit anywhere the students wanted during chapel, a place to eat and listen to music at night, and the freedom to visit girls in the parlor of their dormitory.[42] The protest died down quickly when President Banks called in each of the leaders of the movement and gave them a severe scolding.[43]

With these other events as competition, the Prairie View Bowl disappeared from most fans' interests. As a result, only a few thousand spectators showed up to watch Kentucky State defeat Prairie View nineteen to sixteen.[44] To add insult to injury for Prairie View, the SWAC stripped the Panthers of the conference title after officials discovered Prairie View used an ineligible player during the season.[45]

During the war, college football experienced a tenuous existence. The shortage of cars, tires, and fuel created by war rationing caused football attendance to decrease dramatically, as people found it hard to travel to games. The most significant impact of the war involved the loss of able-bodied athletes to the military. Unable to staff a team, many colleges suspended football from 1942 to 1945. Other schools, though, fielded highly competitive teams made up of men receiving military training at the universities.[46]

During World War II, American colleges played a role in the training program for US soldiers. The military embraced sports as a way to teach discipline, competitiveness, and aggression to soldiers. Federal Security Administrator Paul V. McNutt urged colleges to continue their football programs. McNutt believed football played an important role in America's overall role of preparation.[47]

A major significance of the war was that African Americans distinguished themselves in battle and became heroes to the black community at home. In Texas, the son of a sharecropper, Dorie Miller, became a statewide and national hero for his efforts during the attack on Pearl Harbor. Miller, who worked in the mess of the USS *Arizona*, first moved his wounded captain to safety. Then, he took control of a machine gun and shot down between two and six Japanese airplanes. These actions won Miller the Navy Cross.[48] African American boys then hoped to become sailors and soldiers as much as they wanted to be football stars.

Changes in the attitudes of white colleges towards black football players occurred at the same time. The loss of players turned college football teams into shells of their former selves. As a result, national attention turned to the football teams associated with the major army training stations around the country. Places like Camp Lee in Virginia, the Great Lakes Naval Training Center on Lake Michigan, and McDill Field in Florida all fielded competitive and integrated teams. As a result, many white colleges saw black athletes as a way to continue having winning seasons.[49]

In Texas, the state's black colleges faced the loss of players and coaches to the war effort. Bishop College entered the 1942 football season unsure if the school would field a team. When the Tigers' coach, Jimmy Stevens, left the school and enlisted in the army, Bishop decided to drop its program for the duration of the war.[50] Wiley also felt the stress of the war effort when the army drafted the Wildcats' starting running back, Jimmy Valentine.[51]

During the war, black colleges found good equipment hard to come by. With players and students leaving school by the thousands, both white and black colleges undertook any possible means to stay open and field football teams. For example, in 1940, Lincoln defeated Howard sixty-three to zero. In an effort to fill its roster for the game, Lincoln used a white center named Ralph Oves.[52]

Despite all of the worries concerning the war and colleges dropping football programs, administrators at Wiley and Prairie View assured Texas' black community that the annual State Fair Classic would take place in 1942.[53] Prairie View also announced the absence of several of its star players for the game. The most notable were running backs "Hippo" Hopkins and "Big Train" Moody. According to the *Houston Informer*, the two players found themselves in "training to carry the ball for Uncle Sam."[54]

The number of black colleges that dropped their football programs because of the war increased as the season progressed. In the Southern Intercollegiate Athletic conference, four out of fifteen schools canceled their seasons. LeMoyne, Fisk, Talladega, and Fort Valley State felt the demands of the war on manpower and educational services made football impractical.[55] Shaw University canceled its season following the team's first game. The cancellation came after the draft sent six of the school's fifteen football players into the army.[56]

The loss of football men to the draft was not the only problem faced by black college football during the war. With white males entering the military, industrial jobs previously denied to African Americans suddenly opened. Ted Mumford, the head coach at Texas College, quit his team and moved to Erie, Pennsylvania, to work for General Electric.[57]

Most of the coverage by the black press involved football games at the different army training camps around the country. In Texas, though, the Wiley–Prairie View State Fair game continued to excite the black community. Going into the 1942 game, however, the *Houston Informer* announced the cancellation of the State Fair of Texas for the duration of the war. As a result, the paper stated that the 1942 classic would be the last contest between the two schools in the Cotton Bowl until the war ended.[58]

The "pomp and ceremony" that usually accompanied the game was absent from the 1942 contest. The actual game on Monday night, October 19, still created a considerable amount of enthusiasm. Both schools featured lineups consisting almost entirely of freshmen. Wiley appeared the favorite after defeating Jarvis Christian fifty-four to zero to open the season. Prairie View, on the other hand, lost its first game, falling to Texas College, six to zero.[59] When the two colleges faced each other, however, Prairie View came out victorious by a score of six to zero.[60]

With lineups depleted of quality athletes, black college football in Texas remained virtually absent from the black press's sports pages. Only a few games received mention, such as Wiley's contest against Xavier at the Louisiana State Fair. The black press also followed Texas College's march to the SWAC championship, relaying game scores like the Steers' 106 to 12 victory over Jarvis Christian.[61]

The war also resulted in the cancellation of the celebrations that accompanied black college football games. Wiley announced its 1942 homecoming game would be the last at the school until the end of the war, because the game occurred on November 21, the day before gasoline rationing started in the United States. With rationing in effect, alumni and fans found it hard to travel to cities like Marshall and Tyler.[62]

The 1942 season came to a close with Texas College winning the conference. The war received most of the black populations' attention, with black college football suffering as a result. Neither Bishop nor Paul Quinn fielded teams. Samuel Huston only played three games, all in November and all against military bases, Fort Clark, Fort Sill, and the Waco Preflight Flyers.[63]

At the same time, ten thousand black Houstonians attended a political rally hosted by the city's African American branch of the Young Men's Christian Association. Taking place at Emancipation Park, Houston's black city park, the festivities featured a band and a demonstration by the 181 Negro Tank Destroyer troops from Company "A" of the 827 Battalion at Fort Hood. Citizens found themselves able to meet the black soldiers and inspect the unit's tank destroying guns. The *Informer* described the event as a "We must win the war" meeting.[64]

For black Texans, though, the season still held a few exciting events that offered some escape from the pressures of the war. SWAC champion Texas College received bids to both the Orange Blossom Classic in Florida and the Vulcan Bowl in Birmingham, Alabama. The Steers lost thirteen to six to Florida A&M in the Orange Blossom Classic.[65] They rebounded on New Year's Day, though, to beat Tuskegee thirteen to ten before fifteen thousand fans in Birmingham.[66] These two games again brought national attention to black college football in Texas.

The Prairie View Bowl became the last black college bowl game to take place that season. The annual game in Houston saw Langston score three times in the third quarter to come from behind and beat Prairie View. The contest attracted less than two thousand spectators, a number down dramatically from the previous years.[67]

Even with the war going on, African Americans continued the fight for civil rights. A. Maceo Smith's Texas Council of Negro Organizations pushed for other social changes in Texas. One issue the organization confronted dealt with black higher education. The group decided in 1943 that it was impossible to achieve equal education opportunities between Texas' black colleges and white colleges. As a result, the TCNO focused its attention on desegregating the state's public white colleges.[68]

The 1943 football season suffered even more than the previous year because of World War II. Of the SWAC schools, only Wiley, Prairie View, Texas College, and Langston fielded teams. While still competing against their rivals, these schools faced mostly military teams from the local black army bases, such as when Texas College kicked off its season against the 325th Aviation Squadron.[69] With the exception of Samuel Huston, who only played two games, the remainder of Texas' black college teams failed to field teams.

The schools that continued to play attempted to help the war effort through the contests. Wiley and Prairie View decided to hold their game at the Cotton Bowl in 1943, even though the State Fair was cancelled. In an effort to attract more spectators, the two schools gave servicemen a discounted ticket price of fifty cents. The game served as a war bond drive in an effort to buy a jeep for African Americans in the military.[70]

The war bond drive succeeded as nine thousand fans watched the two schools battle to a zero to zero tie.[71] The large turnout for the Wiley–Prairie View game was an exception, not the norm, for college football during World War II. The average game attendance fell closer to the six hundred spectators who attended Langston's forty-eight to zero route of Samuel Huston.[72]

The most significant event that came out of the 1943 football season involved the resignation of Prairie View's coach Fred Taylor. He left the Panthers to serve as the "Red Cross Club Director for foreign service."[73] The move ended his thirteen-year tenure at the school.

With the number of conference teams decreased to four in 1943, the SWAC announced that no champion would be crowned.[74] Even without a champion, the season ended in traditional fashion with the Prairie View

Bowl. Despite the announcement that the previous year's game would be the last until the end of the war, when Prairie View saw the success of its game against Wiley in Dallas, the Panthers decided to continue their postseason contest. Since New Year's Day fell on a Saturday, servicemen in the Houston area received the day off, thus ensuring a crowd of fifteen thousand to watch Prairie View defeat Wiley six to zero.[75]

By the fall of 1944, events in the war favored the United States. The excitement over the country's success in Europe and the Pacific extended to the home front. African Americans in Texas began to pay more attention to college football. The sport still lagged far below the level of cultural importance it held before World War II, but the modest success Prairie View, Wiley, and Texas College experienced during 1943 showed the other black colleges in the state that football remained viable in a time of war. As a result, more SWAC schools returned to competition. Samuel Huston also took advantage of the lack of conference members to rejoin the SWAC.

The Texas African American community was buzzing with excitement over two upcoming "classics."[76] The first was the annual Wiley Prairie View contest at the Cotton Bowl in Dallas. Even though the State Fair was still cancelled, the two schools again received permission to compete at the Cotton Bowl.[77] The hopes of the contest's promoters that the game in Dallas still might attract large crowds came true as fourteen thousand spectators watched Wiley beat Prairie View twenty-eight to zero.[78]

The second classic occurred two days before the Wiley–Prairie View contest. In what became known as the "Texahoma Classic," Texas College faced Langston at Farrington Field in Fort Worth.[79] The two schools had long histories of competition from their years together in the SWAC. Administrations at both colleges hoped to use the excitement over the State Fair game in Dallas to attract fans to Fort Worth. Texas College came out of the contest victorious, thus setting the Steers up for a showdown with Wiley for the conference championship.[80]

Black college football also returned to a prominent place in the community during the 1944 Prairie View homecoming. Despite the announcement by the black press in 1942 that all homecoming games in the state were cancelled for the duration of the war because of gasoline rationing, Texas' black colleges continued to hold homecoming festivities every year. In 1944, four thousand fans traveled to Prairie View to watch the Panthers lose to Texas College. The *Houston Informer* focused the majority of its coverage on the social aspects of the game, listing the alumni in attendance and what clothing styles the women wore. The paper also covered the top half of its sports page with eleven pictures from the game, the majority of which focused on the crowd.[81]

For coach Long's last game, his Wildcats faced Prairie View in the annual Prairie View Bowl. While the Wiley team prepared for the game, the college administration worked hard behind the scenes to keep Long as the head of the Wildcats.[82] With the excitement over coach Long's possible last game, eight thousand fans attended the Prairie View Bowl, which ended in a Wiley victory.[83] Fortunately for Wiley's supporters, Fred Long decided to stay at the college, even though he already had signed a three-year contract with Kentucky State. The reason Long stayed had nothing to do with the efforts of the Wiley administration or fans. Instead, he turned down the Kentucky job because his wife refused to leave Texas.[84]

As the next season approached, the popularity and cultural role of college football increased. As a result, the 1945 season marked several important events for all of college football. During the war, Congress passed the GI Bill of Rights, in which the government promised to pay veterans fifty dollars each month to cover college expenses. After the US victory in World War II, colleges used the GI Bill to recruit veterans for the schools' football teams. At the same time, colleges used job subsidies, loans, and alumni support to attract younger athletes. The increase in the number of football players on each team allowed colleges to shift to two-platoon football consisting of separate squads for offense and defense.[85]

Black colleges also saw their enrollments increase because of the thousands of soldiers returning from the war. Colleges that had dropped football programs during the war restarted teams. The growth of black college football in Texas increased the sport's role as a form of cultural expression for African Americans.

When returning black veterans in Texas sought to take advantage of the GI Bill and receive a college education, most chose to attend Prairie View A&M. The state-supported school's enrollment almost doubled from 1,400 in 1942 to 2,600 in 1954.[86] The massive influx of students brought Prairie View increased financial resources, which the school in turn used to establish new programs that attracted even more students.

The increase in enrollment at Prairie View also carried over to the school's football team. The Panthers' team numbered more than one hundred athletes.[87] With the financial resources to attract the best black athletes in the state of Texas, Prairie View became a national powerhouse in the postwar period, while the state's private schools found it increasingly difficult to compete.

So many veterans enrolled at Prairie View that the college started a "Veterans' Club" that consisted of 373 members.[88] At the same time, most of Texas' black colleges, unlike their white counterparts, found meeting their financial needs difficult because the new students came from lower economic groups and could only afford to pay a limited amount to attend school. As a result, black colleges in Texas could not raise tuitions to meet budgets. At the same time, philanthropic organizations like the General Education Board that had previously supported African American higher education decreased their assistance. Therefore, the majority of black colleges cut services to make ends meet.[89] Charles Estus, a ROTC student at Prairie View before the war, discussed the problem faced by black colleges. He stated that when he returned from the military, he decided to transfer because "I wanted more and Prairie View made no progress academically."[90] While students like Estus expressed displeasure with the state of black colleges after the war, as the decade progressed, football at these schools regained its place as a defining feature of the black community and African American masculinity.

Several black colleges dealt with the loss of private funds by creating their own philanthropic organization. The new entity, the United Negro College Fund, provided money for colleges to help with student scholarships and to maintain academic programs. Bishop College joined the United Negro College Fund in 1944.[91]

The end of the war led many schools to resume playing football. One Texas school, Butler College, returned excitedly to the college ranks and kicked off its season against Samuel Huston in Austin. Butler's enthusiasm faded as Samuel Huston won the game fifty to zero. Even with the lopsided score, the game attracted a considerable amount of attention from the black community in Austin and the African American press.[92]

The Wiley–Prairie View game at the State Fair really signaled the return of black college football in Texas. With the war over, the Texas State Fair resumed. Even though the two schools continued to face each other during the war at the Cotton Bowl in Dallas, the 1945 contest saw the State Fair Classic back as the central feature of Negro Day at the fair. The black press proclaimed the game the social event of the year, and promoters expected twenty-five thousand people to attend.[93]

The prediction of twenty-five thousand spectators was a little high, but not by much. Nineteen thousand fans filled the Cotton Bowl on October 15 and watched the highest-scoring game in the history of the State Fair Classic. Wiley ran roughshod over Prairie View, winning thirty-five to seven.[94]

The Wiley victory marked the end of Prairie View's optimism for a championship season. The same weekend, Samuel Huston also saw its hopes for a conference championship dashed when the Dragons lost to Southern, thirty to zero. The Southern–Samuel Huston game took place in Houston to capitalize on the large black population in the city.[95]

The practice of colleges playing in neutral cities with large black populations continued. Texas College and Langston faced each other in Fort Worth. The contest marked the second year in a row for the two schools to meet as the "Texahoma Classic." The Steers won the game twelve to seven and put itself in contention for the conference title.[96]

The end of the war allowed colleges to again travel greater distances. For Texas College's homecoming, the Steers chose to play Kentucky State instead of a local school. The attraction of a national powerhouse team from outside of Texas caused a "record breaking homecoming crowd" to flock to Tyler and watch Texas College win twenty to zero.[97]

The black press added to the rebirth of black college football in Texas by hyping upcoming tilts. In a front-page article, the *Houston Informer* called the 1945 Prairie View-Texas College game the "greatest grid spectacle that South Texas has ever witnessed."[98] The *Dallas Express* also participated in the promotion of games, proclaiming that the Wiley and Southern contest possessed the potential of attracting the largest crowd ever to watch a college game in Houston.[99]

One major event in 1945 that strengthened black college football's position in Texas as a defining aspect of the African American community was Wiley College's march to the conference title. The Wildcats went through the season undefeated. The team even beat conference favorite Southern University by a score of thirty-three to zero.[100] The one challenge Wiley received came from Texas College, which led for most of the game, until the Wildcats finally scored in the last minutes of play to win eight to six.[101]

Wiley's SWAC title earned the Wildcats an invitation to face Florida A&M in the Orange Blossom Classic. Eight thousand spectators filled Phillips Field in Tampa to watch Wiley trounce Florida A&M thirty-two to six, thus earning the Texas school the national championship. The victory proved bittersweet for fans of black college football in Texas. While the national championship allowed black Texans to express pride in their race and culture, the game also carried sad emotions, as Harry Long, the brother of head coach Fred Long and an assistant on the Wildcat team, died of a heart attack during the first quarter.[102]

The final indication of the return of black college football in Texas came with the Prairie View Bowl on New Year's Day 1946. The Panthers finished in the middle of the pack in the SWAC. Even so, ten thousand fans filled Buffalo Stadium in Houston to watch Prairie View defeat Tuskegee twelve to zero.[103]

African Americans expressed no less optimism than whites about the United States after the war. Civil rights leaders worked to lay the groundwork for challenges that later brought about change. *Ebony* magazine, which published its first issue in 1946, served as a means of cultural definition and expression for African Americans. In sports, Jackie Robinson broke professional baseball's color barrier when he took the field for the Brooklyn Dodgers in 1947.[104] By dominating Major League baseball, Robinson also disproved stereotypes about black physical and intellectual inferiority, and as a result furthered the image of African American masculinity.

One reason for the newfound optimism came from the fact that World War II produced significant shifts in the size and composition of the black workforce, and African Americans changed from agricultural- to factory-based employment. Many blacks also worked for the first time as skilled and semiskilled laborers in factories. A pay increase accompanied these changes. Some African Americans even moved into white-collar jobs.[105]

The postwar energy surrounding black college football in Texas carried over to the 1946 season. Reaping the popularity of its national championship, Wiley saw fifty athletes report for the first day of practice.[106] The other black colleges in Texas also saw their teams grow, with Prairie View attracting sixty potential football players.[107] The *Houston Informer* summed up the fervor surrounding the football season, stating, "king football bids fair to maintain its place in the sun in the eyes of the pigskin fanatic in and around Texas."[108]

With the increased rosters and the return of veterans from the war, Texas' top teams became some of the most dominant in the country. Prairie View opened its season by beating an army team from Bergstrom Field by a score of 73 to 6. Wiley began its season defeating Philander Smith College 105 to 0. [109]

The 1946 football season also saw Bishop and Jarvis Christian field their first teams since before the war. The two schools faced each other early into the season. Led by right halfback Fred Warbington, Bishop won the game fifty-seven to zero.[110]

With the rejuvenated teams competing in the state, black Texans looked excitedly toward the annual State Fair Classic. Special trains ran from Marshall and Prairie View to carry fans to the game. The game also marked the return of the accompanying "elaborate social calendar" that offered to be "more brilliant than anything ever before attempted at the classic."[111] The enthusiasm held true to promise as the game drew thirty-five thousand fans.[112]

The high fan turnout for the State Fair Classic was representative of all of college football. By 1946 and 1947, the sport's attendance figures returned to prewar numbers. The national average for fans per game at white college football exceeded twenty-seven thousand in 1947. The University of Michigan averaged more than seventy thousand fans a game that year, and the Notre Dame–University of Southern California contest at the Los Angeles Coliseum attracted more than 105,000 spectators.[113]

Black college football in Texas held such popularity that a new bowl game, the Cattle Bowl, emerged to start on New Year's Day 1947. The game, which took place in Fort Worth, sought to become "the outstanding New Year's Day classic for Negroes in the country."[114] The committee of African Americans from Fort Worth that organized the game, as well as the accompanying social activities, hoped to attract more than twenty thousand spectators. Some of the planned accompanying features included the crowning of the "First Queen of the Cattle Bowl" and a high school band contest.[115]

Following the war, the increased importance placed by African Americans on higher education resulted in the Houston black junior college becoming a four-year institution. The new Houston College for Negroes worked to develop national recognition as a school by fielding a competitive football team. The idea worked well since seven thousand spectators attended the college's first annual homecoming game against Prairie View in 1946.[116]

The high level of interest among African Americans toward black college football had nothing to do with the school's win-loss record. The black community in Texas turned out for college football because the games offered a means of celebration and cultural expression. Rooting for college teams like Prairie View and Wiley also created continuity with the past for Texas' African Americans. Even losing teams still possessed cultural importance, as exemplified by Bishop College's homecoming game in 1946. Bishop defeated Tillotson College forty-seven to zero for the Tiger's first victory on the season. Despite the poor records of both teams, the black press reported twenty-three thousand fans attended the contest in Marshall.[117]

The end of the season gave the Texas black community much to celebrate. When Prairie View faced Lincoln in the annual Prairie View Bowl on New Year's Day, the black press stressed that the contest was the oldest bowl game in the Southwest. This fact allowed Texas' African American community to take pride in the fact that its bowl game preceded the Cotton Bowl and other white college bowl games in the state.[118]

The 1946 season also brought a first for black college football in Texas. Wiley received an invitation to face Florida A&M in the inaugural Angel Bowl. Taking place in Los Angeles, the bowl game marked the first time a black college from Texas played in the city. The Angel Bowl was a success as twelve thousand fans watched the two colleges battle to a six to six tie.[119]

The attendance figures of black college football games continued to grow in the postwar period. As more people became interested in the games, black college football grew as a form of cultural expression and pride. The success of African Americans on the football field served as a symbol of equality. For former soldiers who felt they had earned civil rights during the war, football offered a physical rebuttal to the racist attitudes used to segregate blacks in Texas and the South.

Meanwhile, a major event occurred in the late 1940s that changed the history of higher education in Texas. In 1945 Heman Sweatt, an African American mail carrier from Houston, applied for admittance to the University of Texas Law School. When the university denied his application, Sweatt sued the school. Backed by both the local office and the national chapter of the NAACP, Sweatt appealed his case all the way to the Supreme Court.[120]

The case caused the University of Texas administrators to worry that they might have to integrate their school. As a result, the state legislature sought to alleviate the situation by creating a law school for African Americans in the basement of a building in Austin. Sweatt and his attorneys declared this idea unacceptable and continued to pursue the case. When it appeared the University of Texas might lose, the school sought another option as a compromise. The Texas legislature decided to create a new state-supported university in Houston with a law school for blacks. Sweatt rejected this attempt to circumvent integration, and instead waited for the Supreme Court to return its decision. [121]

Despite Sweatt's rejection of the compromise, the state proceeded with its plan to create the university. As a result, Texas State University for Negroes formally opened its doors in 1947.[122] The creation of Texas State University by the state legislature established another outlet for black culture in Texas, as well as a new football team for black Texans to support. Because the university received state funds, its financial resources immediately exceeded those of several of the private black institutions in Texas. Texas State also already possessed a following because of the school's earlier existence as Houston College for Negroes. As a result, Texas State expected an enrollment of 1,500 students in its first year.[123]

The close proximity of Texas State to Prairie View made Houston the center of the black college football world for Texas. Texas State faced every other black college in Texas, but found itself excluded from any championships because it was not a member of the SWAC. To many black Texans, that fact seemed of little importance.[124]

At the same time, the success of African Americans in football caused the Negro Associated Press to call for more integration in college football. Al White, a reporter out of New York, praised the black players at northern colleges, stating, "And on hundreds of campuses large and small, famed and not famed, where color is no hindrance, hundreds of Negro athletes will be straining at the leash."[125] White then listed all of the accomplished African American athletes who played for white colleges. He concluded by chastising southern colleges, Army, Navy, and several prominent Catholic colleges for not recruiting black players.[126]

The movement for the integration of college sports received assistance from black college football. In New York City in 1947, the first football game between a black college and a white college took place. Wilberforce

University, the oldest black college in the United States, defeated Bergen College of New Jersey by a score of forty to twelve.[127]

The growth of black demands for civil rights carried over to the cultural life of the community. In Texas, the State Fair created a second Negro Day in order to capitalize on the increased attendance of African Americans. Since the Wiley–Prairie View football classic served as the central attraction of the original Negro Day, promoters scheduled a second black college football game for the Cotton Bowl the new day. The Dallas Black Chamber of Commerce sponsored the event, and invited Texas College and Samuel Huston to face each other in the "First Annual State Fair Junior Classic."[128]

The introduction of the second State Fair game became only one of the many events that took place during the 1947 season and illustrated the growth in popularity and importance of black college football. Paul Quinn College fielded a team for the first time since before World War II. When Texas College faced Tennessee State in September, ten thousand fans traveled to Tyler to watch the first night football game in Tyler.[129] Finally, for the Wiley–Prairie View State Fair Classic, the promoters raised the prices of tickets to one dollar fifty cents for presale and two dollars for general admission, an increase of almost thirty percent.[130] Black Texans paid no attention to the ticket increase, as 130,762 people attended Negro Day and more than 20,000 watched the football game.[131]

The *Express* proclaimed the State Fair Classic the greatest football game in the Southwest, and the top black college game in the country.[132] Prairie View won the 1947 game twelve to six, with the contest receiving front-page coverage in the *Dallas Express*. While the game marked the major attraction of Negro Day, the other events also received considerable action. For the first time in the contest's history, the accompanying events received more coverage in the black press than the game. The *Dallas Express* put its coverage of the day's social activities, along with five separate pictures of the parade and "Miss Prairie View," on the front page.[133]

The victory in the game carried even more importance for the students of Prairie View than just athletic success. As Earvin Garnett, a Panther halfback from 1946 to 1950, recalled, "If we won, Tuesday was a holiday for the entire student body. If we lost, Tuesday was classes as usual."[134]

The Texahoma Classic in Fort Worth also attracted a large number of spectators. The attendance figures remained smaller than the State Fair Classic, but 6,500 fans still sat through "sweltering heat" to watch Texas

College tie Langston. The popularity of black college football in Texas became stronger because Prairie View, Bishop, Wiley, and Texas College all possessed winning records going into the last month of the season. Of the SWAC colleges, only Samuel Huston failed to win a game.[135]

The non-SWAC colleges, Texas State University, Jarvis Christian, and Paul Quinn all experienced respectable attendance figures and seasons. Texas State even defeated Prairie View by a score of thirteen to twelve.[136] The SWAC still dominated the black community in Texas, though. As Texas College and Prairie View prepared to face each other, the *Houston Informer* promoted the contest as the "game of the year."[137] Wiley's gate receipts for the season from football proved high enough that the school found itself able to purchase lights for its stadium, build a new gymnasium, and construct a 440-yard track.[138]

The season ended with Texas' black colleges building on the success of their football teams. When Wiley defeated Samuel Huston six to zero on November 22, the game took place in San Antonio at the new Alamo Stadium, since no competition existed in the city from any other black college.[139] Many of the African American colleges in Texas also sought to take advantage of Thanksgiving weekend as a means to attract large numbers of fans. Wiley faced Texas College on Thanksgiving Day before 6,500 fans in Marshall.[140] Samuel Huston and Tillotson moved their Thanksgiving Day game to San Antonio to avoid competition with the contest between the University of Texas and Texas A&M in Austin on the same day. Even Jarvis Christian scheduled its homecoming for Thanksgiving to attract as many fans as possible.[141]

As the season came to a close, the Prairie View Panthers accepted an invitation to compete against Wilberforce in the Fruit Bowl. The game, which took place in San Francisco, marked Prairie View's first trip to California, and the first time the city of San Francisco hosted two African American college teams. The game attracted ten thousand fans to watch Wilberforce win twenty-six to zero.[142]

Other signs of change in Texas football took place at the same time. For the first time, the black press in Texas covered the Cotton Bowl on New Year's Day. Coverage focused on the Penn State team which faced Southern Methodist University in the game and brought two African American players. The presence of Wallace Triplett and Dennie Hoggard on the Penn State team marked the first time an African American competed against one of Texas' white colleges, as well as in the postseason bowl game in Dallas.

The Penn State team finished the 1947 season undefeated and ranked fourth in the nation. The organizers for the Cotton Bowl chose economics and prestige over racial restrictions when allowing Triplett and Hoggard to compete. With Southern Methodist University, led by All-American Doak Walker, ranked third in the country among college football teams, the proposed matchup with Penn State offered to make the Dallas bowl game the top attraction in the country on New Year's Day. The football game eventually attracted more than forty-seven thousand fans to watch the two universities play to a thirteen to thirteen tie.[143]

One school, Wiley, fared poorly in 1948. Once a dominant team in the conference, the late 1940s marked a down period for the Wildcats. The team lost potential players to Prairie View, Texas College, and the newly created Texas State University. Wiley even saw its coach of more than twenty years, Fred Long, leave and become Prairie View's field general.[144]

Wiley was not the only Texas black college to start poorly. Samuel Huston watched as "Buzzing Bill" Phillips and Southern University scored in every quarter to defeat the Dragons forty-one to zero. At the same time, Grambling and its star running back Paul "Tank" Younger ran over Texas State for a score of sixty-one to zero.[145]

A losing season did not mean that fans ignored their team or lost pride in their college. Even with Wiley's poor showing over the previous few years, the State Fair Classic continued to draw large crowds. For the twenty-fourth annual contest, twenty-five thousand fans filled the Cotton Bowl to watch the game. The big crowd for the football game mirrored the large number who turned out for the fair's Negro Day. A total of 142,000 people took advantage of the day to watch the special events, including the baby pageant and twin pageant, both of which received front-page coverage and pictures in the *Dallas Express*.[146]

The excitement surrounding black college football received a further stimulant with the development of a new rivalry between Texas State and Prairie View. The two colleges operated in close proximity to each other in the Houston area. Both Texas State and Prairie View received their funds from the state, sparking a strong rivalry. In 1948, the *Houston Informer* added to the energy level surrounding the game. The paper ran advertisements promoting the competition, listing ticket prices of one dollar fifty cents for a gate ticket and two dollars and fifty cents for a box seat. When the game took place, the *Informer* picked Texas State to come out the victor.[147]

The prediction failed to come to pass as Prairie View won the game twenty-one to zero. The contest remained a zero to zero tie until the second half, when Prairie View running back Haywood Young rushed for three touchdowns. The loss left Texas State without a win on the season.[148]

The Prairie View victory over Texas State also served as the Panthers' homecoming. The celebration attracted the largest homecoming crowd in the history of the college. A major draw for homecoming involved the activities that accompanied the game, such as the parade and the crowning of "Miss Prairie View" and "Miss Homecoming."[149]

Prairie View continued its perfect season, much to the excitement of its fans. When the Panthers played Texas College, the twenty to six outcome marked Prairie View's sixth victory for the season. More than three thousand fans traveled to Prairie View for the game.[150]

The popularity of black college football allowed Bishop and Texas College to schedule their game in November 1948 for the Cotton Bowl in Dallas. Texas College's record showed only two losses for the season, while Bishop found itself at the bottom of the conference. Despite the fact that neither team possessed a chance at the conference title, the game still received much attention from the Dallas black community. Major support for the game resulted because Bishop's roster listed fifteen athletes from Dallas. They formed almost half of the entire Bishop team.[151]

For African Americans, the 1948 bowl season created much optimism concerning equality in sports. Black players participated in seven bowl games around the country, a record for college football. Three of the bowl games involved only black colleges, including the Prairie View Bowl. The other games saw African Americans compete for integrated teams. For the second year in a row, black athletes participated in the Cotton Bowl on New Year's Day in Dallas when the University of Oregon faced Southern Methodist University. The University of California fielded two African American players in the Rose Bowl, as did the University of Nevada in the Harbor Bowl at San Diego. Finally, running back Gene Derricotte of the University of Michigan became the first black player invited to the Shrine East-West All-Star game in San Francisco.[152]

The 1948 season came to a close with fans experiencing much to cheer about. Several thousand fans even attended Bishop's twenty-two to nineteen victory over Wiley, despite the fact that neither team had won a game during the season.[153] With its lopsided victory over San Francisco State in the Fruit Bowl, a game noted as the first bowl game matching a black college and a predominantly white college, Southern University finished the season with twelve wins and zero losses and won the black college national championship. The bowl victory and the championship filled black Texans with pride, since a number of Southern's players came from Texas.[154]

At the same time, Lafayette College of Pennsylvania turned down an invitation to compete in the Sun Bowl in El Paso because of the bowl organizers' refusal to let the black players on the Lafayette team compete. When Lafayette students urged the administration at their Pennsylvania school to see if something could be worked out, the Sun Bowl organizers in El Paso informed Lafayette president Dr. Ralph Hutchison that a replacement team already agreed to attend. A subsequent student-led civil rights protest, which included a letter sent to US president Harry Truman, beseeching him for assistance, brought negative national attention to segregation in college sports, as well as negative publicity for the city of El Paso and the state of Texas.[155]

Black college football entered the last year of the 1940s at a high point. The sport weathered the war early in the decade to achieve its highest level of success and popularity to date. Black Texans now looked to sports as a means of achieving equality. With integration at colleges around the country, as well as Southern University's victory over a white college in the Fruit Bowl, the African American population in Texas pointed to the ability of black players on the field as evidence for the integration of the state's white colleges.

The growth of black college football also involved the physical growth of facilities and campuses. Football formed the backbone of the varsity sports program at most black colleges in the late 1940s. It was oftentimes the primary revenue producer for the schools' athletic programs. Many black colleges also relied on the success of their football teams to create positive public images of their schools. The image of a successful football team helped black colleges attract students.[156]

Texas College used the increased revenue from its football team to rebuild the school's stadium. The new Steer Stadium in Tyler became one of the best black college football facilities in the country. It featured five hundred reserved boxes and a total seating of five thousand.[157]

Texas College opened its new stadium against Grambling in September 1949. At the game, the Steers debuted their new head coach, Fred Long.

The longtime coach of Wiley College left Prairie View after one season to take over football at Texas College.[158]

In 1949, Texas State entered the Southwestern Athletic Conference as a probationary member. The Tigers found themselves underdogs in every conference game they played, especially since they failed to win a game the previous season. Still, Texas State and its fans looked to the upcoming season with excitement.[159]

The 1949 season held significance for Paul Quinn. The Tigers existed in virtual obscurity when it came to their football team. For more than two decades, they played without a conference or regular game contracts. As a result, Paul Quinn found it hard to attract athletes, find competition, or even win games. In October 1949, though, the Tigers placed themselves in Texas football history by becoming the first black college from the state to play an all-white team. They faced, and defeated, an infantry team from Fort Hood. The army team consisted of former players from several white college powerhouses, including Penn State and Texas Christian University. For African Americans in Texas, the nineteen to six victory added to the feeling of empowerment brought on by black college football. If the weakest of Texas' black college teams defeated a team made up of former players from some of the best white teams in the country, then it seemed reasonable that black Texans deserved equal opportunity in football and life.[160]

The State Fair Classic drew even more attention as the 1940s came to a close. Part of the increased energy surrounding the game came from the fact that Wiley's team appeared more competitive than in the previous few years, after playing Arkansas State to a thirteen to thirteen tie.[161] The opening of the new Bishop Center in Dallas further added to the excitement of the weekend. The center served as a junior college for African Americans in Dallas. During the State Fair, the center held an open house to attract and inform students.[162]

The State Fair Classic remained the most popular game of the year in Texas, however. The *Dallas Express* summed up the excitement surrounding the game, stating, "All roads lead to Big 'D' this weekend for the gala calendar of social events ushering in the 21st annual Wiley–Prairie View Football Classic."[163] Led by running back Harry Haywood, Prairie View ran roughshod over Wiley, winning the game by a score of twenty-eight to six. The game drew more than twenty thousand spectators for the second year in a row.[164]

Every college in Texas made its homecoming a major cultural event and source of pride. In the Texas College homecoming game, the Steers' opponent, Prairie View, entered the contest undefeated and a challenger for the conference title. Texas College's long-standing rivalry with the Panthers added to the enthusiasm surrounding the game, and as a result attracted ten thousand fans to Tyler to watch the contest.[165]

Prairie View's hopes at a perfect season and the conference championship came to an end as the Panthers lost three games to close out the season. First, Grambling shocked Prairie View fourteen to thirteen.[166] The Panthers then proceeded to lose their own homecoming game twenty-seven to six when they overlooked their next opponent, Langston. The third loss came against conference champion Southern.[167]

The Prairie View losing streak caused the Panthers to limp into their bowl game against Fisk University at the end of the 1940s. Bishop College, though, completed its surprisingly successful season by coming from behind to defeat crosstown rival Wiley twenty to twelve. The winning pass from quarterback Timmie Christian to Edward Morgan gave the Tigers a record of five wins, three losses, and one tie on the season. For the first time in more than a decade, Bishop finished with a winning record.[168]

In 1949, black college football reached a major turning point in the sport's history. Paul "Tank" Younger from Grambling became the first player from a black college to play professional football when he joined the Los Angeles Rams as a free agent in 1949. For African Americans, the Rams' signing of Younger showed that professional football recognized the abilities of athletes at black colleges. Over the next decades, as more players from black colleges joined and starred for professional football teams, African Americans in the South and Texas used the success and integration of the pro leagues as proof that white colleges in Texas and the South needed to integrate. Football became a cultural rallying point for social change.[169]

As the 1940s came to an end, black college football in Texas existed as a major component of the African American community. During the next decade, the cultural importance of black college football grew in Texas as schools like Prairie View experienced new levels of success. At the same time, though, African Americans continued to fight for civil rights. The new civil rights movement changed black college football as African Americans paid more attention to the integration of white colleges in the state.

The increased role of black athletes at northern colleges, along with the success of integrated professional football teams, played a major role in the movement toward integration and civil rights in the South. In Texas, 1950 marked a turning point in African American history as the Supreme Court returned its decision in the *Sweatt v. Painter* case, ruling in Sweatt's favor. Sweatt enrolled at the University of Texas in the fall of 1950; however, John Chase enrolled in the school's graduate architecture program two days (June 7) after the *Sweatt* decision, making Chase the first African American student at the University of Texas as well as the first black student at a major university in the South. In October, Herman Barnett became the first black student at the university's medical school in Galveston.[170]

When the Supreme Court issued its ruling in favor of Sweatt, it argued that a small new segregated law school could not equal the elaborate law library and strong faculty at the University of Texas.[171] With a legal decision to stand on, African Americans in Texas pushed for further integration. As a result, the 1950s marked a new chapter in black college football in Texas.

Historical marker at the former Paul Quinn College campus in Waco. Photograph by author.

Wiley College in Marshall. Photograph by author.

Classroom building at Wiley College. Photograph by author.

Huston-Tillotson University in Austin. (Note that Samuel Huston and Tillotson merged in 1952.) Photograph courtesy of Tommy Dean.

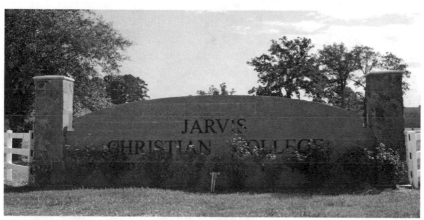

Jarvis Christian College. Photograph by author.

Prairie View A&M football stadium in Prairie View. Photograph by author.

Gomez Administration Building at the previous Paul Quinn College campus in Waco. Photograph by author.

Historical marker at the Wiley College campus in Marshall. Photograph by author.

Jarvis Christian College prayer bell. Photograph by author.

William Decker Johnson Hall at the previous Paul Quinn College campus in Waco. Photograph courtesy of Texas Southern University Archives.

The president's home at Wiley College in Marshall. Photograph by author.

Fair Park in Dallas. Photograph by author.

Hall of State, Fair Park in Dallas. Photograph by author.

Historical marker honoring Melvin B. Tolson at the Wiley College campus in Marshall. Photograph by author.

1947 Texas State College football team. Photograph courtesy of Texas Southern University Archives.

Members of the 1947 Texas State College football team. Photograph courtesy of Texas Southern University Archives.

A Texas Southern football player from 1948. Photograph courtesy of Texas Southern University Archives.

Texas Southern University versus Prairie View A&M University in 1948. Photograph courtesy of Texas Southern University Archives.

Texas Southern University versus Sam Huston College in 1948. Photograph courtesy of Texas Southern University Archives.

1951 Texas Southern University football team. Photograph courtesy of Texas Southern University Archives.

Texas Southern University All-American QB Adolphus Ford. Photograph courtesy of Texas Southern University Archives.

1952 Texas Southern University football team. Photograph courtesy of Texas Southern University Archives.

1952 football game featuring Texas Southern University. Photograph courtesy of Texas Southern University Archives.

1952 Texas Southern University homecoming queen with escorts. Photograph courtesy of Texas Southern University Archives.

1952 SWAC title game. Photograph courtesy of Texas Southern University Archives.

A scene from the 1953 Texas Southern University football season. Photograph courtesy of Texas Southern University Archives.

Scenes from the 1953 Texas Southern University homecoming, including Jackie Robinson crowning the queen. Photograph courtesy of Texas Southern University Archives.

1953 Texas Southern University cheerleaders. Photograph courtesy of Texas Southern University Archives.

Texas Southern University coach Alexander Durley instructs his assistant coaches during the 1955 season. Photograph courtesy of Texas Southern University Archives.

B. W. Cheeks of Texas Southern University runs away from Wiley College defenders during the 1963 contest. Photograph courtesy of Texas Southern University Archives.

Herman Driver of Texas Southern University scores a touchdown against Bishop College in 1963. Photograph courtesy of Texas Southern University Archives.

1963 Texas Southern University offensive line. Photograph courtesy of Texas Southern University Archives.

Willie Ellison of Texas Southern University scores a touchdown against Wiley College in 1965. Photograph courtesy of Texas Southern University Archives.

Prairie View A&M versus Texas Southern University in 1965. Photograph courtesy of Texas Southern University Archives.

Astrodome at night. Photograph courtesy of Texas Southern University Archives.

Texas Southern University versus Grambling University in the Astrodome in Houston during the 1969 season. Photograph courtesy of Texas Southern University Archives.

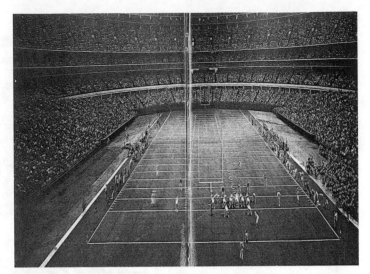

The Astro-dome Classic, 1969. Photograph courtesy of Texas Southern University Archives.

Kenneth Burroughs, Texas Southern University player drafted by the New Orleans Saints 1970 draft. Photograph courtesy of Texas Southern University Archives.

Texas Southern University versus Texas A&I University in 1972. Photograph courtesy of Texas Southern University Archives.

Texas Southern University versus Prairie View A&M University in 1972. Photograph courtesy of Texas Southern University Archives.

Texas College versus Hardin-Simmons University in Abilene 2017. Photograph by author.

Cultural Prominence and Decline

Black college football in Texas entered the 1950s as the premier social event of the state's African American community. Texas' black colleges experienced record attendance numbers at football games. School enrollments increased as veterans returned from World War II and sought higher education degrees. The social events that accompanied black college football games came to play as big a role as the actual games in the development of a black community spirit.

As the decade progressed, however, the position of black college football in the community changed. With the onset of the civil rights movement, African Americans in Texas began to turn their attention away from college football. Game attendance decreased. The top contests, such as the State Fair Classic and the Prairie View Bowl, attracted fewer fans each year. Instead, many black Texans pushed for integration of the state's white colleges. Black college football in Texas never completely lost its role as an institution of African American community pride, but by 1960 many came to see segregated sports as a step backward in the push for equality.

The change in the status and role of black college football in Texas began in 1951 with the integration of the University of Texas Law School. The Supreme Court returned its verdict in the case of *Sweatt v. Painter*, declaring that African Americans should receive admittance to graduate programs at the main state-supported university in Texas. The University of Texas chose to deal with the issue of integration by interpreting the Supreme Court's decision as meaning that African Americans should receive admittance only under special circumstances. This approach allowed the university to slow integration by approaching each application for admittance on a case-by-case basis. As a result, thirty-two African Americans applied for admittance to the University of Texas in 1950 following the *Sweatt* case. The school accepted twenty-two of the applicants, only admitting African Americans into programs not offered by the state's black colleges. The University of Texas' policy thus worked to continue segregation in its undergraduate enrollment because all of the black colleges in Texas offered undergraduate education.[1]

The issue of integration at public white colleges in Texas led the state legislature to commission the Texas Legislative Council in 1950 to study the impact of the *Sweatt* decision on higher education in Texas. The council argued in its findings that making black universities in Texas equal to the state's white universities would require the legislature to appropriate large funding increases to the public black colleges of Prairie View and Texas State.[2]

Since equal funding for African American colleges would prove costly and unacceptable to most of the state's white population, the Texas Legislative Council proposed that Texas integrate its white universities. The council argued that while small numbers of African Americans would enter the white schools, the numbers would not prove significant. Then, with black Texans possessing the opportunity for admittance to white universities, the separate but equal doctrine no longer applied, thus allowing the state legislature to reduce funding to the state-supported black colleges.[3]

African Americans in Texas worked to ensure the success of higher education integration in the state. On September 30, 1950, the *Houston Informer* urged the state's black community to donate money for the "Sweatt Victory Drive Fund." The fund sought to raise fifty thousand dollars to assist Sweatt in his move to Austin and enrollment in the University of Texas Law School.[4]

The African American colleges in Texas also sought to prepare their students to face the economic changes of Texas daily life by educating students to capitalize on new opportunities occurring in industry and technology. The state-supported schools of Prairie View and Texas State took the lead in these efforts. Texas State University for Negroes began its School of Vocational and Technical Education in the 1950s. The program offered on-the-job training, as well as in-school work for skilled trades.[5]

The struggle for civil rights also expanded in earnest in the 1950s. Black Texans challenged the system of segregation in their efforts to integrate sports. In the late 1940s and early 1950s, several African Americans from Houston pushed the city for access to a public golf course. Houston's city council ignored the request, and the black leaders sued. The case went to the federal courts, which ruled in 1951 that Houston must provide a black course under the doctrine of "separate but equal." When the *Brown* decision took place three years later, Houston and the rest of the large cities in Texas integrated their municipal golf courses in an effort to comply with the ruling.[6]

Black Texans received support and motivation from the Supreme Court in the fight for equal rights. The court continued to make decisions in favor of desegregation. In 1950, the court declared segregation in interstate travel illegal. Houston ignored the ruling as the city prepared to open its new airport. The local chapter of the NAACP pushed the issue by protesting the segregation at the airport and in the interstate travel system, attracting negative publicity for the city. As a result of the protests and publicity, Mayor Hofheinz integrated all of the facilities at the airport, except the restaurant, in 1953. Two years later, a federal court ordered the restaurant integrated.[7]

In Texas, the biggest event of the 1950 black college football season involved the decision by Texas State University not to join the SWAC after the school spent the previous year as a probationary member of the conference. Instead, Texas State decided to join the Mid-Western Athletic Conference. Grambling University from Louisiana agreed to join the MWAC along with Texas State. The moves made the conference one of the top football powerhouses in the country, since Tennessee State, Kentucky State, and Wilberforce all already belonged to the MWAC.[8]

The football season in Texas began with much anticipation as Wiley and Texas State sought to "blast the lid off of the 1950 football season."[9] Fans energetically awaited the season opener, even though both schools had accumulated unimpressive records over the previous few years. A celebratory atmosphere surrounded the game regardless of the teams' records—a common thread for all black college football. The *Houston Informer* summed up the state of black college football in Texas when the paper promoted the Texas State–Wiley game, saying, "This could develop into one of the most thrilling games of the new season from the spectator view . . . Both teams will shoot the works to climb out of the football doldrums which they have been in for the past three seasons."[10]

Texas' African American colleges received significant attention in the black press. Football coverage occurred regularly, while world events were often left out of the papers. An article in the *Dallas Express* promoting the upcoming "Texahoma classic" between Texas College and Langston exceeded in size the articles on the integration of the US military by President Harry Truman and Sweatt's fund.[11]

In an effort to capitalize on the increased popularity of black college football, the Texahoma Classic moved from Fort Worth to Dallas for the 1950 contest. The Dallas Black Chamber of Commerce and the black branch of the YMCA worked to promote the game, which occurred two days before the annual Wiley–Prairie View State Fair Classic. Texas College and Langston decided to move their tilt to Dallas because they hoped that by competing in the same city as the State Fair, the Texahoma Classic might attract some of the large number of fans attending that event.[12]

The hopes of the Texahoma Classic's promoters came to fruition as five thousand spectators filled Dal-Hi Stadium to watch Langston trounce Texas College forty-two to six. Two days later, more than twenty thousand spectators attended the State Fair Classic and watched Prairie View defeat Wiley. The Panther's forty-seven to zero victory marked the largest margin of victory in the history of the rivalry.[13] The black press praised Prairie View's effort, declaring, "Joe Washington, Peyton Womack, and Buford Holland, a trio of halfbacks, ripped the Wiley line to shreds with their slashing drives."[14]

Many of the Texas teams experienced success in 1950. Bishop College, a perennial last-place finisher, experienced one of its most successful seasons. The Tigers defeated Prairie View thirteen to zero early in the campaign.[15] Later, Bishop beat Samuel Huston thirty-three to six in Austin.[16]

The winning trend among Texas' African American colleges even extended to Paul Quinn. Paul Quinn competed without conference affiliation. As a result, the Tigers played only a few games each season, most of which they lost. This changed in 1950 when Paul Quinn opened its season by defeating Campbell College of Jackson, Mississippi, eighty-one to zero. The Tigers amassed twelve touchdowns, seven conversions, and one safety.[17]

The success of black college football in Texas translated into financial increases for the schools. The more contests a team won, the more students learned about the college and chose to attend, and the more fans paid to watch the football games. The ticket prices averaged around two dollars during the 1950s. Prairie View used the increased revenue brought in by its football team to improve the school's stadium. As the

Panthers prepared to host their homecoming game against Texas College, the *Houston Informer* ran an advertisement promoting, "The first homecoming game to be played on the improved Blackshear Field."[18] The paper also mentioned the homecoming festivities. For the alumni and fans, accompanying events like the breakfast dance, band concert, ROTC maneuvers, parade, Miss Prairie View crowning, and annual alumni ball all added to the attraction of the weekend. Visitors to Prairie View for homecoming expected and looked forward to the accompanying events because of the celebratory atmosphere they created.[19]

Willie Dunn, a student at Prairie View in the early 1950s, explained the appeal of homecoming for students, alumni, and fans. He recalled that homecoming involved all kinds of activities that catered to a wide array of interests. Most importantly, though, homecoming allowed African Americans to "socialize with people that you know."[20]

The *Houston Informer*'s coverage of the 1950 Texas State homecoming illustrated the social role black college football played in the community. On the sports page, the only mention of Texas State's fourteen to six victory over Texas College was in a listing of the final score. At the same time, the *Informer* dedicated its entire "Social Page" to the thousands of fans in attendance. The paper listed Houston's black social elite who appeared at the game, in addition to giving complete accounts of Laverne Taylor's election as "Miss Texas State," the parade, and the alumni dance.[21]

Even with the success black college football achieved in 1950, problems still occurred. As Prairie View closed out its regular season against Southern University, an on-field incident took place that hurt the image of both institutes. Prairie View tackle John Freeman and Southern tackle Rudolph Gibson got into a fistfight early in the game. The officials restored order and the game resumed, but not before a lengthy delay and the ejection of the two fighting players. Southern came out victorious in the contest, three to zero.[22]

The season concluded in the traditional manner, with the Prairie View Bowl serving as the New Year's Day social event for Texas' black community. For the game, Prairie View chose Bishop College as its opponent. For Bishop, the selection to compete in the twenty-third annual Prairie View Bowl marked the culmination of the school's successful year.[23]

Unfortunately for Bishop, the New Year's Day game attracted a small crowd. Because it took place during a torrential rainstorm, only a few hundred fans attended to view a six to six tie. Even the black press panned the weather, declaring the day more fit for "sitting by the fire and listening to the radio" than for playing football.[24]

For Texas' African American population, the struggle for civil rights increased during the 1950s. One event that showed the growing movement for equal rights occurred in 1951 when the Texas legislature changed the name of Texas State University for Negroes to Texas Southern University. The change occurred after a group of African American students from the school went before the legislature and asked the state to remove the word "Negroes" from the school's name. The students protested the implied segregation of the title.[25]

White Texans expressed their opposition to the name change. They believed the title Texas State University made the black school appear to be on an equal educational level with the University of Texas and Texas A&M. As a result, the Texas legislature agreed to drop the word "Negro" from the University's title, but instead renamed the school Texas Southern University. The legislature felt the name suggested the inferiority of the black college compared with the two premier white universities in the state.[26]

The debate concerning Texas Southern caused more black Texans to pay attention to social issues in the state. At the same time, though, the popularity of black college football continued to grow entering the 1951 season. As students reported to school, each college saw the number of players grow. For example, Texas Southern University, which only won a couple of games the previous year, had thirty-four freshmen come out for the team's first practice. The arrival of new players on college campuses also brought added interest for the African American community as the black press reported which former high school players now attended individual colleges. In 1951, the *Houston Informer* announced that Ernest Lang, a 175-pound all-state halfback from Houston's Jack Yates High School chose to play for Texas Southern.[27]

Texas' African American population further developed a spirit of community pride from football when in 1951 Samuel Huston College became the first black college in the state to compete against a foreign university in a game outside the United States. The Dragons faced Institute Politecnico National of Mexico City. The contest also marked one of the largest crowds ever to watch one of Texas' black colleges play as forty thousand fans filled the Mexico City stadium. Samuel Huston held the lead going into the final seconds of the game, when Institute Politecnico National intercepted a pass on the last play of the game and returned it for the winning touchdown.[28]

With black college football attracting large numbers of fans and holding a place of prominence in the African American community in Texas, the sport began to serve as a platform for people to speak out against problems in Texas society. As fans prepared for the annual Negro Day at the State Fair, Carter Wesley, president and editor of the *Informer* group of newspapers, expressed his opposition to the State Fair day on the front page of his papers. Wesley argued that opposing segregation in schools and buses while accepting segregation at the State Fair only hurt the effort to bring about change in society. As a result, Wesley urged all African Americans to boycott Negro Day and pressure the fair to allow open access to everyone on every day.[29]

While Carter Wesley asked African Americans to boycott Negro Day, the appeal fell on deaf ears. The excitement over the State Fair game ran so high that Prairie View A&M organized a motorcade of fans who traveled to Dallas to support the Panthers. The motorcade included several charter buses paid for by the school, which carried more than a thousand students.[30]

Very few fans listened to Wesley's arguments at the time. According to Lieutenant General Julius Becton, a faculty member at Prairie View in the 1950s, since the fair remained segregated, Negro Day offered the only day African Americans received complete reign of the fair.[31] As a result, Negro Day attendance figures remained high early in the decade.

Wiley College entered the State Fair Classic after defeating Dillard College eighty to zero.[32] Wiley's victory gave the Wildcats momentum going into the State Fair Classic. Wiley's fans hoped that their team might end its four-year losing streak to Prairie View at the Cotton Bowl. Unfortunately for Wiley, Prairie View possessed national championship hopes in 1951 and refused to end its winning ways over the Wildcats. The Prairie View title hopes rested on the Panthers' two lopsided victories of the season, a sixty-four to zero win over Samuel Huston and a seventy-two to zero win over Bishop.[33]

Prairie View showed itself the better team in the State Fair Classic, keeping the Panthers' national championship dreams alive. Led by All-American fullback Ray Dohn Dillon, Prairie View ran roughshod over Wiley, winning thirty-eight to zero. The game was also a success from a social standpoint, as more than twenty thousand spectators filled the Cotton Bowl.[34]

While Prairie View pursued a championship, Texas' other back colleges also experienced success. Texas Southern University notched a winning record for the first time in the school's five years of existence. In one of its victories, Texas Southern upset Kentucky State nineteen to fourteen at the Thoroughbreds' homecoming game in Kentucky.[35]

Paul Quinn also presented itself as a legitimate challenger to the other black colleges in the state. The Tigers' 92 to 0 homecoming victory over Arkansas Baptist marked Paul Quinn's fourth blowout victory of the season. The Tigers previously defeated Mary Allen College 111 to 0, Philander Smith 24 to 0, and Jarvis Christian 70 to 0.[36]

The success of the two schools caused their clash in Houston on October 27 to attract a considerable amount of interest from the black community. Both schools were undefeated. Paul Quinn entered the game having scored 297 points in its four games without giving up a single point. Texas Southern's hopes rested on Adolphus Ford, its quarterback and offensive leader, who completed thirty passes for 444 yards and nine touchdowns during the season, all impressive statistics considering the run-oriented approach of black college football in Texas.[37] When the two teams finally met, the game proved competitive and exciting as Texas Southern defeated Paul Quinn twenty-six to seven.[38]

The popularity of black college football led Bishop College and Grambling College to create a new annual classic. The Latex Classic, which took place in Grambling, Louisiana, marked the final game of the season for both schools. Grambling hoped the classic might eventually turn into a postseason bowl game similar to the Prairie View Bowl. Grambling's coach, Eddie Robinson, even believed that the Latex Classic would reach the same status as the Orange Blossom Classic in Florida.[39] Unfortunately for Grambling, 1951 marked the only year for the Latex Classic.

Despite all of the positives during the year, the 1951 season ended in disappointment for Prairie View. The Panthers saw their hopes for a national championship end with a thirteen to zero loss to Southern University. The season was not a complete loss for Prairie View's fans, though. The Panthers still won the SWAC championship, their first conference title in eleven years.[40]

With the conference season over, two games still remained on Prairie

View's schedule. First, Prairie View faced Texas Southern in the "Sister Bowl." The title came from the close proximity of the two schools, a fact that created an instant rivalry. Also, since Prairie View won the SWAC, and Texas Southern finished with its best record ever, the *Houston Informer* declared the game the "top college football game of the year in the Southwest."[41]

The Prairie View–Texas Southern game also featured a new element in 1951. Representatives from the newspapers of the two colleges met at Prairie View and decided to create a trophy to give to the winner of the annual event. The trophy would reside with the victor for an entire year. The newspaper editors, along with the presidents of schools, decided to make the trophy by bronzing the game ball and one of the winning team's captain's shoes, and mounting them on a wooden base. Every year after, the schools planned to engrave the score of the game on the trophy and have the losing college's queen present the trophy to the queen of the victor.[42] Prairie View defeated Texas Southern, winning the inaugural cup.[43] Unfortunately, the two schools dropped the trophy after the first year, giving no reason for the action.

Prairie View also faced Arkansas State in the Prairie View Bowl. The promotion for the annual contest focused on the celebratory atmosphere surrounding the game. Prairie View's ROTC band and special drill team, pep squad, and other "halftime specialists" announced their readiness.[44] Further building the holiday feel of the game, the Prairie View athletic council called for all departments at the college to help make the twenty-fourth annual Prairie View Bowl the best in the contest's history. The athletic council hoped that each department would develop extra entertainment to go along with the game.[45]

Eight thousand fans attended the game at Houston's Buffalo Stadium. To the delight of the African American community in Texas, Prairie View won, edging past Arkansas State, twenty-seven to twenty-six, on a last-minute pass from quarterback Charlie Brackens to Charlie Wright.[46] The *Houston Informer* published a play-by-play account, but the paper also wrote an article discussing the social importance of the game. The *Informer* declared that the Prairie View Bowl continued to be popular and successful because the contest offered two teams of "conscientious lads" who always gave the fans "clean entertainment."[47] The impor-tance of the game centered on the fact that while white college football throughout the country experienced scandals, no such scandals existed in black college football in Texas.[48]

Along with the growth in popularity of black college football, the early 1950s also marked a period of physical growth for Texas' African American colleges. By 1952 the Prairie View A&M campus consisted of thirty-three permanent buildings, fifty-five teachers' cottages, two trailer villages, a 1260-acre farm, a canning shop, a dairy barn, and a yarn shop.[49] The university grew to the point that it served as the largest employer in Waller County.[50]

The popularity and success of college football in Texas caused Giles Miller, a Dallas textile mogul, to buy the New York Yankees of the National Football League and move the team to Dallas in 1952. With visions of professional football becoming a national pastime, Miller changed the team's name to the Dallas Texans and scheduled them to play at the Cotton Bowl in Dallas. Miller's vision was ahead of his time. Despite Governor Alan Shiver's proclamation of a "new era in sports in Texas," only five thousand fans attended the first game, leaving seventy thousand empty seats at the stadium.[51]

College football was far too popular for the Texans to make any money. The team drew so poorly that the league took over the Texans three-fourths of the way through the season and made them a traveling team. At the end of the season, the NFL's commissioner, Bert Bell, moved the Texans to Baltimore and changed the team's name to the Colts. During the Dallas Texans' one year of existence, black Texans paid a modest level of interest in the team since the Texans fielded several African American players, including star running backs Buddy Young and George Taliaferro.[52] Though the Dallas Texans left the state, the team foreshadowed the future integration of football in Texas, especially since white Dallasites appeared not to have problems with the Texans' African American players.

Another major event involving the integration of sports in Texas occurred in the summer of 1952 when Dave Hoskins, a pitcher from Dallas, became the first African American to play in the professional Texas League. Hoskins, who starred for the Dallas Eagles, received ample coverage from the black press and the African American community in Texas. He eventually went on to play for the Cleveland Indians of the American League.[53] Hoskins' integration of baseball in Texas served as the first major sports desegregation in Texas, and opened the door for the Dallas Texans and future desegregation in the state.

Despite these events, college football remained segregated. Even so, the 1952 college football season began with every black college in Texas expressing its optimism and hopes for success. Texas College, which finished the previous season in second place in the SWAC, hoped for a conference championship in 1952. Fred Long, the Steers' head coach, saw more than forty athletes report for the first day of practice. Unfortunately, he lost two players—Stanley Griffin, a guard, and Lennin Tolbart, a fullback—to the draft.[54]

The draft offered a formidable foe for black college football teams. The black press in Texas announced at the start of each football season the names of former football players that were taken by the military. Paul Quinn College, which recently joined the South Central Intercollegiate Association, lost eleven players to the draft before the 1952 season began.[55]

Prairie View found itself threatened most by the military service of its players. The college required all freshmen and sophomore men to serve in the school's ROTC.[56] This training made the students better candidates for military service than their peers at other colleges. Also, Lt. Gen. Julius Becton, who was the head of the ROTC program in the late 1950s, actively sought the captains of the football and other sports teams to serve in advances ROTC since the sports captains already were the leaders on campus.[57]

Before the 1952 season, one of the founding members of the SWAC, Samuel Huston College, ceased playing football. The first black college in Texas to permanently drop its program, Samuel Huston joined with fellow Austin school Tillotson College to form Huston-Tillotson College. The merger became the culmination of almost ten years of negotiations between the two.[58] The new college decided to drop its football program in an effort to focus all its financial resources on academics.[59]

Even with the loss of Samuel Huston, black Texans passionately awaited the football season. The *Houston Informer* expressed the emotions of the African American community. The paper announced the beginning of the season by stating, "Screaming crowds, cheering sections and tearing down of goal posts will be with us once more this weekend when the nation's broad shouldered young behemoths open the 1952 college football season."[60]

Texas Southern entered the season with high hopes. Following the Tigers' eight-win season in 1951, fans of the school believed that 1952 offered a chance at national success. These hopes grew when Texas

Southern defeated Butler College sixty-three to zero in the first game of the season. The *Informer* praised Texas Southern's effort, exclaiming, "The passes were on the money and the timing on the Tiger ground plays was like a Swiss watch."[61]

Texas Southern's hopes of football glory ran into a tough challenge the next week when the Tigers faced the Southern University Jaguars. Southern won the contest the previous year, but in 1952 Texas Southern came out on top. Competing at Houston's Public School Stadium, Texas Southern used a strong defensive stand in the closing minutes of the game to win fourteen to seven. The victory not only marked Texas Southern University's first win over Southern; it also marked the first time the Tigers scored a point against the Jaguars.[62]

Texas Southern's victory, according to the *Houston Informer*, made the Tigers a "sleeper" for 1952 as a team that "defies experts, predictions, fans' opinions, and coaches' woes."[63] Texas Southern was not the only Texas black college to express optimism for a winning season. Prairie View opened its season by defeating Bishop fifty-eight to zero. Led by quarterback Charlie "Choo-Choo" Brackins, the Panthers eagerly awaited the State Fair contest against Wiley. Prairie View looked to easily defeat Wiley after the Wildcats lost twelve to seven to Arkansas AM&N.[64] The *Houston Informer* went as far as to predict a lopsided Prairie View victory would make all previous Wiley–Prairie View State Fair Classics "look like a Monday afternoon sewing circle."[65]

The State Fair Classic continued to be an important event at Negro Achievement Day. Both Prairie View and Wiley, along with the State Fair officials, sent out invitations to the winners of interscholastic league contests for African American schools as part of the Negro Achievement Day events. The winning students and schools received free admittance as honored guests to the State Fair and the football game. Overall, 138 black schools from around the state, including twenty-six state champions, received invitations based on efforts in literary arts, track and field, band, football, basketball, and tennis. In addition to the special guests, the fair expected fifty thousand public school students to attend the regular achievement day events.[66]

Among the African American community, excitement also ran high for the Texahoma Classic. The ninth annual contest in Dallas again took place two days before the State Fair game. The Texas College and Langston contest added to the excitement of black college football in

Texas as the second weekend in October experienced a holiday-type atmosphere with the two classics taking place.[67]

The publicity and excitement concerning the two black college football classics were justified, as Texas College upset Langston seventeen to six, and then two days later, Prairie View easily defeated Wiley, fifty-three to zero. [68] The *Dallas Express* summed up the victory, stating, "The Prairie View Panthers did everything but drop the seats of the Cotton Bowl on the Wiley Wildcats Monday night in Dallas."[69]

Not every black college in Texas fared as well. Wiley's loss to Prairie View represented the pattern of defeat of the Wildcats' season. Paul Quinn College also lost, falling to Southern University fifty-one to six.[70] Bishop College suffered the worst defeat of the early season, losing to Texas Southern by a score of eighty-five to zero.[71]

For the black community in Texas, though, the season revolved around Prairie View and Texas Southern. The two schools entered the last week of October nationally ranked and prepared to face two other contenders for the national championship. Prairie View traveled to Tallahassee, Florida, to play the number one team in the country, Florida A&M. Texas Southern, meanwhile, stayed at home to face number four ranked Lincoln University of Missouri.[72]

The Texas black press declared the Texas Southern–Lincoln contest the game of the week for black college football in Texas. Not only did the contest possess national title implication, but Texas Southern also made the game its homecoming. The university scheduled festivities to last over the entire weekend, including a pep rally, a bonfire, a parade, and three separate dances. As a result, black Texans flocked to Houston to show their support for the Tigers.[73]

The *Houston Informer* expressed the high level of emotion felt by the Texas African American community concerning the two games: "In every good team's season there comes a Saturday on the schedule where a successful season or a fair one is decided, where a coach finds out if those late hours . . . were fruitful or whether he will know the frustration of having his foot on the threshold of greatness and not being able to get through the door."[74]

The two contests were as closely matched and as exciting as predicted. Prairie View failed to beat Florida A&M, but only lost ten to seven. Texas Southern, meanwhile, played Lincoln to a thirteen to thirteen tie. The positive showings by the two Texas schools caused Texas Southern to rise in the national standings to fourth while Prairie View remained at number six.[75]

The regular season came to a close with black college football at the pinnacle of popularity in the community. The sport served as a cultural definer for black Texans. The accomplishments of the athletes allowed African Americans to express pride in their race, as well as to argue against the segregation present in Texas society.

The cultural role of black college football reached a new level with the Prairie View Bowl on January 1, 1953. In the 1953 edition of the annual bowl game, Prairie View chose as an opponent its neighboring college, Texas Southern. The game promised to determine the national champion since Texas Southern entered the game with a record of ten wins, no loses, and one tie, while Prairie View's record stood at eight wins and one loss.[76]

Thirteen thousand fans sat through a torrential rainstorm to watch Texas Southern defeat Prairie View thirteen to twelve. The Tigers' All-American quarterback Audrey Ford threw for two touchdowns in the first two minutes of play. Texas Southern then held the lead as Prairie View fought back to score two touchdowns of its own. The fact that the Panthers missed both of their extra points while the Tigers connected on one of their points after multiple attempts marked the difference.[77]

As a result of its victory, Texas Southern tied for the 1952 black college national championship with Florida A&M, Lincoln, and Virginia State. The title was Texas Southern University's first national championship in only its sixth year of existence. The victory also earned head coach Alex Durley the award for coach of the year, given by the Negro Coaches Association.[78]

The 1953 Prairie View Bowl carried the same heavy cultural importance as always, with the black press in Texas devoting more coverage in their social pages to the halftime festivities than the football game received on the sports page. The 1953 halftime show played a specific role in community aid as Prairie View used the opportunity to raise money for the March of Dimes. With a large crowd in attendance, numerous events occurred to present the March of Dimes message. Several prominent citizens gave speeches on behalf of the organization, including Dick Gottlieb, general chairman of the Harris County Polio drive, and "Killer" Kowalski, a white professional wrestler. Prairie View's ROTC members circulated through the stands with donation buckets and collected $1,363.37 to help fight polio.[79]

Along with the fund raiser, numerous social activities took place at the New Year's Day contest, including performances by the Tiger and Panther bands and drill teams. Phi Beta Sigma fraternities at both schools held a dance to raise funds for scholarships at their respective colleges. Finally, the black press made sure to list all of the local citizens in attendance at the game, along with descriptions of the spectators' attire.[80]

Texas' black colleges all expressed optimism for the 1953 season. Texas College proclaimed its team the best the school fielded in several years, and therefore ready to challenge for national glory. The Steers backed up their claims when Texas College opened against Florida A&M in Jacksonville. Paul Quinn also announced that it planned to exact revenge on fellow Texas colleges for the past years of defeats; the team's optimism stemmed from the end of free substitutions in college football. The Tigers hoped that since the rule change limited the number of players a team could use in a game, schools with smaller rosters might be more competitive.[81]

At the same time, African Americans in Texas experienced some success in their struggle for equal rights when Del Mar Junior College in Corpus Christi became the state's first white college to integrate its undergraduate student body. The same year, Wayland Baptist University in Plainview and the Southwest Theological Seminary opened their undergraduate classes to African American students. Through their actions, Wayland Baptist and the Southwest Theological Seminary became the first four-year institutions in the state to desegregate.[82]

In 1953, San Angelo Junior College became the fourth white college in Texas to admit African Americans. For black Texans, the move further opened the idea of integration at the state's white colleges. The black press praised the actions of San Angelo Junior College, but the school's president, Dr. Rex Johnson, downplayed the events, stating, "We do not feel that we need to be patted on the back for doing the right thing. That is what we ought to do and that is what we are doing. We have accepted one Negro boy and two Negro girls and will accept others as they come to us."[83]

The steady integration of Texas' white colleges caused African Americans to focus more on the struggle for equal rights and less on black college football. The decline in support for the sport occurred gradually, though. Fans still expected exciting contests as Texas Southern kicked off its season against Southern University. While the Tigers hoped to repeat as national champions, Southern exacted revenge for the defeat it suffered the year before, winning twenty-eight to six. The contest between the two national contenders attracted twelve thousand fans to Baton Rouge's new War Memorial Stadium.[84]

The year 1953 saw an attempt at creating a new annual football classic for black college football. The "Texiana Classic" featured Bishop College and Grambling College. By playing in Fort Worth, the two schools hoped to attract as much attention as the State Fair Classic and the Texahoma classic.[85]

While Bishop and Grambling worked to form a new classic, Texas College and Langston cancelled the Texahoma Classic. The two colleges still faced each other, but they played in Tyler at Texas College's Steer Stadium instead of in Dallas. The two schools found it hard to compete against the Wiley–Prairie View Classic at the Cotton Bowl. While fan attendance dropped because of the venue change, the game still showed reasonable success as 3,500 fans watched Texas College defeat Langston twenty to seven.[86]

The Texiana Classic also proved moderately successful, with two thousand fans attending the game. The game did face several problems, however. One problem came from the name of the classic. Fans found the name *Texiana* confusing, so the promoters changed the name to the Cow Town Classic a week before the event. The other problem involved the competitiveness of the two teams involved. Grambling defeated Bishop thirty-two to six. The only bright spot for Bishop involved the return of Mitchell Johnson to the football field after serving two years in the Korean War. The problems were too great to overcome, and the colleges cancelled all future Cow Town Classics.[87]

Meanwhile, the State Fair Classic continued to dominate black college football in Texas. The game attracted more than twenty thousand fans to the Cotton Bowl. With the 1953 contest, though, African Americans around the state began calling for a change. Prairie View's thirty-two to zero victory marked the Panthers' seventh straight win over the Wildcats. As a result, people like Lloyd Wells, a syndicated black sports columnist from Houston, called for the game to replace Wiley with Texas Southern or another competitive team. Wells predicted that a Prairie View–Texas Southern contest at the State Fair would attract forty thousand fans.[88]

For many African Americans in Texas, the State Fair game ranked second in importance to Negro Achievement Day. As usual, the *Houston*

Informer provided more coverage of the day's events than the football game itself. While no pictures existed of the football players on the paper's sports page, the *Informer*'s social page ran nine pictures showing the parade and contest winners, including the winners of the twins pageant, the baby contest, the best parade floats, and the crowning of the Negro Day Queen.[89]

Homecoming games played a major role in the cultural importance of black college football in Texas. The homecoming games continued the pageantry and excitement of the State Fair contest. At the same time, each college's homecoming festivities focused fan attention on the actual school itself and the school's hometown. As a result, homecoming served as a major source of revenue, in addition to promoting the school's academic mission.[90] For Texas Southern University's 1953 homecoming against Xavier, the Tigers expected ten thousand fans.[91] The highlight of the homecoming weekend, though, was not Texas Southern's victory. Instead, the fans expressed the most excitement over the fact that Jackie Robinson of the Brooklyn Dodgers attended and crowned Lenora Norris homecoming queen.[92]

Prairie View continued its unbeaten season when it defeated Texas College twenty-seven to seven.[93] The next week, Prairie View defeated Langston College twenty-seven to zero. The victories gave the Panthers the number one national ranking for black colleges.[94] As a result, Prairie View looked for its first national championship.

Before Prairie View could claim the title, the Panthers first had to play Southern University. Five thousand fans attended the game at Baton Rouge's War Memorial Stadium. Thanks to the play of its offensive line, "the strongest and most rugged" in the country, Prairie View won the game twenty to zero.[95]

The Panthers then received an invitation to face the number two ranked Florida A&M Rattlers in the Orange Blossom Classic in Florida. The national title implications attracted forty thousand fans to the game. Prairie View took a thirty-three to seven lead going into the fourth quarter. Florida A&M then came back and scored three touchdowns and a safety to close the gap to thirty-three to twenty-seven. At that point, Prairie View buckled down and stopped the Rattlers. The victory gave Prairie View its first national championship in school history.[96]

The black community in Texas rejoiced over Prairie View's achievement.

Being the largest of Texas' black colleges, Prairie View received the most fan support. The Panthers chose to celebrate their national championship by facing Texas Southern in the annual Prairie View Bowl on New Year's Day. The game was a huge attraction for Texas' black community since the contest featured the past two national champions.[97]

More than twenty thousand fans filled Buffalo Stadium to watch the game. The fans expressed no disapproval in the game, as Prairie View won thirty-three to eight. The only complaints focused on the halftime performance. According to Lloyd Wells, the halftime show at the Prairie View Bowl was "something that has in the past become as important as the game itself."[98] Wells went on to describe the performance at the game as "the saddest I've ever witnessed."[99]

On May 17, 1954, American society changed dramatically. The Supreme Court returned its decision in the case of *Brown v. Board of Education of Topeka*, unanimously ruling against segregation in education. For African Americans throughout the United States, the action by the court served as validation for equal rights. The integration of education inspired more people to become involved in the civil rights movement, and eventually brought about the desegregation of most facets of life in the United States, including higher education in Texas. As a result, African Americans not directly connected to the schools now gradually focused much of their attention on desegregating Texas' white colleges, while decreasing interest in black colleges and black college football.[100]

For the 1954 football season, Prairie View coach Billy Nicks expressed hopes that his team again would finish the season undefeated, winning a second national championship.[101] The other black colleges in Texas sought to overtake the Panthers. Texas Southern expressed its optimism for a successful season as the Tigers began their first year as members of the SWAC.[102]

These hopes turned upside down when Paul Quinn upset Texas Southern to open the season. Playing its third game in ten days, Paul Quinn beat Texas Southern fourteen to twelve before six thousand spectators in Houston. The game proved doubly special for Paul Quinn since the victory marked Paul Quinn's first ever win against Texas Southern. The next week, Paul Quinn built on its success by playing Grambling to a scoreless draw.[103]

The outstanding effort by Paul Quinn earned the Tigers an eighth place national ranking going into October. Other Texas schools also made the national black college football rankings. Prairie View came in at second, and Wiley received recognition in ninth place.[104]

While the other black colleges in Texas experienced successful seasons, Prairie View continued its dominance. Led by All-American quarterback Charlie "Choo Choo" Brackins, the Panthers destroyed Bishop College fifty-three to zero. The Prairie View–Bishop game showed the decline in interest in segregated football following *Brown v. Board*. At the contest only one thousand fans appeared in Marshall.[105]

Prairie View looked excitedly toward the State Fair Classic against Wiley, which was expected to attract forty thousand.[106] A particularly large crowd was predicted because both Prairie View and Wiley entered the game undefeated. Prairie View came in as the number one team in the country while Wiley was ranked number six. The high level of talent exhibited by both colleges further increased the energy surrounding the game.[107]

Prairie View coach Billy Nicks expressed fear concerning his team's chance in the State Fair Classic because starting running backs John Payton and Johnnie Price had been lost to injuries. Fortunately for Nicks, the Panthers never missed the two running backs, as William "Cowboy" Clark and "little midget size halfback" John Oliphant performed the ball-carrying duties. The team fought hard and defeated Wiley nineteen to six. The victory gave Prairie View an eighteen-game winning streak and an eight-year streak against Wiley at the State Fair. At the same time, the twenty thousand fans in attendance fell well below projected numbers.[108]

By the end of October, Texas' black college teams saw their hopes for an outstanding season diminished. Paul Quinn lost to Texas College thirteen to zero. At the same time, Florida A&M seemed to knock Prairie View out of the hunt for the national championship. Ten thousand stunned fans traveled to Prairie View and watched the Panthers fall nineteen to seven, ending the college's eighteen-game winning streak.[109]

Even with the loss to the Rattlers, Prairie View still found itself in contention for the SWAC championship. As a result, ten thousand fans attended Prairie View's homecoming game against Texas College. The homecoming weekend served as the social highlight of November for Houston African Americans. Unlike the previous year, fans found nothing to complain about concerning the halftime show or accompanying events.[110]

The season came to an end with all attention placed on the Prairie

View–Southern contest on November 27. The two colleges entered the game undefeated in their conference and nationally ranked. Playing at Prairie View's Blackshear Field, the Panthers defeated the Jaguars twenty to thirteen, costing Southern an unbeaten season and sole possession of the national championship.[111]

As Prairie View prepared for their New Year's Day Bowl game against Texas Southern University, the Panthers received some exciting news. Prairie View tied for the 1954 black national championship. The Panthers shared the title with Tennessee State, Southern, and Florida A&M, since all of them had one loss during the season.[112] The championship marked Prairie View's second consecutive, making them the first college in Texas, black or white, to win back-to-back national titles.

The African American community anxiously awaited the New Year's Day game. The black press published advertisements promoting the game that included a picture of Prairie View quarterback Brackins, as well as a listing of all of the events accompanying the game. The "one-hour pregame band and drill show" featured high school bands from Yates High in Houston, Central High from Galveston, Beaumont's Charlton-Pollard High, and Lincoln High from Port Arthur. The Prairie View and Texas Southern bands also performed. Overall, according to the press, the game offered "plenty of fun and holiday entertainment."[113]

All of the pregame publicity worked, as more than ten thousand fans filled Houston's Public School Stadium to watch the Prairie View Bowl. The fans witnessed an exciting game, as Prairie View defended its national championship by defeating Texas Southern fourteen to twelve. The Panthers put together an impressive eighty-five-yard drive in the closing minutes of the fourth quarter that resulted in the winning touchdown.[114]

Texas' African American community shifted even more toward integrated football following the 1954 season. The reason for the change of interest involved four players from Prairie View A&M signing contracts with professional football teams. Tackle Elijah Childress and halfback William Clark signed with the Detroit Lions, while Charlie Brackins joined the Green Bay Packers as the first black college quarterback to play in the National Football League.[115] The fourth player was Charley Wright.[116] While none of these individuals had significant careers in the NFL, the fact that professional teams signed black college football players served as reason enough for many African Americans to follow integrated football.

Despite the changing landscape of college football, Prairie View maintained its dominance by attracting the best athletes. The school recruited the football players by finding a way to pay for the students' school, even though Texas' black colleges gave no official scholarships.[117] Football players received working scholarships, identical to the assistance provided to nonathletes at the school. The athletes seldom carried out the duties of their assigned jobs, however. According to Tommy Williams, who played for Prairie View in the late 1950s, "We seldom worked. We were supposed to pick up the locker room, but we never did. Our job was football."[118]

The integration of undergraduate enrollment in Texas' premier white universities also took place in 1955. The University of Texas and Southern Methodist University became the first of the Southwest Conference schools to admit African Americans. By 1958, integration had occurred at thirty-eight of fifty-seven white colleges in Texas. Not every college in Texas went along with desegregation, though. Texas Tech, Baylor, Rice, and Texas Christian all delayed integrating their undergraduate population until the early 1960s.[119]

Early in the 1955 season, black college football fans found themselves treated to an outstanding game when Texas Southern faced Prairie View. The contest was referred to as the "Texas College Classic" by the black press and attracted more than ten thousand fans to Houston's Public School Stadium. The game also proved important because the twenty-seven to eighteen final score marked the first time in several years that Texas Southern defeated Prairie View.[120]

The Texas College Classic offered an entertaining and popular event for the Texas black community, but the game did not compare to the cultural importance of the State Fair Classic. The year 1955 marked the thirty-first edition of the game. Negro Achievement Day had become so popular among the African American community that the *Houston Informer* again dedicated more space on the social page to the day's events than it gave to the game on the sports page. The paper published accounts and pictures of everything involved including the parade, twins contest, and the Boy and Girl Scouts exhibits. The football game received no mention in the *Informer*.[121]

Even though the *Houston Informer* failed to mention football, the paper made sure to cover a protest by the Youth Council of the Dallas Branch of the NAACP. The Youth Council opposed the segregation at the State Fair. Young people went in groups of five and attempted to make use of the amusements and receive services on days other than Negro Day. The Youth Council also chastised the Black Chamber of Commerce in Dallas for going along with the segregation. The protestors ended by challenging black Texans to stand up against segregation at the fair.[122]

One major trend of black college football in Texas involved the major disparity between the public and private colleges. This difference in the caliber of play always existed, but it became more obvious after World War II. The public colleges possessed more than two thousand students each and fielded large football teams at the same time the private schools watched their athletic numbers dwindle. While both Texas Southern and Prairie View won national championships in the 1950s, Bishop and Wiley struggled to stay out of the bottom of the conference. Along with Wiley's loss to Prairie View at the State Fair, Bishop College lost to Grambling, a state-supported college from Louisiana, eighty to zero. Paul Quinn College also lost on the same day, falling to Tennessee State, eighty-five to zero.[123]

Even as the smaller private schools suffered losing seasons, Texas' African American community still supported the schools, albeit less than the past. Paul Quinn agreed to face Alcorn College in Dallas on Thanksgiving Day. The game took place in conjunction with the State Teachers Association meeting, thus ensuring a large turnout. The two colleges played at the Southern Methodist University stadium, making Paul Quinn and Alcorn the first two African American colleges to use the facilities.[124]

The disparity between the private and public black colleges in Texas caused some of the private colleges to leave the SWAC. Bishop College left the SWAC after 1955 and joined Philander Smith, Tougaloo, and Dillard in forming the Gulf Coast Intercollegiate League. The new conference consisted only of private colleges, thus offering the members a chance at a title. As Tommy Wyatt, a tackle on the Bishop team from 1956–60, recalled, "We were a small school and the conference only consisted of small, church-based schools like us."[125] Wiley originally planned to join, but the school changed its mind and stayed in the SWAC after the alumni pledged better support for athletics.[126]

The defection of Bishop cost the SWAC another one of its original members. In the last game of the 1955 season, Texas Southern reminded African Americans why Bishop chose to join a new conference. The Baptist college from Marshall entered the game with a record of zero wins and nine losses. With a team consisting of less than thirty total players, Bishop lost to Texas Southern by a score of eighty-four to zero. The game proved so lopsided that both schools agreed to only play ten-minute quarters in the second half in an effort to slow Texas Southern's scoring.[127]

Along with Texas Southern, Prairie View continued its dominant ways in the conference. The Panthers failed to win the SWAC title in 1955, but they did upset conference champion Southern University in the last regular season game. Led by freshman running back William Stell, Prairie View defeated Southern nineteen to thirteen.[128]

Prairie View ended its year with the annual Prairie View Bowl. Since the game was considered the main New Year's Day event for African Americans in Texas, the publicity for the matchup focused mostly on the surrounding social activities. For the 1956 contest, the advertisements stressed the pregame one-hour band performance featuring five African American high school bands from around the state.[129]

At the bowl game on January 2, the band performances were popular, but the attendance numbers came in below the previous year's figures. Only six thousand fans journeyed to Houston's Public High School stadium for the contest. Even with the low turnout, the game offered the Texas black community a measure of pride and success as Prairie View scored an easy victory over Fisk University.[130]

With the civil rights movement heating up, white southern universities and politicians opposed integrated athletic events as a means of defiance against federal mandates for integration. One example of the resistance took place in November 1955 when Georgia Tech received a bid to face the University of Pittsburgh at the Sugar Bowl in New Orleans. Georgia governor Marvin Griffin, a staunch segregationist, pressured the board of regents at Georgia Tech to prevent the football team from facing Pittsburgh and its black halfback, Bobbie Grier.[131]

The Georgia Tech students and alumni failed to see Governor Griffin's point of view. Recognizing the importance of the bowl game for creating national exposure for the school, two thousand students marched through downtown Atlanta, turned over cars, and hanged effigies of the governor in protest of the ban on competing. Because of the negative publicity he received, Griffin backed down and the board of regents allowed the team to compete in the Sugar Bowl.[132]

At the same time, major changes came to Texas football. In 1956, Abner Haynes and Leon King enrolled at North Texas State University, and subsequently joined the football team. These actions made Haynes and King the first African Americans to integrate a four-year, white university athletic team in Texas. The two players and their team faced moderate racial prejudice during the late 1950s, but by 1959 Haynes earned All-American recognition and lead North Texas to a nine win, one loss season and a spot in the Sun Bowl. After graduation, Haynes went on to a distinguished career in professional football with the Dallas Texans and Kansas City Chiefs of the American Football League.[133]

The hopes of Prairie View to again dominate black college football decreased some with the Panthers' first game. Prairie View lost to Jackson College, twenty to twelve. The loss was even more devastating to the Panthers since the army drafted Prairie View's starting quarterback, Leon Brooks, along with halfback Edgar Johnson and utility back Warren Maryland, all before the first game.[134]

The Prairie View defeat hurt the school's title chances and thus made Texas Southern the favorite to win the conference. The hopes of Tigers fans increased when Texas Southern easily defeated Southern University to open the season. The two colleges chose to compete in Galveston, creating a bowl game atmosphere. Eight thousand fans journeyed to watch Texas Southern win nineteen to seven. The Tigers' backfield so dominated the game that the trio of Johnny Felder, Lloyd Gardley, and Ernest Lang combined for twenty-five first downs.[135]

Despite Prairie View's loss to Jackson College, as well as the drafting of its starters, the Panthers still possessed the biggest following in Texas. When Prairie View faced Texas Southern, the game served as the premier football match between two black Texas schools.[136] According to the black press, the attendance exceeded the previous contests between the two schools. Texas Southern won the game thirteen to seven.[137]

Wiley also experienced on-field success early in the season. The Wildcats defeated Arkansas State twenty to thirteen in Marshall. The victory served as Wiley's second straight conference win. Despite this early success, Wiley still found little to cheer about because the State Fair decided to remove the Wildcats from the annual State Fair Classic. Even though Wiley had been one of the two original teams to compete, the State Fair and the Dallas Negro Chamber of Commerce chose Tennessee State to face Prairie View. The game's promoters hoped the switch to a nationally ranked opponent would attract more fans.[138]

The change of opponents for Prairie View created a sense of disappointment among Texas' black community for several reasons. Tennessee

State defeated Prairie View forty-five to zero. Furthermore, the loss of the traditional rivalry between Prairie View and Wiley caused the black press to virtually ignore the football game. The only reference to the game in the papers was the score.[139]

The poor showing by some African American college teams in Texas caused the black press to limit its reporting of games. Schools like Jarvis Christian or Butler were not mentioned as the 1956 season progressed. Only Texas Southern received major coverage. After winning their homecoming game over Lincoln before nine thousand fans, the Tigers hoped to win the SWAC. Texas Southern then faced Langston in Fort Worth at Farrington Field. Both schools entered the contest with just one loss.[140]

Even with the decreased press coverage, homecoming games always generated interest. When Prairie View announced its homecoming in the black press, the college expressed its plans to make the event the biggest in the school's history. Festivities were set to include a parade, dances, and the crowning of homecoming and university queens. The game received little promotion other than the announcement of the kickoff time and that Prairie View faced Texas College.[141] Still, 8,500 people journeyed to Prairie View to watch the Panthers win twenty-six to twelve.[142]

As African Americans turned their attention toward the civil rights movement, black college football responded by stressing its role as a social and cultural event to attract fans. When Texas Southern faced Paul Quinn College, fans expressed the most excitement about the fact that local students got in free, and that the game was "local merchants' night."[143] The promotion promised free gifts to "lucky ticket holders."[144]

The one surprise of the 1956 season for black Texans came from Wiley College. The Wildcats, who had failed to finish in the top of the conference since their national championship in 1945, held first place by late November. Unfortunately for Wiley, its twenty to three loss to Southern in Baton Rouge cost them the SWAC title. Still, for the African American community in Texas, the return of success at Wiley provided something to cheer about.[145]

As the annual Prairie View Bowl rolled around, the Panthers discovered that their unimpressive record for the season made it hard to find an opponent. After receiving criticism from fans for attempting to book a weak team to ensure a Prairie View victory, the Panthers chose Texas Southern as an opponent. Since the Tigers were co-champions of the SWAC, and from neighboring Houston, the game received a considerable amount of interest. A local Houston radio station, KCOH, even broadcast the game live.[146]

The Prairie View Bowl proved to be one of the best football games of the year. Texas Southern took a six to zero lead into halftime, but Prairie View came back in the second half to win twenty-seven to six. Unfortunately, the game only attracted 5,500 fans, a decrease from the previous year's attendance.[147]

One reason for the decrease in the number of fans came from the appearance of Syracuse University at the Cotton Bowl in Dallas. In 1956, Texas A&M won the Southwest Conference, but Texas Christian played in the Cotton Bowl because of the Aggies' probation.[148] As a result, Texas Christian faced Syracuse University and its All-American running back Jim Brown in the Cotton Bowl on January 1, 1957. Brown dominated the game. He rushed for 132 yards and scored twenty-one points. Unfortunately for Brown, TCU won the contest by a score of twenty-eight to twenty-seven following a bad snap on a Syracuse point-after-touchdown attempt. Sixty-eight thousand spectators filled the Cotton Bowl in Dallas to watch the game.[149] The *Dallas Express* declared that African Americans in Texas "could take great pleasure in Brown on the field."[150] The *Express* also argued that since Brown was a senior and only twenty years old, he must be smarter than the rest of the white seniors on both the Syracuse and Texas Christian teams because the white players were twenty-one and twenty-two years old.[151]

By the end of the 1950s, African Americans in Texas watched a steady stream of black high school football players accept scholarship offers from white colleges outside the state instead of playing for Texas' black college teams. Charley Taylor played for Grand Prairie's Dalworth High School in the late 1950s. When it came time to choose a college, he picked Arizona State. Taylor became one of the top wide receivers in the country and eventually played professional football, where he caught 649 passes for the Washington Redskins.[152]

The effort to integrate white colleges reached the football teams in the late 1950s. The Southwest Conference schools still followed strict segregation football, but Texas' smaller white colleges possessed fewer restrictions. Besides Haynes at North Texas, Leford Fant played wide receiver for Texas Western University in El Paso in 1958.[153] The integration of white college teams marked a major milestone for college football in Texas.

The African Americans who served as the pioneers of integration in white colleges faced many trials along the road to equality. Black players on white Texas teams served as constant targets of abuse from opposing players and fans. Refusing to compete against Haynes, the University of Mississippi, Mississippi State, and Chattanooga University all cancelled their games against North Texas State. The problems faced by the black football players also extended beyond their opponents to the black athletes' own schools. Haynes found himself forced to live with relatives in Denton's black neighborhood while attending college because North Texas State refused to integrate its dormitories.[154]

At the same time, the civil rights movement won a significant victory. Congress passed the Civil Rights Act of 1957. The act marked the first civil rights legislation by the federal government since Reconstruction. The actual bill possessed little power. It created a civil rights commission to monitor violations of African American civil rights. The commission also suggested solutions to protect African Americans, but received no power to carry out its proposals.[155]

Despite all these changes, the black colleges in Texas looked excitedly toward the new season. No team expressed more optimism for the 1957 season than Wiley. The Wildcats sought to build off of the previous year's success. After finishing seventh in 1955, Wiley won its way into a tie for first place in the conference in 1956. This success caused sixty students to come out for the team in 1957.[156]

The other co-SWAC champion from 1956, Texas Southern, found itself challenged early in the 1957 season. The Tigers' first two opponents, Southern University and Wiley, both appeared to be contenders for the conference title in the upcoming season. Texas Southern's worries were unfounded in regard to Southern University, though, as the Tigers defeated the Jaguars nineteen to six.[157]

Texas' other black colleges all experienced favorable outcomes in their first games. Prairie View, Wiley, Texas College, and Jarvis Christian all won. Bishop, the only African American college in Texas not to win its opening game, lost to Wiley by a score of twenty-six to zero.[158] For black college fans the loss brought little importance since the game marked the return of the Bishop College band. After being without one for several years, the school reinstated the band, which made its marching debut at the Wiley game.[159]

Wiley continued its surprising success. The Wildcats followed up their season-opening victory over Bishop by defeating Texas Southern twelve to six.[160] Wiley then beat Grambling by a score of forty to twelve.[161] These victories resulted in Wiley leading the conference going into the last month of the season.

Even with all of Wiley's success, the Wildcats still found themselves excluded from the State Fair Classic. Prairie View decided to face Texas Southern at the 1957 contest. The change to Texas Southern took place because of the poor attendance the previous year when Tennessee State thoroughly defeated Prairie View in the game. Prairie View came out of the contest victorious in 1957, winning seven to six. Unfortunately, only three thousand fans journeyed to Dallas to watch the game. While the black press blamed the low turnout on bad weather, the *Dallas Express* pointed out that the three thousand fans were significantly fewer than when Wiley and Prairie View faced each other at the fair.[162]

Attendance figures declined rapidly the late 1950s. Black college football responded by promoting the social elements of the sport. For Prairie View's game against Grambling on October 26 in Prairie View, the Panthers declared the day "Dad's Day." The college encouraged the fathers of all the schools' students to attend the game and the special reception afterward.[163]

Black college football in Texas sought other ways to attract fans to games. When Prairie View faced Arkansas AM&N at the Golden Lions' homecoming game, the Panthers' fans back in the Houston area found themselves able to watch the game on television. Broadcast over KATV out of Houston, the game was the first live broadcast of an all-African American football game. Two black-owned businesses in Pine Bluff, Arkansas, the PK Miller Funeral Home and the College Grocery Store, paid for the cost of showing the game. Also, the broadcast did nothing to hurt ticket sales, as seven thousand people attended.[164]

Meanwhile, Wiley continued its march to a second consecutive conference title. The Wildcats defeated Texas College by a score of forty to twenty. A "large crowd" filled Wiley Stadium on Thanksgiving Day to watch Wiley continue its unbeaten season.[165]

Wiley wrapped up its successful season and the conference championship by defeating Prairie View fourteen to six. Prairie View entered the contest ranked second in the conference, with the Panthers' only loss coming against Southern University. Led by quarterback Ike Iglehart, who passed for both of Wiley's touchdowns, the Wildcats dominated the Panthers. Prairie View's only points came with seven minutes left in the game when Thomas Daniels returned a kickoff eighty yards for a touchdown. The conference title implications of the game attracted eight thousand fans to Prairie View's Blackshear Field.[166]

Because of Wiley's undefeated season, the Wildcats received an invitation to face the Military Academy of Mexico in the first ever International Classic. The new classic took place in San Antonio at Alamo Stadium on December 16.[167] Unfortunately for Wiley, the black press in Texas never reported how the Wildcats performed against the Military Institute, and the International Classic never occurred again.

Prairie View rebounded from its loss to Wiley by facing Texas Southern in the thirtieth edition of the Prairie View Bowl. The game marked the third straight year the two schools competed and the second time they faced each other that season. The game ended in a six to six tie. The contest sent mixed messages about the state of black college football in Texas. The *Houston Informer* made the game its front-page story on January 4, 1958. At the same time, only a few thousand fans attended. The *Informer* blamed the poor fan turnout on the cold weather that hit Houston on New Year's Day, but Prairie View Bowl attendance had decreased steadily over the previous few years.[168]

The late 1950s witnessed several changes in black college football. The costs faced by private African American colleges in Texas to field competitive football teams extended to other private colleges around the country. Langston University of Oklahoma found the price of competition too high and left the SWAC in 1957. The next year, the SWAC responded by adding two state-supported schools, Grambling College of Louisiana and Jackson State of Mississippi. The change left Texas College and Wiley as the only two private schools remaining in the conference.[169]

Texas Southern became involved in the movement to integrate Texas' universities. Ralph Lee, a white member of Texas Southern's board of directors and an ardent segregationist, publicly stated that he voted to keep Texas Southern an all-black institution to maintain the all-white status at Texas' public white universities. In response to Lee's actions, Reverend E. A. Munson, an independent white Baptist minister, enrolled at Texas Southern and was accepted as a student. Munson's action negated the "separate but equal" argument made by white Texans concerning higher education in the state.[170]

Paul Quinn, which joined the weaker South Central Athletic Association in 1958 in an effort to increase revenues through affiliation with a conference, played fewer games and attracted less qualified athletes than the other African American colleges in Texas. Paul Quinn's home attendance also fell far below that of other colleges, averaging less than one thousand fans per outing. All of these factors made competition next to impossible for the private institution. The *Houston Informer* addressed the situation, asking fans and the state to come up with a plan to assist the small colleges since the private schools projected a combined athletic budget deficit of $250,000 in 1958.[171]

All of the black colleges in Texas addressed declining attendance figures by focusing their efforts on specific contests, usually in cities with large African American communities. Black college football in Texas originally used this practice in the 1920s to build its fan base. In the late 1950s, the schools found themselves forced to return to the idea to meet increasing athletic budgets. For example, the Wiley-Bishop contest in 1958 took place in Dallas at Southern Methodist University's Ownby Stadium. Wiley routed its rival institution forty-two to eight before three thousand fans. Both schools believed the three thousand spectators exceeded the number that would have attended if the game took place in Marshall.[172]

Tommy Wyatt of Bishop recounted the rivalry between the two Marshall schools. "It was a friendly rivalry," Wyatt said. "We wanted to beat them, but we were not playing for the same accolades. Whoever lost, it did not affect their position in the conference."[173] Wyatt went on to state that "no animosity" existed between the two schools, with students visiting each other's campus, supporting the other institution's teams, and also dating students from the opposite school.[174] These interactions provide a good example of the role of black college football at the time. The rivalries and competitions remained important, but community identity as a whole superseded the physical contests.

In 1958, black college football continued to feel the growing impact of the civil rights movement. The Texas black community focused its attention on integrating white institutions. Black athletes who played for white colleges in the state became increasingly popular. Many black youths also expressed anger over African American acceptance of segregated facilities and institutions. This aspect of the civil rights movement caused the Black Chamber of Commerce in Dallas to change Negro Day at the State Fair. Protests over the segregated day had gone on for several years leading up to that point. In 1958 the Black Chamber of Commerce and the State Fair dropped the separate days but kept the facilities segregated. As a result, when Prairie View and Texas Southern met for the State Fair Classic on October 13 in the Cotton Bowl, the game took place as part of "Higher Education in Texas Day."[175]

The decline in attendance figures affected the black public colleges the least. Prairie View maintained a competitive football program throughout the late 1950s. Supported by state funds and the largest enrollment of any black college in Texas, exceeding two thousand students, Prairie View contended for the SWAC title annually. The year 1958 saw the Panthers open the season with one win and one tie entering the State Fair Classic. Prairie View's winning streak continued as the Panthers defeated Texas Southern twenty-six to nineteen at the Cotton Bowl. Texas Southern held a nineteen to eighteen lead with three minutes left in the game, but Prairie View rallied for the win.[176]

Prairie View went on to an undefeated season in 1958. The Panthers dominated the SWAC, defeating Grambling forty-four to six and Southern twenty to fourteen.[177] While black college football in Texas watched its role in African American culture decrease in the late 1950s, Prairie View showed that through success the sport still maintained community spirit and pride. When Prairie View played its homecoming game against Texas College, the contest involved the first and second place teams in the conference. As a result, more than ten thousand fans traveled to Prairie View to watch the Panthers win forty-three to zero.[178]

The success of the Prairie View football team helped increase the school's finances through football ticket sales and alumni donations. This improved economic situation led the college's board of directors to approve the construction of a new student center in 1958. The two-story, air-conditioned building included a snack bar, cafeteria, post office, lounges, and other means of recreation for students. The proposed cost of the building project reached one million dollars.[179]

Texas' other black colleges refused to give in to the declining attendance and importance of football. Texas Southern attracted attention for its football program when the Tigers faced white Corpus Christi University. Since Texas Southern already had lost three games that season, its twenty to zero victory over Corpus Christi appealed to the members of the community fighting for the end of segregation in Texas. The victory by the Tigers further pushed the issue that African Americans deserved equal access and treatment in the state.[180]

Texas College also experienced success in 1958. Picked to finish last, the Steers surprised the sportswriters and fans, finishing second. The season marked the best year by Texas College in more than a decade. The Steers also showed that though private and public schools in the SWAC had very different resources available, a small school still possessed the ability to occasionally defeat a large one. An example of this occurred when the Steers knocked undefeated Southern University from the conference lead. Down six to zero at halftime, Texas College capitalized on eight Southern turnovers to win thirteen to six. Furthermore, the game served as the Texas College homecoming, and as a result attracted five thousand fans to Tyler.[181]

The non-SWAC colleges in Texas also experienced success in 1958. With Paul Quinn's victory over Alcorn College, the Tigers won the SCAC title. The conference championship marked the first for Paul Quinn in thirty-four years, dating back to the college's 1922 SWAC championship.[182]

Also in 1958, Prairie View agreed to face Florida A&M in the Orange Blossom Classic. The game showed that black college football still possessed a national following as more than thirty-nine thousand fans filled Miami's Orange Bowl. Prairie View won the contest twenty-six to eight and earned the national championship.[183] The national title marked the third for coach Billy Nicks since his arrival at Prairie View in 1949.[184]

Prairie View concluded its successful season by beating Langston twenty-four to six in the Prairie View Bowl. The thirty-first edition of the New Year's Day game attracted a "cheering crowd" that totaled less than ten thousand fans.[185] While the African American community followed the Prairie View Bowl, the 1959 contest lost some spectators to the local CBS affiliate in Houston that broadcast three national bowl games—the Cotton Bowl, Orange Bowl, and Gator Bowl—on New Year's Day. All three contests featured integrated teams.[186]

As the integration of big-time white college football continued, many kept a close watch in hopes that Texas would soon heed the call. In 1956, Charles "Bud" Wilkinson, the head coach of the University of Oklahoma, signed Prentiss Gault, an African American quarterback, to a football scholarship. In 1957, he made the varsity team, lettered three years, and made the all-conference his senior year. The recruitment of Gault made the University of Oklahoma the first major university in its area to sign a black athlete to play football. Then, in 1958, the University of Missouri, which had previously refused to compete against teams fielding African Americans, integrated its football team.[187]

As the civil rights movement grew in intensity by 1959, football in Texas got caught up in the fight. The city of Houston hosted a preseason game between the Chicago Bears and Pittsburgh Steelers of the National Football League. The game's promoters announced ahead of time that African Americans would receive "choice seats." Come game time, the black Houstonians who purchased tickets found themselves relegated to the end zones, regardless of the seat printed on the ticket. As a result, Lloyd Wells of the *Houston Informer* urged all African Americans to "never attend a segregated game under any conditions."[188] Wells went on to state that many African Americans tore up their tickets over the segregation, leaving only two hundred black Texans in attendance at the game. Wells expressed his hope that next time no African Americans would purchase tickets, thus forcing Houston to desegregate its facilities to avoid losing money.[189]

Prairie View again dominated the 1959 season. The team's lopsided victories put the Panthers in first place for scoring among both black and white small colleges in the United States. Prairie View also placed fifteenth in total defense. For black Texans, both of these accomplishments served as evidence that black college football players in Texas were equally as talented as white players in the state.[190]

The black press continued to devote less attention to the smaller schools than to Prairie View and Texas Southern. In 1959, Paul Quinn faced Jarvis Christian in Hawkins at Jarvis Christian's stadium, the Mosquito Bowl. Paul Quinn won the game thirty-seven to two. An article in the *Houston Informer* covering the game took up two inches of copy. At the same time, the Prairie View–Texas Southern game at the State Fair covered more than half the sports page.[191] Even without much support, Paul Quinn continued to play well. The Tigers followed up their victory over Jarvis with a win against Rusk College.[192]

The State Fair Classic, the premier black college football game in Texas, experienced a slight increase in fan attendance to close out the 1950s. A total of twelve thousand fans watched Prairie View defeat Texas Southern thirty-four to fifteen, yet attendance was still far below that of the contest's peak years. The passing offensive strategy used by both schools made the game exciting for the fans. John "Bo" Farringon of

Prairie View also built the excitement while playing wide receiver and defensive back. He held the title as the fastest man in the SWAC after setting the conference record in the one hundred–yard dash the previous spring. Farrington scored two touchdowns on the day and "played a whale of a defensive ball game" as he showed off for a professional scout from the Chicago Bears who came to watch the contest.[193]

As the season progressed, the press coverage given to colleges like Jarvis Christian and Paul Quinn decreased. The black press in Texas instead chose to cover Prairie View's unbeaten streak. The Panthers' thirty-five to six victory over Grambling received a large banner in the paper and an article covering the majority of the sports page.[194]

For the remainder of the black colleges, homecoming offered the best chance of attracting fans. The schools continued to offer extra events such as dances, dinners, and parades to entice alumni and fans to campus for the football game. Texas Southern expected five thousand spectators as the Tigers sought to keep their homecoming record perfect.[195] Nothing helped a college inspire its fans more than a homecoming win. Jarvis Christian won its homecoming game over Philander Smith. That contest attracted over two hundred more fans to Hawkins than had attended the previous Jarvis Christian games.[196]

Meanwhile, Prairie View continued its winning streak, finishing the regular season undefeated and ranked first nationally. The Panthers once again accepted a bid to face Florida A&M at the Orange Blossom Classic in Miami. The game received more attention than a regular game because Florida A&M entered the contest ranked second in the nation, making the classic a fight for the national championship.[197]

Unfortunately for Prairie View, Florida A&M defeated the Panthers twenty-six to seven. The loss dropped Prairie View from first to third in the nation.[198] Even with the loss, the decade ended with some positive notes for black college football in Texas. As his team prepared to face Texas Southern in the Prairie View Bowl on New Year's Day, the Washington, DC, Pigskin Club named Prairie View coach Billy Nicks the coach of the year for small colleges. Nicks beat out coaches from white colleges for the award. The Pigskin Club flew Nicks to Washington, DC, and put him up in a hotel. Nicks's victory countered the racial prejudice used to keep blacks segregated. Whites argued African Americans were not intelligent enough to perform skilled jobs in big-time college football—certainly not coaching. Nicks offered living proof of the inaccuracy of this racist ideology.[199]

The 1950s marked a period of both profound success and a decline in significance for black college football. Prairie View won two national championships and Texas Southern won one. Several African American football players joined the National Football League. Early in the decade, large crowds watched the state's black colleges compete, including more than twenty thousand annually for the State Fair Classic.

At the same time, Texas' private black colleges found it difficult to compete. Schools like Jarvis Christian and Paul Quinn watched their attendance figures fall well below the other colleges in the state. The disparity between the private and public black colleges was so great that when Samuel Huston joined with Tillotson to form a new college, the school cancelled its football program altogether in order to focus on academics.

As the importance of black college football declined, so did interest in the State Fair Classic. With protests over segregation at the State Fair, promoters of Negro Day and the State Fair Classic watched as attendance figures plummeted. African Americans began to view the segregated day and sporting event as counterproductive to the enhancement of civil rights and positive images of black masculinity. The idea that self-governing black groups and events allowed for healthy expressions of African American culture and masculinity disappeared as civil rights protests became the norm.

The onset of the civil rights movement marked a further decline in the importance of black college football for the African American population of Texas. As African Americans fought throughout the state and the nation for equal rights, the popularity of segregated teams and institutions decreased. Thus black college football found itself in a tenuous position entering the 1960s as integrated sports and civil rights pushed black college football further from the minds of the African American community, both in Texas and around the nation.

The 1960s marked a turbulent time for African Americans. The civil rights movement dominated people's actions and thoughts. The quest for equal rights received the majority of coverage by the black press. As African Americans fought to end segregation throughout society, traditional black institutions fell by the wayside. Black college football became one such institution.

Despite the significant athletic success of Prairie View A&M and Texas Southern University in the 1950s, black college football in Texas watched its attendance figures decrease. In the 1960s, fans became less and less interested in black college football as integrated football reached Texas. When professional football began in Texas, and the state's white college football teams started recruiting African American athletes, black colleges in Texas found themselves unable to compete. As a result, by the end of the decade, only Prairie View, Texas Southern, and Bishop still fielded football teams.

The arrival of professional football in Texas played a major role in the declining popularity of black college football. In March of 1959, Houston oilman Bud Adams met with Dallas oilman and shipping magnate Lamar Hunt. The two men previously had attempted to acquire National Football League (NFL) franchises but were denied. They then decided to create their own competing league, the American Football League (AFL).[1]

The AFL featured eight teams, including the Houston Oilers and the Dallas Texans, all of which fielded integrated teams. The new league found itself unable to compete with the older, established NFL for star players from white colleges. As a result, the AFL looked all over the country for talented players. Black college football offered a largely untapped market for the AFL. For example, Al Davis, an assistant coach with the San Diego Chargers, signed Ernie Ladd, a defensive tackle from Grambling. Ladd, who was born in Rayville, Louisiana, but grew up in

Orange, Texas, went on to play for more than thirteen years in professional football.[2] Also, the Dallas Texans signed Abner Haynes, the star running back from North Texas State University.[3]

The NFL responded to Adams and Hunt's threat by creating its own team in Dallas in an effort to maintain a monopoly of the market. The Dallas Cowboys began play in 1960. The NFL rushed the Cowboys into existence for them to compete for fans and ticket money with the AFL. To fill out the roster, a player pool was established at the league meeting in Los Angeles. Each of the twelve NFL teams froze twenty-five players on their rosters. The Cowboys then picked three players from each of the other teams, for a roster of thirty-six veterans. The Dallas team entered its first season so inadequately prepared to compete that the Cowboys lost every game they played in its first year, with the exception of one tie. With the NFL's financial backing and television contracts, though, the Cowboys soon dominated Texas football. The team developed a huge following, especially among the state's black population, since the Cowboys continually fielded African American star players.[4]

Black college football also lost fan support and cultural significance in the 1960s as college students around the country became even more involved in the civil rights movement. In cities like Greenville, North Carolina, and Atlanta, Georgia, students from black colleges focused their attention on integrating public facilities like lunch counters. Students would enter a counter, sit down, and wait for service. Receiving none, and sometimes being treated violently by white patrons, the students would remain until the counter closed. The students would repeat the process the next day and continue the protests for several months, as in the case of Greenville in 1960, until the white businesses gave in and desegregated the lunch counters.[5]

Nonviolent protests involving African American college students also took place in Texas in 1960. That year, African American students from Wiley and Bishop met to fight racial prejudice in the city of Marshall.[6] At Prairie View in the early 1960s, students, including members of the football team, marched to nearby Hempstead and integrated the town's cafés.[7] Since Prairie View was the largest employer in Waller County, the protests quickly achieved the intended results.[8]

Texas Southern University's students became some of the most actively involved in the civil rights movement among black college students in the state. This high level of involvement stemmed from the location of Texas Southern in Houston's Third Ward, as well as direct, daily contact between students and the problems faced by the urban poor.[9] On March 4, 1960, more than fifty students from Texas Southern protested at Weingarten's Supermarket near the university campus. The students held a sit-in, seeking to integrate the store's lunch counter.[10]

Over the next two weeks, the Texas Southern students expanded their protests to include other Houston stores, such as Walgreen's Drugstore and Woolworth's Department Store. The owners of the targeted stores responded to the protests by closing their lunch counters.[11] The protests attracted enough attention that Texas Southern University students joined with white students from Rice University and the University of Houston to form the Progressive Youth Association (PYA). The PYA used nonviolent protests and sit-ins to push for integration in Houston. The association listed among its purposes and objectives the total integration of American society, improved economic status, better employment opportunities, and good will among the races.[12] The protests worked, as nine downtown department stores agreed to integrate their lunch counters on September 1, 1960.

At the same time, the integration of white college football expanded in Texas. One particular event at the start of the decade brought the issue of integration to the attention of a wide range of Texans. In 1960, Ernie Davis, an African American, led the Syracuse Orangemen to the Cotton Bowl to face the University of Texas. The All-American running back dominated the game as Syracuse defeated the Longhorns twenty-three to fourteen to win the national championship.[13]

The active involvement of Texas' African Americans in the civil rights movement, combined with integration at white colleges in Texas, caused black college football to decrease in importance to the African American community. The general black population in Texas cut back on the amount of support it gave to football as fans without a direct connection to the colleges shifted their interests to other activities. Even with decreased interest among the general population, the state's black colleges only saw marginal declines in overall enrollment. Enrollments at the public colleges of Prairie View and Texas Southern increased as a result of the cheap tuition offered by the two schools.[14]

While still important, the black colleges provided a deep sense of identity for those people with a direct relationship to the colleges.

However, professional football teams in Texas began to fill the cultural position formerly held by black college football, receiving more coverage in the state's African American newspapers than the black colleges. The *Houston Informer* focused the majority of its August 27 sports page to the six black players on the Dallas Texans' roster.[15] Integrated football created a new source of cultural identity for black Texans because the sport fit into the goals of the larger civil rights movement, equality in all aspects of American society. When Dallas defeated Houston on September 3, fifty-one thousand fans, including several thousand African Americans, filled the Cotton Bowl.[16]

The large African American turnout at the Cotton Bowl resulted in part from the Texans integrating the seating in their stadium. The black press praised the organization for its actions, while lambasting the Houston Oilers for continuing segregation in their stadium. The segregation resulted in only fifty black fans attending the team's game against the Oakland Raiders in September 1960. The *Houston Informer* called for a boycott of Oiler games until the team changed its seating practices.[17]

In this evolving environment, state-supported institutions dominated black college football. The favorites to win the SWAC in 1960 included Prairie View, Texas Southern, Grambling, and Southern. Meanwhile, the black press picked the two private colleges, Wiley and Texas College, to finish seventh and eighth, respectively, out of eight teams.[18]

Other changes took place as black college football in Texas sought to cope with its new status. In 1960, Prairie View replaced Texas Southern with Wiley College as the Panthers' opponent for the State Fair Classic. Wiley, an original competitor in the classic, had been absent for several years. Prairie View still competed against Texas Southern, but the two schools played in Houston where the bulk of their fan base lived.[19] As a result of the venue change, eleven thousand spectators watched Prairie View hold off Texas Southern thirty-five to twenty-eight in 1960.[20]

The next week when Prairie View and Wiley prepared to face each other at the State Fair, the two colleges found their contest lost support to the civil rights movement. Althea Simmons, a black attorney and the executive secretary of the Texas State Conference of the NAACP, led a demonstration against the State Fair's discriminatory practice of limiting African American access to only one day. The protesters formed a picket line around the fair grounds to pressure the city into granting African

Americans access to the midway on a year-round basis.[21] The segregation of the State Fair appeared even more hypocritical to black Texans since the Dallas Texan's games in the Cotton Bowl were integrated.

While the protest attracted a considerable amount of attention, the black press in Texas failed to report on the football game the following week. Instead, the *Houston Informer* discussed the eight thousand five hundred African Americans who attended the Dallas Cowboys–Cleveland Browns game the day before the Wiley–Prairie View contest. Black fans were particularly interested in the professional game because Dallas fielded two black players, while Cleveland's roster contained seven African Americans, including the best player in the league, running back Jim Brown.[22]

The interest in black college football among the general African American population of Texas began to decline throughout the state. The same weekend as the Dallas-Cleveland NFL contest, Texas Southern easily defeated Texas College by a score of twenty to six. The game, which took place in Tyler, drew "only a small crowd" according to the *Dallas Express*.[23] As November rolled around, Texas' black colleges found themselves in poor shape in regard to football. Prairie View entered the month undefeated, but after losing to Grambling twenty-six to zero, the Panthers' chance at the conference title appeared slim.[24] Meanwhile, Texas Southern, Wiley, and Texas College held the last three places in the conference. To make matters worse, neither Wiley nor Texas College had yet won a game.[25]

The regular season came to a close with Prairie View facing Southern University at Houston's Jeppesen Stadium. The game held conference and national title implications since Southern entered the game undefeated while Prairie View had only one loss, to Grambling. Twenty thousand fans watched the Panthers upset Southern twenty-three to fifteen. As a result, Prairie View, Southern, and Grambling all shared the SWAC title.[26]

Meanwhile, black Texans also found themselves able to point to college football as proof that African Americans deserved equality with whites. In 1961, "Pistol" Pete Pedro, an African American running back at West Texas State University in Canyon, led the nation in scoring with twenty-two touchdowns as a sophomore. He even scored six touchdowns in one game against Texas Western University from El Paso. [27]

At the same time, professional football in Texas developed an even bigger following when the Houston Oilers won the first AFL championship in 1960. The team featured two African Americans, Julian Spence and John White. Spence also made the league's all-star team as a defensive back.[28]

The civil rights movement continued to intersect with football. In 1961, for example, students at UCLA threatened a boycott of the Rose Bowl on New Year's Day if their school consented to play the segregated team from the University of Alabama. The student opposition to racial prejudice stemmed directly from their firsthand exposure to the situation in the American South from participation in the Freedom Rides of 1961 and other civil rights activities. The prejudice faced by African Americans no longer existed as an abstract concept, but a very real situation.[29]

The changes in American society that resulted in declining numbers of fans attending football games increased financial concerns for athletic departments. The financial questions related to intercollegiate football created a difficult problem for the state-supported universities of Prairie View and Texas Southern. For the private black colleges in Texas, though, the decline in fan attendance and interest became catastrophic. The cost of fielding a competitive football team in the 1960s proved too high. As a result, other aspects of the colleges, like academic programs, suffered. Bishop College sought to improve its situation by moving from Marshall to Dallas in 1961. By positioning itself in one of the state's largest cities, Bishop attracted enough students to remain financially viable and field a football team for close to thirty more years.[30]

The change of location kept Bishop going financially, but the college's football team continued to struggle on the field. The Tigers lost to their longtime foe, Wiley, by a score of twenty-four to twelve. Wiley, one of the weaker teams in the SWAC, dominated Bishop, showing that the difference in the level of play still existed between the SWAC colleges and the rest of Texas' black colleges.[31]

The struggles for civil rights and for black college football again came together at the State Fair Classic in 1961. According to the *Dallas Express*, a record number of visitors journeyed to the fair on the day of the State Fair Classic. The visitor turnout, which exceeded that of the previous few years, came about because the State Fair organizers and the city of Dallas acquiesced to African American protests and integrated the fairgrounds. Starting in 1961, black Texans received access to Fair Park at all times, instead of just the two days a year as previously occurred.

With the integration, though, the celebratory atmosphere that existed on Negro Achievement Day disappeared as the fair organizers cancelled the African American parade, giving no reason for the action.[32]

The many different competing events in the early 1960s caused the black college football season to receive little publicity in 1961. The professional games of the Houston Oilers, Dallas Texans, and Dallas Cowboys attracted the majority of attention from black newspapers in Texas and the state's community. Only Texas Southern and Prairie View found it possible to attract a following among people with no affiliation to an African American college as the two schools competed for the conference championship. Not every game played by the Texas schools received interest from African Americans, though. The casual fans only followed the games against the SWAC's other top teams. For example, Texas Southern's twenty-three to nineteen loss to Grambling attracted ten thousand fans in Louisiana.[33] Twelve thousand spectators attended Prairie View's homecoming victory over Bishop College. At the same time, Wiley's twenty-one to nineteen upset victory over Southern University only generated a listing of the score and no mention of the attendance in the black press.[34]

Texas College received its only press coverage of the season when the Steers lost their final game of 1961 to Wiley by a score of fifty-six to zero. For Texas College, the loss was more troublesome, as the college announced plans to leave the SWAC following the season. One of the original members of the conference, the Steers, found it impossible to compete physically and financially against the state-supported institutions.[35]

The 1961 season also was eventful for Paul Quinn College. Despite being the oldest black college in Texas and one of the founding members of the Southwestern Athletic Conference, the Tigers found it too expensive to remain competitive in intercollegiate football. As a result, Paul Quinn cancelled its program entirely following the 1961 season. The move made Paul Quinn the second black college in Texas to drop football.[36]

The number of people involved in the civil rights movement continued to increase during the early 1960s. Activists stepped up campaigns to integrate public facilities in Texas, which soon involved efforts to integrate sports facilities in the state. Inspired by the desegregation of the Cotton Bowl and Dallas Texan's games, African Americans in Houston fought to end segregated seating at the Oilers' games. The publicity garnered by the protests generated support throughout the country for the desegrega-tion efforts in Houston. When the Oilers played the New York Titans in New York on December 10, 1961, several hundred members of New York's chapter of CORE picketed the contest. The protesters in New York handed out flyers detailing the segregation in Houston and urged people to boycott the Titans-Oilers game in an effort to show support for Houston's black community and to bring about change.[37]

George Preston Marshall, owner of the Washington Redskins, further incorporated the NFL into the civil rights movement by refusing to sign African American players. One of the founding members of the league, by 1961, only Marshall's Redskins continued to field all-white teams. The Redskins' location in the nation's capital made them a point of contention regarding race relations. Newly elected President John F. Kennedy openly sought to integrate the Washington team, including having Secretary of the Interior Stewart Udall warn Marshall in 1961 of impending federal intervention unless integration occurred. The public stance by Kennedy regarding football foreshadowed a stronger government presence in the realm of racial integration.[38]

The challenges to segregation in the NFL stadiums in Texas mirrored other challenges to segregation that still existed in sports. In baseball, the majority of professional teams still undertook spring training in Florida. In the cities that hosted the baseball teams, integration moved slowly, with black players still residing in segregated housing while training. By the early 1960s, civil rights protests decried the injustices faced by African American ballplayers during spring training in cities like St. Petersburg, Florida.[39]

While protests concerning segregated seating in Houston continued, the Oilers still fielded black players, a fact that caused the team to grow in popularity. Assistance for the successful growth of Texas' professional football teams came from the fact that in 1961 the Houston Oilers again won the AFL championship. In the championship game, the Oilers defeated the San Diego Chargers, featuring native Texan Ernie Ladd, by a score of ten to three.[40]

The following summer, black Texans experienced another step forward in the fight for equal rights. In 1962, the US District Court, Southern District, returned a decision in favor of Houston's African American community. Responding to a lawsuit brought by community activists of the Charles A. George Dental Society in Houston, the court ordered Harris County to integrate the public swimming area at Sylvan Beach, in La Porte, one of the Houston area's main public beaches.[41] A second civil rights victory took place for African Americans in Texas during that year. The city of Houston reached an agreement with black protesters over the issue of integrating city facilities. The city government agreed to integrate all public facilities. Other large cities in Texas, such as Austin and Dallas, soon followed Houston's example.[42]

Despite the success the civil rights movement experienced in Texas and around the country in the early 1960s, problems still existed. The Houston railroad station chose to fight the decision of the city government to integrate. Students from Texas Southern University and Rice University held sit-in protests at the station in response. The protest grew and achieved more attention when the Congress on Racial Equality joined the struggle. The effort for integration at the train depot failed when the city police arrested five of the student activists for unlawful assembly and a court fined them five hundred dollars.[43]

The effect of the civil rights movement and integrated football on black college football appeared evident at the start of the 1962 season, when the *Houston Informer* announced it planned to only cover the "big game of the week." With fans more interested in integrated sports, the *Informer* made a financial decision to cover games that brought the most readership. In an effort to reduce expenses, the paper focused its efforts on just one black college game each week, usually involving Prairie View, Texas Southern, Grambling, or Southern University. As a result, the *Informer* saved money on reporters and travel to isolated games in Marshall and Louisiana. The newspaper then spent the savings to cover integrated professional football.[44]

The coverage of only one football game a week left Bishop College and Jarvis Christian College in a predicament. Neither school belonged to the SWAC. As a result, the *Houston Informer* published almost no coverage of the two schools' games. The *Dallas Express* covered Bishop, but only because the Baptist college had moved to Dallas the previous year. Despite the lack of attention toward athletics, Bishop College saw its enrollment and financial stability increase in the larger city.

At the same time, the black press announced another casualty of the decline in interest toward black college football. Texas College, which left the SWAC following the 1961 season, cancelled its football team entirely before the 1962 season. The Steers, who won the black college national championship in 1935, announced they still planned to compete in the less expensive sports of basketball and track, but not football.[45] For black college football fans in Texas, the death of Arnett Mumford compounded the heartbreak of losing Texas College. Mumford, who coached at Southern University for more than twenty years, began his career at Jarvis Christian College, then landed at Bishop before heading at Texas College and guiding the Steers to their only national championship.[46]

With the loss of Texas College, the SWAC brought in Alcorn College from Mississippi as a new member. The addition of Alcorn left Wiley as the only private college in the conference. While competing as a private college left Wiley at a disadvantage in regard to player talent and team size, the Wildcats welcomed Alcorn to the SWAC with a twenty-eight to seven victory.[47]

Black college football continued to push on in the 1960s. Rivalries such as Prairie View–Texas Southern and Wiley-Bishop still attracted fans. While the attendance figures in the 1960s fell compared to the number of fans who attended in the 1930s and 1940s, the games remained popular. When Wiley faced Bishop in 1962, their fans expressed excitement over the fact that the two schools would play the contest for the first time at Bishop's new campus in Dallas.[48]

The biggest rivalry in the state remained Prairie View–Texas Southern. The game at Houston's Jeppeson Stadium attracted 18,500 fans in 1962. Prairie View entered the game picked to lose, but almost pulled off an upset. Texas Southern responded to the Panthers' challenge, though, and came back from a fourteen-point deficit to win twenty-one to fourteen.[49]

The State Fair Classic between Prairie View and Wiley also attracted a considerable number of fans with more than eighteen thousand spectators attending the game at the Cotton Bowl. While the attendance numbers fell below the twenty thousand mark set in the late 1940s, the crowd exceeded the average number of fans from the previous ten years. The increased attendance came from the integration of Fair Park the previous year. Since African Americans received admittance to the fairgrounds any day of the year, civil rights activists stopped their boycotts of the State Fair Classic, thus attracting fans.[50]

Black college football teams maintained fan interest and support primarily by winning games. As Jarvis Christian and Wiley continued play poorly, they became increasingly less popular in the black community, who lost interest. At the same time, Texas Southern renewed black community interest by challenging for the SWAC title. The Tigers set themselves up for a conference showdown with the number one ranked team in the country, Jackson State, by beating Grambling forty-two to twenty-five. Against Grambling, Texas Southern fell behind by thirteen points in the first quarter, but came back to win thanks to five touchdown passes by quarterbacks Carl Zenn and Charlie Green.[51]

All of the excitement over the possible conference championship faded when Texas Southern lost to Jackson State. But despite finishing second in the SWAC, the Tigers received a bid to travel to Florida and face Florida A&M in the Gateway Classic on December 1. The Gateway Classic represented a new postseason contest which Florida A&M felt complemented the school's already existing Orange Blossom Classic. Florida A&M hoped for twenty thousand fans to attend the contest in Jacksonville.[52] Unfortunately the Gateway Classic only took place the one year, and then was dropped.

Inspired by its move to Dallas, Bishop also created its own postseason contest, the Dallas Bowl. Bishop faced Fisk University in the new bowl game that took place on December 1.[53] The new postseason contests excited fans of Texas Southern and Bishop, but the majority of interest given to these games went to Prairie View's annual postseason bowl game. The 1962 edition of the Prairie View Bowl was eventful, because the Panthers moved the contest from New Years' Day to December 1. Held at Houston's Jeppesen Stadium, Prairie View faced Central State College of Wilberforce, Ohio.[54]

Meanwhile, a rally held at Houston's City Auditorium on Sunday, December 16, attracted more attention from Texas' African American population than any of the postseason football games. The meeting featured civil rights leaders Dr. Martin Luther King, Jr. and Dr. Ralph Abernathy. The two men spoke on the need for civil rights legislation and nonviolent protest. Organized by the Baptist Pastors Fellowship conference, the event filled Houston's City Auditorium.[55]

Professional football also received more attention from the black community in Texas than the college bowl games in December. Much to the excitement of Texas football fans, the 1962 AFL championship game was an all-Texas affair. Lamar Hunt's Dallas Texans faced Bud Adams' Houston Oilers. The game went into double overtime before Dallas finally won, twenty to seventeen. The game attracted almost thirty-eight thousand fans in Houston, and many more on television.[56]

The end of the 1962 football season also saw a first for sports and African American opportunity in the United States. The Dallas Texans selected Junious "Buck" Buchanan with the first pick in the draft. A six-foot, seven-inch tall, 272-pound defensive lineman from Grambling, Buchanan became the first player from a black college to be taken first overall in a professional football draft.[57]

The civil rights movement remained a main focus of interest among black Texans going into 1963. In January, Dr. Martin Luther King followed up his appearance in Houston by speaking before four thousand people in Dallas—a racially mixed crowd far larger than those that attended the majority of the black college football games in Texas the previous season.[58]

Fans of professional football in Texas experienced some heartbreak on May 14, 1963, when the Dallas Texans announced their plans to move to Kansas City. The move came because of the financial losses the team incurred while trying to compete with the NFL's Dallas Cowboys. Even with the loss of the Texans, the Oilers and Cowboys remained competitive in Texas, giving the state two strong professional teams.[59]

Major events during 1963, including the March on Washington and the Birmingham marches, made the civil rights movement the main focus of interest for the United States. All over the country, African Americans and the black press followed the national struggle for equality, while actively participating in local protests. The national focus on civil rights carried over to the Texas black community, which placed even less importance on black college football. The lack of interest in the sport caused Jarvis Christian to disappear from the African American papers in Texas. Wiley and Bishop also received almost no attention from the general black population unless the two private schools faced one of the state's public institutions. Prairie View found itself able to attract a decent-sized following and maintain some cultural importance in 1963, however, as the Panthers pursued their fourth black national championship.

Prairie View's success made Houston native Otis Taylor, the starting flanker of the Panthers, a star. Every week the black press praised Taylor for his athletic accomplishments. When Prairie View faced Texas Southern, the *Houston Informer* published Taylor's picture and proclaimed him "the man to watch."[60]

Prairie View's success on the football field brought other positive changes to the campus. When the Panthers played Texas Southern in Houston in October, almost all of Prairie View's 3,300 students attended.

The Texas Southern contest also marked the first performance by Prairie View's larger one hundred–piece marching band.[61]

The thirty-ninth State Fair Classic attracted sixteen thousand fans to Dallas. Attendance was lower than the previous year, but the fact that Prairie View entered the game undefeated was an attraction to fans who normally possessed no connection to the school. The contest also offered a break from the national struggles for civil rights. The Panthers' twenty-seven to ten victory over Wiley left Prairie View in first place in the conference.[62]

While the Prairie View football team maintained its unbeaten streak in 1963, the student body actively worked for civil rights. In November, the Prairie View students went on strike from school following the administration's refusal to back a boycott of merchants in nearby Hempstead. The strike at the college resulted from the protesters' belief that the Prairie View faculty and administration "failed to go along with the boycott that had reached the ninety percent effective range."[63]

The striking students issued a list of demands to Prairie View's administration one week later. The main demand of the students involved the removal of Dr. T. R. Solomon as director of student life. The protesters charged that Dr. Solomon insulted students, possessed a bad attitude, opposed the civil rights movement, and opposed all social functions. The strike received more attention than Texas Southern University's homecoming game against Jackson State that took place at the same time.[64]

The Prairie View students furthered their protest by boycotting the Panthers' homecoming game against Bishop College. Without the students in attendance, only a few hundred spectators watched. The *Dallas Express* supported the students by publishing a wide-angle picture that showed the empty stands.[65] Unfazed by their classmates' protests, the Prairie View football team continued to win. The Panthers pushed their record to eight wins and no losses by the end of November.[66]

Several significant events occurred at the end of the 1963 football season that illustrated the changes taking place in black college football and American society. First, Prairie View cancelled the Prairie View Bowl. The cancellation marked the end of the second longest running bowl game in the country behind the Rose Bowl. One reason for the end of the Prairie View Bowl involved the game's failure to attract large crowds as in previous years.[67]

The second major event involved Prairie View's invitation to compete in the National Association of Intercollegiate Athletics (NAIA) playoffs. The NAIA was a national athletic governing body for small colleges. Prairie View became the first black college from Texas to compete in the predominately white college organization's football postseason. The Panthers defeated Kearny State University from Nebraska twenty to seven in the semifinals to advance to Sacramento, California, and the national championship game. In the Camellia Bowl, Prairie View faced St. John's College of Collegeville, Minnesota.[68]

Excitement ran high among Prairie View alumni and students as the Panthers prepared to face St. John's. With the contest taking place in California, though, Prairie View's band and students expected to miss the game and remain in Texas because of the travel expense involved. In a showing of good faith and solidarity, Prairie View's student body collected money to send the marching band and majorettes to Sacramento to cheer on the Panthers.[69]

Unfortunately, the game ended in disappointment for the Panthers and their fans. The week before the game, Prairie View's star quarterback Jim Kearney broke his left hand and missed the contest. Without Kearney, Prairie View lost thirty-three to twenty-seven.[70]

The Camellia Bowl also disappointed the game's promoters. Only 12,200 fans attended the contest, a much smaller number than the promoters had hoped for. The game also lost money for the second year in a row. As a result, the city of Sacramento and the executive board for the Camellia Bowl decided to sever ties with the NAIA and to host an NCAA bowl game in 1964.[71]

Despite the loss in the NAIA title game, Prairie View still won the 1963 black college national championship. The football team received other accolades that were a source of pride for black Texans. The NAIA recognized Billy Nicks as coach of the year. Jimmy Kearney, the Panthers' star quarterback, also won the NAIA player of the year award. Both Nicks and Kearney beat out white competitors for their awards.[72]

While Prairie View prepared to compete in the Camellia Bowl, five Southwest Conference colleges, including the University of Texas, announced plans to integrate their football teams.[73] The white press in Sacramento asked Prairie View head coach Billy Nicks what impact he felt integration would have on black college football. Nicks responded: "It won't hurt us for three or four years. After that, though, I think members of our SWAC, made up of Negro schools, will lose quite a few players."[74]

One month later, professional football's rise to prominence among sports fans became solidified on January 29, 1964, when the American Football League signed a television contract with NBC. The deal paid the AFL thirty-six million dollars over five years. The new contract made the AFL financially sound and allowed the league to compete on an even level with the NFL. As a result, the two leagues went into negotiations and merged in 1970. With the merger, professional football presented a unified league that further attracted African American fans.[75]

The civil rights movement achieved a monumental victory in 1964 when President Lyndon Johnson pressured Congress to finally pass the Civil Rights Bill that had been floundering for more than a year. The Civil Rights Act of 1964 existed as a major piece of social legislation. The act enforced the Fourteenth Amendment, declaring it illegal to deny anyone his or her rights as citizens because of race, creed, color, or gender. The Civil Rights Act of 1964 also desegregated all public facilities, ordered schools to stop delaying integration, and made discrimination in hiring illegal.[76]

The civil rights victory carried over to the state of Texas, where in the spring of 1964, the University of Texas hired Ervin Perry as a professor of engineering. Perry, who had taught part-time at the university since 1960, received a full-time position, much to the elation of the black community in Texas. Perry became the first African American professor hired by a white university in Texas. The appointment served as a rallying point for Texans to fight for further integration in the state's higher education system.[77]

To maintain fan support and interest, Texas' black colleges focused their efforts on specific, high profile games. The schools also used the established practices of scheduling games in neutral cities with large African American populations and hosting "classics" to attract casual fans to games. When Texas Southern faced Southern University in 1964, the contest received billing as the "Gulf Coast Classic." The game took place at Galveston's Public School Stadium. The black press also ran advertisements promoting the contest as a major social event of the year.[78]

When the State Fair Classic took place, the decreased role of black college football in the African American community was apparent. The 1964 contest served as the fortieth consecutive game. With the end of Negro Achievement Day, the accompanying events that once received a considerable amount of fan interest no longer took place. Gone were the many pageants and contests. The pregame and halftime shows only involved performances by the Wiley and Prairie View bands. The State Fair also raised ticket prices to three dollars a person.[79] When the game took place, only five thousand fans paid the increased ticket price to watch the contest. Prairie View also showed its superiority over the other black Texas colleges, beating Wiley thirty-nine to thirteen. The Prairie View All-American quarterback Jimmy Kearney threw for two touchdowns in the game and rushed for another.[80]

By the middle of the season, the main attention given to black college football in the *Houston Informer* involved publicizing upcoming contests. The press actively praised events, such as the Texas Southern homecoming game against Grambling, in an effort to attract fans to the contests.[81] The only accounts of the previous week's games occurred in the "SWAC Conference Round-Up" section of the newspaper each week. The top teams, Prairie View and Grambling, received the majority of the space in the two-column article, while Wiley usually only received mention as the losing opponent of the other schools. At the same time, the paper ignored Bishop and Jarvis Christian completely.[82]

Prairie View again dominated the conference. The Panthers looked for their eighth straight victory of the year as they prepared to face Alcorn A&M on November 14. The contest, which served as the Prairie View homecoming, included a parade before the game at noon, the crowning of "Miss PV," and a performance by both schools' bands at halftime.[83]

The homecoming contest gave Prairie View fans much to cheer about. The Panthers won the game thirty-seven to zero. In winning, Prairie View's defense held Alcorn to only forty-one yards of total offense. Twenty-seven of Alcorn's yards came from the running back, Smith Reed. Prairie View running back Hyman Alexander scored three of the Panthers' touchdowns.[84]

Bishop College finally attracted some interest among the Texas community when the Tigers played Texas Lutheran University in 1964, a white college from Seguin. Bishop, which won the Gulf Coast Conference in 1964, designated the contest its homecoming game. Even with the publicity and the cultural importance of a black Texas college facing a white Texas college, only 2,500 fans attended the game at Bishop's stadium in Dallas. Despite the low fan turnout, Bishop played well, winning the game forty-two to seventeen.[85]

Prairie View worked hard to maintain a place of importance in

African American society. The college found itself able to hang on to that position in 1964 when the Panthers won their second consecutive black college national championship. After not losing a conference game for more than two years, Prairie View presented itself as one of the greatest dynasties in the history of black college football. Prairie View's reputation for greatness was backed up by the fact that the Panthers won five national championships in a period of less than fifteen years.[86]

The 1964 season marked a turning point for black college football in Texas. During the early part of the decade, African American college football teams in Texas worked to retain some of their cultural importance while being challenged by the civil rights movement and integrated professional football in the state. Starting in 1965, the major white colleges in Texas began to integrate, taking even more attention away from African American college football. At the same time, Prairie View coach Billy Nicks, who possessed a career record of 185 wins, 54 losses, and 9 ties, retired from coaching. After Nicks left Prairie View, the Panthers' level of success decreased dramatically. As integrated football came to dominate the state, Prairie View fell into a level of mediocrity and did not win the SWAC title again for almost fifty years.[87]

With the passage of the Civil Rights Act of 1964 and the Voting Rights Act of 1965, African Americans achieved major victories, with the end of segregation and disfranchisement in the country. Entering the last half of the 1960s, United States underwent further dramatic changes. The escalation of the country's effort in the Vietnam War diverted attention from the civil rights movement. Some activists who previously participated in civil rights protests shifted their attentions to publicly opposing the war. At the same time, many African Americans gave up hope that the government and American society would bring about change. As a result, some black leaders began supporting the black power movement.[88]

Black power constituted a major change from the nonviolent protests of the late 1950s and early 1960s. Stokely Carmichael, the head of SNCC, expressed in 1966 the ideas held by a new group of black activists. He stated that black power meant the "coming together of black people to elect representatives and to force those representatives to speak to their needs."[89] Another major component of black power was black nationalism. Militant groups like the Black Panthers in Oakland, California, expressed the new black nationalism. The Black Panthers reflected the alienation and anger felt by African Americans in many urban areas. As a result, the Black Power movement turned away from the earlier inter-racial approach to civil rights, and instead embraced a practice of black exclusiveness.[90]

At the same time, Texas Southern University began the Manpower Resource Project. The program offered African American youths an opportunity to receive training both on the job and in school. The students attended classes at Texas Southern, while also working at sponsoring businesses, such as Humble Oil and Refining Company, Southwestern Bell Telephone Company, and the Marathon Oil Company. Texas Southern hoped to provide its engineering students with cooperative education, thus enabling the students to get high paying jobs upon graduation.[91]

Fans were further distracted from an interest in black college football when the first integration of a football team at a major white college in Texas occurred. The achievement came to be in 1965 when Warren McVea joined the University of Houston football team. McVea, an all-state running back out of Brackenridge High School in San Antonio, received more than seventy scholarship offers from colleges around the country. He even received a personal letter from former President Harry Truman, urging McVea to attend the University of Missouri.[92] McVea wanted to attend the University of Texas, which had just won the national championship in 1963, but found himself denied because of the Southwest Conference's refusal to sign black players. As a result, he chose the University of Houston, an independent college, and therefore not under any pressure from the SWC to remain an all-white team.[93]

Starting in 1964, the black press covered Warren McVea on a weekly basis. The African American community was so interested in integrated football at a major white college in Texas that the *Informer* gave play-by-play accounts of McVea's games for the University of Houston's freshman team. The university's educational television station, KUHT-TV, broadcast the Cougars freshman team's victory over the Air Force Academy. Normally, freshman football received no attention whatsoever in the press or on television, but since McVea scored two touchdowns in the Air Force game, KUHT sought to capitalize on his popularity among the state's African American community.[94]

The excitement over McVea ran so high that in 1965, before he ever played in a varsity football game, the San Antonio Friends of Houston University took out a full-page advertisement in *Texas Football* praising his talents. The San Antonio group called him a "living legend in San Antonio," and the "most exciting running back in UH history and the finest runner in Texas high school history."[95] The advertisement also included a full-page artist's drawing of McVea carrying a football.[96]

Competing for the Cougars from 1965–67, McVea became the highest profile athlete on the team. He performed well, especially after switching positions from running back to wide receiver. Despite being limited by a groin injury, McVea played well enough to earn second team All-American honors in his senior season.[97]

As the 1965 football season began, integrated football in Texas received the majority of the black community's attention. The *Houston Informer* discussed the beginning of the University of Houston's season. The Houston Oilers also received a significant amount of coverage each week, while the paper made no mention of the opening of practice at the Texas black colleges.[98] In the past, the black press had always publicized the beginning of practice at the black colleges, how many players reported, and what chance of winning each college coach felt his team possessed.

Prairie View opened the season by losing its first game in over two years. Prairie View also lost the next week to Grambling by a score of forty-four to seven. The victory by Grambling represented a power shift in the SWAC away from the Texas colleges and to the colleges from Louisiana and Mississippi.[99] This shift of dominance in the SWAC presented some irony, though, since the white universities in Louisiana and Mississippi integrated more slowly than the universities in Texas, offering African Americans less choice to play college football.

Wiley also experienced significant setbacks to start the 1965 season. Fred Long, who coached the Wildcats and other Texas colleges for over forty years, suffered a stroke before the season began. Unable to coach from the sideline, Long continued to attend games and watch from the stands. When Wiley faced its old rival Bishop in Dallas in early October 1965, the Wildcats dedicated the game to Long. Wiley defeated Bishop fourteen to six for one of the Wildcats' few victories for the year. Overall, the 1965 football season served as a disappointment for Wiley and the other black colleges in Texas.[100]

Black college football teams in Texas watched as white college football game attendance set records nationally. Almost six hundred thousand fans attended white college football games in the state the first week in

October. The steady increase of African Americans in professional football also took fans away from black college football. During 1965, Dallas, as well as a large portion of the state's black population, followed the Dallas Cowboys and the team's "Rookie of the Year candidate," "Bullet" Bob Hayes. Hayes, who played college football at Florida A&M and won the gold medal in the one hundred–meter sprint at the 1964 Olympics in Tokyo, became a major football star in Texas and throughout the nation.[101]

As the Black Power movement grew in Texas and across the country, the efforts of segregated colleges also came to be viewed by activists as inconsequential. Despite the decreasing significance of black college football, the State Fair Classic between Wiley and Prairie View still attracted a crowd. For the 1965 contest, the Dallas Black Chamber of Commerce brought back the pregame parade as a way of opening the celebration.[102]

Prairie View defeated Wiley sixteen to seven. The victory marked the first conference win for Prairie View for the season. The poor records of both teams attracted fewer than ten thousand fans.[103] The *Houston Informer* chose not to publish the score of the State Fair Classic, or anything else about the actual football game. Instead, the *Informer* only published pictures of the two schools' queens and their escorts.[104]

Texas' black colleges closed out the season in competitive fashion. Prairie View won its homecoming game in early November. Homecoming remained an important enough cultural event for alumni and fans that twelve thousand spectators filled Blackshear Field at Prairie View to watch the Panthers defeat Bishop nineteen to zero.[105] The same day, Texas Southern defeated Jackson State twenty-six to fourteen. The Texas Southern victory provided a major upset since Jackson State entered the contest ranked third in the conference, coming off a seventy-seven to zero victory over Wiley.[106]

The 1965 black college football season came to a close with almost no mention in the black press or the community. Prairie View finished with the best record of any of the Texas African American colleges, winning five games, losing three, and tying one, placing the Panthers fourth in conference. Meanwhile, Texas Southern finished in fifth place and Wiley came in last. Bishop and Jarvis Christian received no mention in the black press after early November.[107]

At the same time, the integration of Texas' educational system increased. By the 1966–67 school year, 47 percent of Texas' African American children attended integrated public schools. The students who attended integrated high schools looked to integrated colleges in the state instead of black colleges for higher education.[108]

With more students wanting to attend white colleges, the potential for success from integrated college athletics became evident in 1966 when Texas Western University from El Paso became the first white university to win the college basketball national championship with an all–African American starting lineup. In winning the championship, Texas Western defeated an all-white University of Kentucky team. The prominence of black athletes at Texas Western allowed the athletes to exert their masculinity and speak out against social problems on campus. They expressed dismay over the social isolation of African Americans, the restrictive interracial dating policies, inadequate housing, and the lack of employment for African Americans.[109]

On September 10, 1966, integration came to Southwest conference football when John Westbrook competed for Baylor University in a game against Syracuse University. With Baylor leading twenty-eight to six in the fourth quarter, Westbrook entered the game. He rushed for nine yards on his first carry. After the Bears advanced to the eleven-yard line, a white player replaced Westbrook to score the touchdown.[110]

The week after John Westbrook played for Baylor, Jerry Levias played for Southern Methodist University. Unlike Baylor, which begrudgingly accepted Westbrook on its team, Southern Methodist coach Hayden Fry actively sought an African American player to integrate the team. Fry chose Levias as his pioneer.[111] On May 22, 1965, he became the first African American to receive an athletic scholarship from a Southwest Conference university.[112]

In 1966 as a sophomore, Levias joined the Southern Methodist University varsity football team. The previous year, SMU compiled a record of one win and nine losses. With Levias at wide receiver, the Mustangs won the Southwest Conference and earned a ninth-place national ranking. Levias also earned SWC player of the year honors after scoring more than 30 percent of his team's points.[113]

As a star on the football field, Levias received better treatment than other African American students at white universities, but he still faced racial prejudice. He received racial taunts from both opponents and his own teammates. SMU's fraternity system remained segregated during the late 1960s. From African Americans involved in the Black Power movement, Levias received criticism as a sellout for his accommodating approach toward civil rights. Black activists expressed their disapproval of Levias's refusal to speak out on social and political issues.[114]

While the level of interest given to black college football decreased in the 1960s, the colleges themselves grew and maintained an important role in the culture of Texas. The majority of black college students in the state attended an African American college. Prairie View expected its largest enrollment ever in 1966—3,518 students. Since an increase in student enrollment meant an increase in financial resources and operating budgets, Prairie View expanded its physical plant in the 1960s. In 1966, the college administration announced plans to build a new library, costing half a million dollars.[115]

Football at Texas' African American colleges proved a different story. Prairie View and Texas Southern, the two colleges with the largest student populations and alumni bases, continued to attract decent-sized crowds. As the fans decreased in number, though, the black press stopped publishing attendance figures for African American college games.

Still, the black college football teams in Texas continued to work hard. Texas Southern began the 1966 season on a high note, defeating Southern University twenty to fourteen. For its second game of the year, Texas Southern played Wiley College in Galveston, hoping the neutral site would attract fans.[116]

Prairie View did not fare as well in its opening contest. Playing with a new head coach, Hoover Wright, following the retirement of Billy Nicks, the Panthers lost to Jackson State fourteen to seven.[117]

Prairie View's disappointment about the season continued as the team lost to Southern by a score of thirty-five to zero. Playing in Baton Rouge, Southern scored twenty-one points in the first quarter, including a ninety-three-yard punt return for a touchdown. Prairie View failed to accomplish anything on offense, punting the ball eleven times in the game.[118]

The Prairie View losses received little attention from people other than the students and alumni directly attached to the school. Articles on professional football and Warren McVea and the University of Houston occupied the majority of space in the sports pages of the Texas black newspapers. The *Houston Informer* even failed to mention the Texas Southern University victory over Wiley.[119]

Large crowds occasionally turned out for black college football games if the contest involved prominent teams. When Prairie View faced Grambling in October 1966, seven thousand spectators filled Prairie

View's Blackshear Field. Prairie View played competitively in the contest, tying Grambling ten to ten. Since the Prairie View student body exceeded 3,500, a large amount of the fans in attendance were current students. The remainder of the crowd consisted of alumni, the parents of current players and students, or Grambling students who traveled from Louisiana.[120]

The same day as the Prairie View–Grambling contest, Bishop played Wiley in Dallas. Less than one thousand spectators watched Bishop score a touchdown and two-point conversion in the last few minutes of the game to beat Wiley fourteen to thirteen. The small number of fans in attendance still celebrated enthusiastically since it marked Bishop's first victory over Wiley in six years.[121]

The 1966 football season gave one clear example of the decline in importance of black college football for the majority of Texas' African American population. The state's black newspapers failed to report on the State Fair Classic between Prairie View and Wiley. No articles, pictures, or mention of any type appeared in the *Houston Informer* on the game or its accompanying events. The *Dallas Express* ran one three-paragraph article, explaining that only five thousand fans attended the contest and that Prairie View won twenty-one to nothing.[122] Even Prairie View's own yearbook, *Pantherland*, only printed the minimum amount of information instead of giving a detailed game summary.[123] The neglect was significant since the State Fair Classic once served as the premier annual social event for African Americans in Texas.

At the same time, the Texas Southern University homecoming game against Grambling received front-page coverage in the *Informer*. Since the contest offered to determine the conference champion, interest in the event ran high.[124] The attention given to the Texas Southern–Grambling game presented a new situation for black college football in Texas. To remain popular, colleges had to field winning teams. Gone were the days when schools that continually lost could count on spectator attendance and fan support. By the late 1960s, if a football team failed to win, it made no money and eventually ceased to exist.

Texas Southern lost to Grambling, but their hopes of a conference championship remained alive when Southern University defeated Grambling forty-one to fourteen to close out the regular season. Unfortunately for the Tigers, the football team lost its chance at a first-place tie when Prairie View defeated them thirty-one to eighteen. As a result, Texas Southern finished third in the conference, with Prairie View fifth. Wiley went the entire season without a victory, yet again finishing last in the SWAC.[125]

For Bishop College, the 1966 football season ended on a high note when the Tigers won their homecoming game over Texas Lutheran. Led by George Merchant, a defensive lineman drafted by the Los Angeles Rams, Bishop put together a goal-line stand in the final minutes of the game to win twenty-eight to twenty-seven. The contest also marked the second year in a row that Bishop faced and defeated the white institution.[126]

The biggest surprise of the football season came out of Dallas. Jerry Levias led Southern Methodist to a Southwest Conference championship. As a result, Levias and his team faced the University of Georgia in the Cotton Bowl on New Year's Day, 1967.[127] SMU's accomplishment was a significant milestone for the black community in Texas, since it marked the first time an African American player competed for a white Texas college in the Cotton Bowl. Tommy Williams, who worked as a scout for the Houston Oilers and as a high school football coach after graduating from Prairie View, expressed the feelings of Texas African Americans regarding Levias's accomplishments and the integration of the Southwest Conference: "It allowed blacks who were very, very gifted to achieve notoriety and success. It was a great thing. Finally, black athletes were recognized as gifted and talented people. If the opportunity had been available at the time, I would have gone because of my talent."[128]

As the Black Power movement grew around the country, it spread to African American athletes at white colleges. In 1967, several members of the Texas Western football team, including All-Americans Fred Carr and Charlie West, protested the treatment they received from their coach, Bobby Dobbs. The black athletes held a sit-in in the lobby of the college's athletic dormitory and demanded such things as an end to racial jokes by teammates and coaches, better living conditions, and the opportunity to compete for any position on the team instead of being forced into specific positions, like running back and wide receiver. Nothing ever came of the protest.[129]

In 1967, black college football also received an increased amount of attention from black Texans. Unfortunately, the circumstances surrounding the publicity proved negative. The previous season, Southern University and Grambling both used ineligible players when they faced and defeated Arkansas AM&N. As a result, Southern and Grambling forfeited their games against Arkansas AM&N, causing the SWAC final standings from the year before to change. Arkansas AM&N saw its record go from two wins and four losses to four wins and two losses, raising the college from seventh in the standings to a tie for first. Texas Southern, which finished second with two losses, found itself a part of a four-way tie for first place with Arkansas State, Grambling, and Southern. The black press gave more coverage to the scandal than the papers gave to the upcoming Dallas Cowboys–Houston Oilers preseason football game.[130]

The tensions and violence existing throughout the country hit home in Texas in the late 1960s. In 1967, the African American community in Houston found itself on edge following the drowning of a black youth in a city garbage dump. The situation became more heated when black parents issued complaints against the Houston public school system over unequal discipline practices toward black and white students. After false rumors circulated concerning the shooting of an African American by whites, students at Texas Southern held a mass meeting in one of the school's dormitories to discuss a means of response.[131]

The Houston Police arrived at the Texas Southern dorm in an attempt to stop any protests before they started. With tensions already high, the presence of the police on campus ignited the students' anger and frustration and led to violence. The Texas Southern students first threw rocks and bottles at the police. After 10:00 p.m., someone fired a gun and the police began shooting toward the dormitory. The fighting lasted for several hours until the police finally stormed the building. In the end, the police arrested 448 students. The students fired between forty and sixty shots, while the police fired two thousand. The fighting also caused between ten and thirty thousand dollars in damage to the school.[132]

The incident resulted in one serious injury. A ricocheting bullet killed Louis Kuba, a white policeman. A Houston grand jury that investigated the incident found the city's police not guilty of any violence or damage to property. At the same time, the grand jury indicted five Texas Southern students for murder. The jury argued that by starting the riot, the students were responsible for Kuba's death.[133]

The violence at Texas Southern seized the interest of the African American community in the fall of 1967, taking further attention away from black college football, which celebrated several milestones. The 1967 season marked the forty-sixth year of the SWAC. To mark the occasion, the *Dallas Express* printed a list of all past championship teams and the season's schedule for the current conference members. The only article on current black college football in the paper discussed the upcoming Wiley-Bishop clash in Marshall. Bishop College also announced 1,341 students had enrolled for the upcoming academic year—the largest count in the school's history.[134]

Soon, the 1967 State Fair Classic found itself affected by the Texas black community's loss of interest in black college football. The Dallas Black Chamber of Commerce reported a steady decline in attendance over the previous three seasons. As a result, the chamber removed Wiley from the contest and replaced it with local Bishop College. The switch in competitors excited Bishop, which prepared for its first appearance at the Cotton Bowl.[135] Unfortunately for Bishop and Prairie View, no account of the State Fair Classic appeared in the black press. The *Houston Informer* only published the score, a thirty-one to twelve victory for Prairie View.[136] Prairie View's yearbook, *Pantherland*, also neglected the contest, only printing the score.[137]

Texas Southern, meanwhile, expressed excitement over its new starting quarterback, David Mays. Against Mississippi Valley State College, Mays completed twenty-two of thirty-one passes to lead the Tigers to a sixty-four to zero victory. In the game, Mays passed for six touchdowns, rushed for a seventh touchdown, kicked seven extra points, kicked a thirty-nine-yard field goal, and handled all of his team's punting duties.[138]

Thanks to the accomplishments of Mays, Texas Southern found itself tied for first place in the conference with Grambling and Jackson State entering the last month of play. The football seasons of the other black colleges in Texas did not proceed as positively. Wiley continued as the worst team in the SWAC. Bishop received no mention in the press other than the Tigers' loss to Prairie View in the State Fair Classic.[139] Jarvis Christian, also largely ignored by the black press and Texas' African American community, found the entire experience too much to take and cancelled its football program at the end of the 1967 season.[140]

Integration spelled the end of other African American sports institutions besides black college football. The desegregation of Texas' public schools led to the demise of the Prairie View Interscholastic League. The PVIL, which had existed since 1920, beginning as the Texas Interscholastic League of Colored Schools, offered black high schools a chance to compete for a state title in everything from football and basketball to speech and drama. In 1967, though, Texas' black high schools began joining the white University Interscholastic League. By 1970, the PVIL no longer existed.[141]

More heartbreak occurred for fans of black college football in Texas as Prairie View found itself humiliated during the 1967 football season. The Panthers lost for only the second time ever to Arkansas AM&N, ending a winning streak that lasted more than thirty years. Arkansas AM&N dominated Prairie View for the entire game, winning the contest in an easy fashion, sixty-five to seven.[142]

Another controversy hit college football in Texas in 1967. The problem centered on an interview in *Sports Illustrated* given by Darrell Royal, the head coach of the University of Texas, concerning Warren McVea and the University of Houston's success. Royal stated: "It has been proven in a lot of sports that the Negro athlete simply has more speed. Now he is getting good coaching in our part of the world because of integrated schools. The result is a lot more spectacular backs."[143]

African American coaches in Texas took offense at Royal's statement. They felt that Royal questioned the ability of black coaches to teach and develop players.[144] Tommy Williams responded, saying: "Royal was a hypocrite. I attended Royal's coaching clinics and I was not impressed with him. When I was at Prairie View, we were doing things more advanced than the white colleges. We did close coverage and bump-and-run defenses first. The Oakland Raiders got it from us. They came and scouted us in 1960 and took our defensive schemes back with them."[145]

The negative racial attitudes still faced by black athletes, as well as reluctance by some whites to give up on segregation in spite of the changing world of race and sports, continued to appear throughout the country. The experiences of Charlie Scott, the first African American to sign a scholarship to play sports at a member college of the Atlantic Coastal Conference, mirrored those of African American athletes at white colleges in Texas. A basketball player for the University of North Carolina from 1966 to 1970, Scott found himself ignored for most of his career by the major white newspapers in the South. In 1969, after leading UNC to an ACC championship, Scott missed out on ACC player of the year when five white sportswriters left Scott off of their ballots completely.[146]

The majority of Texans, though, focused their attention on professional football in 1967. As the AFL and NFL held their first combined playoff system, the possibility existed for an all-Texas Super Bowl.

Unfortunately, Dallas lost to Green Bay in the NFL championship game, while Houston lost to Lamar Hunt's Kansas City Chiefs in the AFL title game. As a result, Green Bay went on to win the Super Bowl, in the first combined NFL-AFL championship.[147]

In the late 1960s, the Black Power movement affected higher education as African American students at white colleges fought for the creation of black studies departments. The students wanted to study their own culture and history, as well as promote better race relations on their campuses. Afro-Americans for Black Liberation (AAFBL) became one group that pushed for changes at the University of Houston. The AAFBL actively participated in the Black Power movement, working with Houston's black population to fight poverty. Like other such groups, the AAFBL found itself faced with charges of violence by its detractors.[148]

Texas Southern University students became actively involved in the Black Power movement as well. The school's position as an urban university played a major role in garnering that support. Following the violence at the university the year before, more black Houstonians chose to support Texas Southern University student protests. The violence at Texas Southern also increased hostility toward the Houston police department among the city's black community.[149]

For African Americans, not much else was of any importance after James Earl Ray assassinated Dr. Martin Luther King Jr. in Memphis on April 4, 1968. King's murder marked the end of nonviolent protest for civil rights in the United States. African Americans around the country expressed grief and despair over King's death. The sadness and anger among African Americans led to riots and protests in more than one hundred American cities.[150]

Other events also occurred in 1968 that took attention away from black college football and pushed more African Americans in Texas to support the Black Power movement. In September, Lee Otis Johnson, an activist associated with the Houston chapter of SNCC, received a thirty-year jail sentence on a charge of possession and sale of marijuana. Only one witness testified against Johnson, and the jury in the trial consisted entirely of whites.[151]

The *Houston Informer* claimed that Johnson's conviction stemmed from the serious problem of harassment of African American activists in the city following the 1967 riot at Texas Southern. The paper stated that the harassment of activists included arrests, the loss of jobs, and evictions from living facilities. In Johnson's trial, the main piece of evidence presented by the prosecution involved Johnson's work for SNCC.[152]

Meanwhile, integration expanded. The University of Texas included walk-on Leon O'Neal Jr., the school's first African American football player, in February 1968. O'Neal played well as a freshman but flunked out of school at the end of the year, never competing for the varsity. Sammy Williams and Hugh McElroy walked on the Texas A&M football team in the late 1960s. Rice University also signed several black players to scholarships in 1968, including Stahle Vincent, a quarterback from Greensboro, North Carolina.[153] As white colleges integrated throughout the state, the black press covered these colleges for the first time. The *Houston Informer* discussed the "many Negro athletes" who played for East Texas State in 1968. With such players' help, East Texas won the Lone Star Conference championship in 1966.[154]

With black athletes attending white colleges throughout the country, a few African American colleges attempted to also improve themselves through integration. In 1968, Grambling signed its first white athlete to a scholarship. James Gregory, who hailed from California, served as the backup quarterback behind All-American James Harris.[155]

Meanwhile, Texas' African American colleges prepared for the upcoming year. Wiley kicked off the 1968 football season by beating Langston College of Oklahoma twenty to ten. The Wildcats dominated their opponent. Wiley's defense intercepted six passes during the game, while only eleven yards rushing for Langston.[156] Prairie View sought to build fan support by moving the school's homecoming game against Grambling to Washington, DC, in 1968. The fans of both Prairie View and Grambling expressed excitement about the possibility of competing in the new "DC Classic." Unfortunately, the plans fell through and the game returned to Blackshear Field.[157]

Integrated football continued to receive a considerable amount of coverage in the black press. Players like Arthur James, a running back at East Texas State University, became stars in the African American community. In one game against Abilene Christian College, James rushed for 323 yards, outgaining the entire Abilene Christian offense.[158]

While integrated football attracted attention away from black college football, African American colleges around the country still fielded quality, competitive teams in the late 1960s. In the 1968 AFL-NFL combined draft, professional teams took thirty-one players from the SWAC. This number marked the second highest amount of players taken from any white or black athletic conference in the country. Only the white Southeastern Athletic Conference had more players drafted, with thirty-six athletes taken by the professional teams.[159]

The biggest game of the season for black college football in Texas occurred on November 2 when Texas Southern faced Grambling. Texas Southern progressed through the season undefeated, and as a result, the Grambling game offered the potential of deciding the conference champion. Even more exciting than a possible championship, the game took place at the three-year-old Astrodome. Nicknamed the "eighth wonder of the world," the Astrodome was Houston's air-conditioned domed stadium. Texas Southern's president, Granville Sawyer, summed up the excitement, stating: "The Astrodome meeting of these two schools begins a new era in the Southwestern Athletic Conference. It's a great thing for the SWAC and we at TSU will utilize the total resources of the university to ensure the success of the game."[160]

The social consciousness of black athletes led many to play a leading role in the Black Power movement. In 1968, Harry Edwards, an African American professor at San Jose State and a former track athlete, organized the Olympic Project for Human Rights (OPHR). The OPHR consisted of several top college and Olympic athletes who sought to alleviate the racial prejudice existing in athletics in the United States. The committee issued several demands, including the reinstatement of heavyweight champion Muhammad Ali, a ban on the participation of South Africa and Southern Rhodesia in the Olympic games because of the two countries' racist political policies, and the inclusion of African Americans as coaches and administrators in the US Olympic Committee. To bring about the group's goals, Edwards proposed a boycott of the 1968 Olympic Games in Mexico City.[161]

One prominent athlete to receive national attention for his actions regarding sports and race was Lew Alcindor (who later changed his name to Kareem Abdul-Jabbar). Alcindor led UCLA to three national championships in basketball during his college career, including an undefeated season in 1967–68. The best college basketball player in the country, Alcindor chose to boycott the 1968 Olympics completely. At the OPHR meeting organized by Edwards, Alcindor stated: "Somewhere each of us has got to take a stand against this kind of thing. This is how I make my stand-using what I have. And I take my stand here."[162]

Even with Alcindor's statement, the OPHR changed its plans when the members found it impossible to agree on a unified plan for a boycott. Instead, the black athletes decided to compete in Mexico City, but not to participate in any victory celebrations. Many of the athletes involved in the protest backed down, though, when the Olympics occurred.[163]

Two athletes did go through with the protest. Tommy Smith, who won the gold medal in the two hundred–meter event, and John Carlos, who came in third, received national attention for their actions. The two men marched out to the awards podium without shoes as an expression of the system of slavery in which black athletes existed. When the flags were raised and the US national anthem played, the two men lowered their heads and raised single, gloved fists as a symbol of the Black Power movement. The action caused Avery Brundage, the president of the US Olympic Committee, to send the two athletes home.[164]

Nationally, many African American athletes chose not to conform to the prescribed role of passive nonparticipants in the civil rights debate. In some cases, protests led to athletes being kicked off of their college teams, costing them an education and years of training. At the same time, the African American athletes' prominent positions in the communities where they lived, as well as coaches' and schools' desire to win, coupled with the large amounts of money connected to intercollegiate athletics, gave these players a strong voice to effectively advocate for racial change.[165]

As the decade neared an end, the football teams of Bishop, Wiley, and Prairie View were all missing from the state's black newspapers. The three colleges found themselves in the middle of poor seasons. As a result, Bishop, Wiley, and Prairie View experienced difficulty competing with integrated colleges and professional teams for attention from the fans. Even the State Fair Classic received no mention in 1968. The lack of coverage of the State Fair Classic proved more disappointing for Bishop, since the twenty to thirteen win marked the Tigers' first victory over Prairie View in more than twenty years.[166]

Texas Southern lost its 1968 homecoming contest to Grambling, twenty-eight to eighteen.[167] Since the Texas Southern–Grambling game took place in the Astrodome, it attracted thirty-five thousand fans. The large turnout for Texas Southern's game came more from the attraction of the Astrodome than the on-the-field contest.[168]

Texas Southern's loss placed its team in a three-way tie for first place in the conference. Grambling and Alcorn also had only one conference loss for the season. As a result, the Texas Southern-Prairie View game provided extra excitement, since Texas Southern had the opportunity to tie for the SWAC title. Prairie View, on the other hand, sat in third to last position, but the school's fans expressed excitement over the possibility of spoiling the championship dreams of Texas Southern.[169]

Prairie View's hopes for an upset almost came true, as the Panthers only lost by a score of twenty-two to fourteen.[170] The Tigers came from behind twice to take the lead late in the fourth quarter. As a result, Texas Southern shared the SWAC title.[171]

Following the Texas Southern contest, Prairie View still had one more game on its schedule. The Panthers and Wiley faced off in Marshall. Playing in rainy weather, Prairie View managed to defeat Wiley twenty-two to fifteen. Since no Texas black college received an invitation to a postseason game, the 1968 football season ended for Wiley, Prairie View, Texas Southern, and Bishop on December 7.[172] The lack of post-season play by the state's black colleges allowed the story of Jerry Levias at the Bluebonnet Bowl in Houston with Southern Methodist University to dominate the black press.[173]

As the 1960s came to a close, football in Texas presented a different face than at the beginning of the decade. The Houston Oilers, who only had two black players when the team began play in 1960, featured a large number of African Americans by 1969, including an entirely African American defensive backfield. Led by former Prairie View Panther Ken Houston, the group of five players became known as the "Black Blanket."[174]

African American football players from Texas competed for integrated football programs throughout the state and the country. Leo Taylor, who played for Jack Yates High School in Houston, finished fourteenth in the nation in scoring as a running back at North Texas State University. The Associated Press named another former Yates player, Lucius Blair Jr., of the University of Tulsa, college football's outstanding defensive sophomore for the 1968 season. Texas A&I's team included several African Americans, including quarterback Karl Douglas. Even Texas A&M, whose 1967 team had been all-white, featured Tommy Reaux on defense.[175]

While the further integration at white colleges received the most attention from black Texans, the state's black colleges still played a significant role in higher education for African Americans. In the 1960s, more than half of African American college students still attended black colleges. The schools offered many black students the best opportunity to achieve a degree since the black colleges relied on high school records for admittance instead of national standardized test scores like white colleges.[176]

At the same time, black college football attempted to compete with integrated football. Prairie View and Texas Southern found themselves able to attract decent players, as exhibited by the Tigers' two conference championships in the previous three years. The two colleges also received access to play some games at Houston's Astrodome. The use of the domed stadium worked to attract larger crowds than normally attended black college football games.[177]

For many schools, though, the struggle became too difficult. As a result, the 1969 football season was the last for Wiley College. An original member of the SWAC and a five-time national champion in 1921, 1924, 1928, 1932, and 1945, the Wildcats left the SWAC following the 1968 season, and played one more year as an independent before canceling their football program.[178]

Black college football in Texas suffered further because the state only possessed one major black newspaper by the end of the decade. The Informer Group, which owned the *Houston Informer*, purchased the *Dallas Express* in the late 1960s. In 1969, the company sought to reduce costs by publishing only a single supplement section for both papers that included the sports page. As a result, the supplement focused on Houston area sports and the professional ranks, neglecting Wiley and Bishop.

Since the *Houston Informer* existed as the lone remaining significant black newspaper in the state, Prairie View and Texas Southern received most of the coverage. Led by new coach Alexander Durley, who formerly coached at Texas College, Prairie View looked to return to the winning ranks in 1969. The Panthers' fans were optimistic about the chances of their team after Prairie View opened the season defeating Jackson State twenty-one to thirteen. [179] Unfortunately, the Panthers lost their next game fourteen to six to Southern University in the Astrodome.[180]

Changes also occurred on African American college campuses in Texas that brought an increase in student and alumni interest in their football teams. The increase came as a result of the Black Power movement's focus on African American exclusiveness and cultural pride. Students saw their universities as important institutions in the black community. Texas Southern declared 1969 "the year of the Tiger." The college pointed to feelings of unity among students and faculty that had not existed during the previous few years. Texas Southern also praised its academic improvements, like a new music building and the creation of a black studies program. According to the college administration, the excitement and congeniality on the Texas Southern campus was enhanced by the fact that the Tigers' football team had scheduled three games for the Astrodome.[181]

The new attitude was evident when Texas Southern faced Tennessee State at Rice University's stadium in October 1969. The Tigers sought to attract community support by granting free admission to all children under the age of twelve, as well as declaring the contest "Boy Scout Night." With two nationally known teams facing each other, the Texas Southern administration expected fifty thousand spectators at the game.[182]

The excitement among African American fans also extended to the Prairie View and Bishop College matchup. Led by running backs Alvin Barnes, Ed Smith, and James Hayward, Bishop began the season by winning three straight games.[183] The State Fair Classic between the schools also received a considerable amount of interest among fans in 1969. After the black press completely ignored the previous classics, the *Houston Informer* printed large advertisements each week promoting the upcoming game. While accompanying festivities like the parade and baby contest no longer took place, the paper stressed the halftime performances by each school's marching band as an added attraction to the game.[184]

Bishop won the State Fair Classic by a score of thirty-six to twenty-one. The victory marked the Tigers' second consecutive triumph over Prairie View. While the Panthers lost, the highlight of the game occurred when Prairie View defensive back Bivian Lee returned an interception 105 yards for a touchdown.[185]

Texas Southern sought to create its own bowl game in 1969. The Tigers scheduled Morgan State College for the first "Astrodome College Bowl" on December 6.[186] First, however, Texas Southern faced Grambling in the Astrodome. The high-profile nature of the game caused the Astrodome to charge ticket prices ranging from three dollars to seven dollars, a dramatic increase over the two to three dollars black college football tickets usually cost in Texas.[187]

The Prairie View season provided highs and lows for the Panthers' fans. After losing to Grambling fifty-eight to twenty-three, Prairie View returned the next week to defeat Mississippi Valley State College.

Mississippi Valley, which joined the SWAC in 1969 to replace Wiley, fumbled the football four times in the game, allowing Prairie View to take the twelve to ten victory.[188]

The average attendance numbers for Texas' black college football teams held steady in the low thousands. Bishop attracted seven thousand fans to its homecoming game against Langston, a game that Bishop won. This figure proved higher than Bishop's other home games, but the Tigers still attracted enough alumni and student support in Dallas to continue to compete.[189]

The Texas Southern–Grambling contest attracted more than thirty thousand fans to the Astrodome. The game provided one of the most exciting black college football games in 1969. Grambling came from behind in the fourth quarter to defeat Texas Southern twenty-eight to twenty-six.[190]

Two weeks later, national attention turned to white college football in Texas. On December 6, 1969, the University of Texas faced the University of Arkansas in the "game of the century." Broadcast nationwide on the American Broadcasting Network, the game decided the national championship as the number one ranked Longhorns overcame a fourteen-point deficit in the fourth quarter to defeat the number two ranked Razorbacks. The game proved so popular that President Richard Nixon traveled to Arkansas to bestow the national championship trophy on the victor. For the African American population of Texas, the victory by the University of Texas proved meaningless since the Longhorn football team possessed no African American players. With the integration of white college football spreading rapidly across Texas and the nation, the University of Texas' championship gave the school the ignominious record of being the last all-white college football team to win the national title.[191]

The highlight of the 1969 football season for Texas' black colleges became the Prairie View–Texas Southern contest. Held at the Astrodome, the two colleges sought to revive the traditional Thanksgiving Day football game that had been a major part of black college football in the state during the 1920s and 1930s. The game proved a major success as Texas Southern defeated Prairie View ten to zero before twenty thousand fans.[192]

Texas Southern closed out the 1969 season by defeating Morgan State College in the first annual Astrodome College Bowl. The Tigers thoroughly trounced Morgan State, forty-four to twenty. Despite the high-scoring affair, the game only attracted five thousand fans to the

Astrodome. The disparity in crowds between the Texas Southern–Grambling game and the Texas Southern-Morgan State game illustrated the role played by black college football in Texas going into the 1970s. Only the prominent teams in the SWAC, like Grambling, attracted fans to their football games.[193]

As the 1960s ended, black college football in Texas found itself in a reduced state. Texas had seven black colleges fielding football teams at the beginning of the decade. By 1970, only three remained. Black college teams in Texas experienced some success, such as Prairie View's national championships in 1963 and 1964, but by the end of the 1960s, even Prairie View struggled to compile a winning record each season.

Integrated football, both at the college and professional level, attracted the attention of the Texas black community away from African American college football. Successful black players, like Jerry Levias of Southern Methodist University and Bob Hayes of the Dallas Cowboys, became heroes to the black population in the state. Their success in integrated football made them champions and symbols of African American masculinity.

As Texas and the United States entered the 1970s, more and more star African American football players bypassed black colleges for integrated universities that possessed more money and opportunities. For these individuals, life in integrated football created different problems. The pioneers faced racial prejudice and social exclusion in the community and on their own campuses. At the same time, the majority of black college students in Texas attended African American colleges. Furthermore, the national struggle for civil rights faded as individuals focused on their own rights and interests. As a result, black college football in Texas took on a new position as an independent yet secondary social entity. The sport became a self-sufficient social event, attracting people directly connected with the black colleges, but was no longer a cornerstone of community or culture for the entire state.

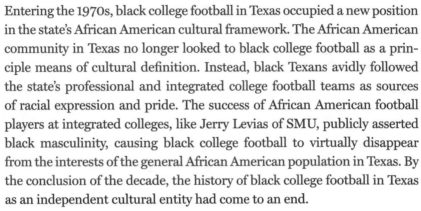

7

Loss of Independence

Entering the 1970s, black college football in Texas occupied a new position in the state's African American cultural framework. The African American community in Texas no longer looked to black college football as a principle means of cultural definition. Instead, black Texans avidly followed the state's professional and integrated college football teams as sources of racial expression and pride. The success of African American football players at integrated colleges, like Jerry Levias of SMU, publicly asserted black masculinity, causing black college football to virtually disappear from the interests of the general African American population in Texas. By the conclusion of the decade, the history of black college football in Texas as an independent cultural entity had come to an end.

The integration of college football teams in Texas increased dramatically during the 1970s as the top African American athletes chose the state's major white colleges over their African American counterparts. In 1970, Julius Whittier became the first African American to letter in football at the University of Texas. Following Whittier, black star players dominated the Longhorns' football team. One such player, fullback Roosevelt Leaks, became the University of Texas' first black running back and an All-American.[1]

While black college football no longer occupied a prominent place in the African American culture of Texas, the state's black colleges continued to provide the main opportunity for black Texans to receive a college degree. In the 1970s, African American colleges in Texas changed their academic programs to meet the educational needs of the black community. By the 1970s, Texas Southern University focused its mission on serving the urban population. The university started a weekend college that offered classes on Friday, Saturday, and Sunday. Texas Southern sought to allow working people an opportunity to receive a college degree.[2]

Black college football in Texas experienced some positive changes during the 1970s, as the state's white newspapers covered black college football for the first time. The fact that the *Dallas Morning News* chose to print anything on football games involving Bishop, Prairie View, and Texas Southern marked a major turning point for the sport. Unfortunately, the newspaper never published articles on the games. Instead, the *Dallas Morning News* included scores of the games, listing each week all college football contests from around the country.[3]

These changes caused black college football to take on a new identity. The sport continued at three of Texas' black colleges—Texas Southern, Prairie View, and Bishop—despite the fact that the football teams of all three schools lost consistently during the 1970s. Attendance numbers reached figures well below the peak years of the late 1940s and early 1950s. With the *Dallas Express* no longer in existence, Texas only had one major black newspaper, the *Houston Informer*, which limited the exposure black college football teams received. Still, the games remained popular enough among the students and alumni that the programs survived.

At the same time as the decline in status of black college football, the Texas African American community underwent changes of its own. With the 1970 census, the state realigned some of its political districts to reflect urban growth. As a result, African Americans in such communities found themselves with more political power. Redistricting resulted in several large, all-black communities in Texas, such as Houston's fourth and fifth wards, developing an African American majority vote. This led to the election of Barbara Jordan to the United States House of Representatives. Jordan, the first African American from Texas elected to the US Congress, served with distinction for six years. She received national acclaim for her leadership in the investigation into the Watergate break-in and the Nixon tapes.[4]

With the changes in the African American community and higher education in the 1970s, black Texans questioned the role of black college football. Texas Southern University expressed the problem of poor funding and low fan interest for intercollegiate football at Texas' black colleges in the 1970 edition of the school yearbook, *The Tiger*. The student editor opinioned that "[t]he role of athletics at Texas Southern has come under increasing questions in the past few years, from both the spectator-student and the athlete himself."[5] The editor blamed the lack of competitiveness and low fan interest on the inadequate funds the colleges received, which made it difficult to acquire equipment and facilities equal to those of integrated colleges in the state.[6]

Not every quality African American athlete in Texas competed for an integrated college during the 1970s, however. For some of the football players at Texas' African American colleges, football provided a stepping-stone to entering the National Football League. As the Texas Southern Tigers prepared for the 1970 football season, the team boasted thirteen seniors, all of whom, according to the *Houston Informer*, expected to sign professional contracts after the college football season ended. The top prospect at Texas Southern, quarterback David Mays, a four-year starter, held every one of the Tigers' passing records, including 657 attempts, 343 completions, and 4,140 yards passing.[7]

Despite the success of Mays and others, black college football still took a back seat to professional football. The Houston Oilers dominated the *Houston Informer*'s sports page. Before the 1970 season, the *Informer* published a listing of the Oilers' depth chart for both offense and defense, along with pictures of the African American starters.[8]

In another shift, the Prairie View Panthers and the Texas Southern Tigers received more attention from the black press during the 1970s than in the late 1960s because of the decline of the civil rights movement. As Prairie View prepared for its football season in 1970, the *Informer* published a full-page article on the Panthers' upcoming game with McMurry College of Abilene. Large pictures of three unnamed Prairie View players accompanied the article.[9] Overall, the interest given to black college football in Texas fell far below the sport's peak years in the 1940s and 1950s.

Black college football in Texas still generated a decent, if diminished, following. At Texas Southern, excitement existed among fans for a successful year when the Tigers defeated Southern University to begin the 1970 football season. The twenty-nine to six victory marked a major upset in the SWAC. The excitement among Texas Southern students and alumni was so high that the *Houston Informer* dedicated an entire page in the newspaper to the game, complete with a full team picture of the Tigers and seven individual pictures, including one of team captains Nathaniel Allen, Fred Hill, and Julius Adams.[10]

While Texas Southern received attention from black college football fans in Texas, Prairie View and Bishop College experienced neglect. The *Houston Informer* failed to give the outcome of Prairie View's thirty to thirteen loss to McMurry College, a predominantly white institution.[11] Bishop College disappeared almost entirely from the sports page.

Prairie View's football team found itself able to attract some interest, though, as the Panthers prepared for the first annual Grambling Football Classic on October 3. The two colleges scheduled their game for Comiskey Park, the home of major league baseball's Chicago White Sox, in an effort to attract fan support.[12] The move worked moderately well, as twenty-three thousand spectators filled the forty-five thousand seat stadium to watch Grambling easily defeat Prairie View fifty-seven to six. The twenty-three thousand fans composed one of the largest crowds to watch one of Prairie View's games in 1970, but the attendance figure fell well below what the two colleges had expected.[13]

The two losses set the tone for Prairie View's season. The Panthers managed to tie Southern University, but failed to achieve a winning record for the year. Prairie View, therefore, focused its attention on two football games as a means of attracting fans in Texas, in addition to building excitement among students and alumni: The first game was the State Fair Classic on October 24, where Prairie View hoped to exact revenge on Bishop College, which had beaten the Panthers the previous two seasons. In the other important football game, Prairie View faced Texas Southern University in the Astrodome on November 26.[14]

Bishop entered the State Fair Classic on a hot streak. The Tigers won their first two games of the season, defeating Texas Lutheran College thirty-four to twenty-one and Langston University thirty-six to six.[15] The early season victories filled the Tigers' fans with hopes of more success when their football team faced Prairie View. Unfortunately, Bishop's optimism proved unfounded as Prairie View came out victorious in the State Fair Classic.[16]

In Texas, the most viewed black college football game of the year took place on Thanksgiving Day, November 26. Now exceeding the State Fair Classic in popularity, the Texas Southern–Prairie View clash at the Astrodome attracted almost thirty thousand fans. For Texas Southern, the seventeen to seven victory assured the Tigers of a third-place finish in the SWAC.[17] Prairie View finished the year with yet another losing record, winning four games, losing five, and tying one.[18]

The less than stellar play on the field by Prairie View's football team disappointed Panther fans. Supporters found some solace in the fact that defensive back Bivian Lee earned All-American honors for the second year in a row. Lee also received an invitation to participate in the North-South All Star Football Game in Miami, Florida, on Christmas Day.[19]

As integration became the norm around the country, African Americans found themselves faced with a new set of racist ideas designed to keep black athletes limited in their opportunities. One particular example of this ideology can be found in Martin Kane's 1971 *Sports Illustrated* article entitled "An Assessment of Black Is Best." Kane argued that physical differences existed between whites and blacks, and that these physical characteristics gave African American athletes an edge in sports and enhanced blacks' athletic ability.[20] This focus on physical ability and racial characteristics afforded white Americans a new approach to the idea of racial superiority. If a black athlete outperformed a white athlete, the black athlete had inherited the talent rather than developed it through dedication and practice. At the same time, white athletes received recognition for their intelligence and hard work instead of inherited talent, thus promoting white athletes as smarter and more dedicated than black athletes.

Nationally, college football also underwent changes in the 1970s. In 1971, Walter Byrnes, the executive director of the NCAA, proposed limits on the number of coaches and scholarships for college football teams. The move came as a result of an economic downturn experienced by the sport as a result of an increase in competition with professional football and other leagues.[21]

To compensate for the decreased number of scholarship athletes on teams, the NCAA ended its ban on freshmen competing for varsities. The changes by the NCAA regarding college football caused large colleges in the United States to fear their dominance of the sport might disappear as smaller schools received an equal shot at recruiting top high school athletes. As a result, the NCAA created a three-level classification system for college athletic programs—Divisions I, II, and III. The new system created a hierarchy in college football, with the Division I teams holding the place of honor. Of the 667 NCAA colleges, only 126 schools received Division I status.[22] The changes did not affect black college football since African American colleges belonged to the NAIA rather than the NCAA.

For black college football in Texas, fans continued to only be interested in special games throughout the 1970s. When Prairie View and Southern University played each other on September 25, the game attracted fan interest. The *Houston Informer* helped increase support for the contest by running advertisements that declared "Black Is Beautiful" and "Bone-Crushing Football in the Astrodome."[23]

In the game, the Prairie View defense, nicknamed the Purple People Eaters because of the school's colors, led the Panthers to a twenty-one to three win. Southern University only accumulated a total of seventy-five yards rushing and fifty-seven yards passing. The attendance at the game in the Astrodome remained unknown, though, as the black press made no mention of the spectators.[24]

Texas Southern's football season also began favorably. The Tigers opened play by winning their first three games. The early highlight of the season for Texas Southern involved the Tigers' upset victory over Tennessee State. Tennessee State entered the contest in Houston ranked fifth in the nation for small colleges by United Press International. When Texas Southern won, many of the Tigers' supporters called for their team to receive a national ranking, though. It was not to be this year.[25]

In the State Fair Classic, Prairie View again changed opponents. The Panthers dropped Bishop and instead chose to face Tennessee State University. By having national powerhouse Tennessee State play in Dallas at the Cotton Bowl, the state of Texas hosted one of the top football games of the year involving black colleges. The main attraction of the contest, though, was the "greatest half-time show ever," including the Prairie View and Tennessee State college bands.[26]

At the same time, Texas Southern and Bishop clashed in Dallas on Friday, October 22. The 1971 game proved a major piece of Texas sports history, as Texas Southern and Bishop became the first two teams of any kind to play a game in the new Texas Stadium in Irving. Since the stadium seated more than sixty-five thousand people, the opportunity to see the new home of the Dallas Cowboys attracted fans that might not have normally watched Texas Southern or Bishop.[27]

Unfortunately for black college football in Texas, the sport continued to lose support to professional football and integrated college teams. The Texas black press coverage of the Houston Oilers or Texas A&I University of Kingsville greatly exceeded that of Prairie View, Texas Southern, and Bishop. Events such as Prairie View's 1971 homecoming, which served as the fiftieth anniversary celebration of the SWAC, still attracted fans. Football games between recognized black colleges, such as Texas Southern University's twenty-one to seven loss to Grambling in 1971, also proved popular. At the same time, Bishop's football games, along with contests between Prairie View or Texas Southern and a weak opponent like Mississippi Valley State, tended to go unnoticed.[28]

The popularity of black college football in Texas continued to decline, as evidenced by a November 13, 1971, *Houston Informer* article in its women's section entitled "Football Food Has a Special Flavor." The paper offered recipes and food selections ideal for eating at a football game or while watching a game on television. The *Informer* declared its "Madras Crackers" and "Banana Chiffon Cup Cakes" perfect for the "100 million arm chair quarterbacks" following the National Football League. The same week, no mention of black college football occurred in the newspaper.[29]

The Texas Southern–Prairie View contest again took place on Thanksgiving Day in the Astrodome in 1971. The two colleges competed on Thursday night to allow more fans the opportunity to attend the game. The three-dollar and five-dollar ticket prices for the game also represented only a slight increase over prices from the 1950s and 1960s. The black press in Texas actively promoted the contest but failed to give the final score.[30] The *Informer* only acknowledged the football game with a picture of state senator Barbara Jordan, who attended.[31]

The fans of the black college football squads that still existed in Texas received some excitement with the announcement of the First Annual College Black All-Star Football Game, scheduled for the Astrodome. The all-star game received even more publicity than the Texas Southern–Prairie View game on Thanksgiving. Taking place December 4, the contest involved senior football players from all fifty-eight black colleges in the NAIA.[32] Unfortunately, local newspapers did not record the outcome of the game.

Black college football in Texas lost more support to professional football as the Dallas Cowboys asserted themselves as one of the dominant teams in the NFL. In 1971, Dallas faced the Baltimore Colts in Super Bowl V. Even though the Cowboys lost sixteen to thirteen, the team still proved highly popular among black Texans because of African American star players on the team like "Bullet" Bob Hayes.[33]

While black college football existed in a diminished state in the 1970s, African Americans as a whole experienced increased opportunities and political power. In 1972, US Congress contained thirteen African Americans. A total of 2,427 black elected officials held political offices throughout the United States. The increase in elected officials corresponded with a rise in the number of black mayors around the country. From 1971 to 1975, the number of black mayors in the United States rose from 8 to 135. These changes in the number of African Americans elected to political offices stemmed from an amendment in 1975 to the Voting Rights Act of 1965 that allowed minorities to fight at-large voting laws. An end to at-large voting created predominantly black voting districts, and thus gave African American neighborhoods and communities the ability to elect representatives that supported black issues.[34]

Within this framework, Texas' black college football teams settled into a steady, though less prominent, reality in the African American community. With only one major black newspaper in Texas, black college football shared print space with integrated college football, professional football, and other sports, such as professional basketball. Bishop College, the lone private African American college in Texas to still field a team, rarely received any attention, attracting around one thousand fans per game. At the same time, the state-supported institutions of Prairie View and Texas Southern averaged between five and ten thousand fans.[35] When Prairie View lost sixteen to three to Jackson State in Mississippi on September 16, 1972, ten thousand spectators filled Mississippi Memorial Stadium in Jackson.[36]

Special football games at venues other than black college campuses still presented an opportunity for the occasional large crowd. Texas Southern began its 1972 football season by defeating Southern University thirty-seven to zero. The contest attracted thirty-two thousand fans to Rice Stadium in Houston.[37] Texas Southern University usually competed at the city of Houston's Jeppesen Stadium.

One change that took place in the 1970s, though, was a decreased interest among African American students in their colleges' football games and traditions. The Texas Southern University student newspaper *The Herald* addressed the declining interest in homecoming among the school's students. The paper referred to homecoming as "a flower that was once in bloom but has now faded out . . . the warmth and feeling for this annual tradition is gone."[38] *The Herald* then reported student opinions on the topic. One Texas Southern student, Al Collins, exclaimed, "Homecoming means absolutely nothing to me. It is just another day of the week."[39]

The Tiger, Texas Southern's yearbook, responded to the school newspaper on the issue of homecoming and the role of athletics. *The Tiger* staff declared that an opportunity for creating unity among African Americans existed via athletics. Athletics allowed African Americans an opportunity to do their own thing while also establishing mutual respect, especially on college campuses.[40]

Despite the decline in the importance of homecoming for Texas Southern students, the 1972 game still attracted more than eleven thousand fans and alumni to Jeppesen Stadium. Texas Southern easily won the contest over Mississippi Valley State College, forty-four to seventeen. At the same time, Prairie View promoted its own homecoming, which featured a "gala halftime show" with the coronation of the homecoming queen and a performance by the school band.[41]

Following the two homecoming games, the black press in Texas neglected to print any more articles concerning the 1972 black college football season. The State Fair Classic, once the dominant social event for African American community, was not mentioned in the *Houston Informer* in 1972. Bishop College also played in obscurity as far as the general black population of Texas was concerned. Part of the reason for the lack of interest in black college football came from the level of play put forth by Texas teams. For example, Prairie View finished with a record of five wins and five losses, the school's first nonlosing season in several years, but the Panthers only won one conference game and finished last in the SWAC.[42] As a result, Prairie View lost much of the support it received from the general black population in Texas during the Panthers' heyday of the 1950s and 1960s.

African American athletes also continued to distinguish themselves in professional football in Texas, further taking attention away from black college football in the state. During the 1972 professional football season, Calvin Hill, a black running back from Yale University, became the Dallas Cowboy's first one thousand–yard rusher. Hill also earned the NFL Rookie of the Year award.[43] Furthermore, Dallas returned to the Super Bowl in 1972. This time, the Cowboys won the game, defeating the Miami Dolphins twenty-four to three.[44] Hill, along with the other African American stars on the Cowboys, solidified integrated professional football as an image of black masculinity, further relegating black college football to a secondary status.

Meanwhile, Texas' African American colleges continued to grow and provide more services. In 1973, the number of students involved in the Manpower Resources Project at Texas Southern University reached 173.[45] At the same time, Prairie View A&M College officially became Prairie View A&M University on Monday, August 27, 1973. The establishment of university status for Prairie View was the top priority of the Centennial Council, a group organized by Prairie View to celebrate the school's upcoming one hundredth birthday. The new status of Prairie View as a university also excited the schools' alumni and students, who felt the title placed their school on an equal plain with other Texas universities.[46]

Black college football adapted in order to survive in the new world of college football. One trend that existed in the 1970s involved Texas' black college football teams annually competing against integrated colleges. In 1972, Texas Southern faced Texas A&I before 17,850 fans at the Astrodome. The next year, the Tigers scheduled a football game at the Astrodome against Sam Houston State University of Huntsville, Texas.[47]

Other changes that black college football in Texas made to adapt to the new role played by the sport involved the football schedule. From the 1920s through the 1960s, the black college football season in Texas began in October after students reported to campus and ended with the Prairie View Bowl on New Year's Day. In 1973, Texas Southern began its football season on September 8 and concluded when the Tigers faced Prairie View on November 17. The change allowed the black college teams to minimize their competition with professional football, whose season lasted into January.[48]

Another way Texas' black college football teams distinguished themselves was via their style of play. The Texas Southern–Sam Houston State contest on September 8, 1973, illustrated the difference in the style of play among black colleges and formerly white colleges in Texas. Sam Houston used the Veer-T, a running-oriented offense. Texas Southern, on the other hand, employed an offense based around the passing game. The passing-oriented game of Texas' black colleges made for an exciting brand of football.[49] In this game, Texas Southern proved itself the better team, defeating Sam Houston twenty-four to fourteen.[50]

Meanwhile, Prairie View continued to struggle. Led by running back Walter Payton, Jackson State defeated Prairie View by a score of thirty-two to seven in 1973. The contest proved an embarrassment for Prairie View fans as the Panthers accumulated minus forty-seven total yards of offense, using five different quarterbacks. The *Houston Informer* summed up Prairie View's play, stating, "By rule of thumb, when you have to use more than two quarterbacks in a game, you are dead and a loser."[51]

The Texas Southern University football team fared slightly better than Prairie View. After defeating Sam Houston State, the Tigers lost to Southern University and Tennessee State. The Texas Southern foot-ball players and fans quickly forgot these two losses as the Tigers faced their second white college of the year, the University of Hawaii. Texas Southern traveled to Honolulu, Hawaii, for the first time in the college's history.[52]

The travel distance and time zone changes involved with flying to Hawaii caused Texas Southern to play sluggishly and commit errors in the football game. The Tigers only amassed sixty-six total yards of offense in the first half. Texas Southern came back to score twenty-one points in the fourth quarter, but still lost to the University of Hawaii Rainbows, twenty-four to twenty-one. The Texas Southern school news-paper declared that the Tigers "did not look like a football team."[53]

The game against the University of Hawaii caused more problems for the Tigers. One night in Honolulu, after a 2:00 a.m. curfew, six Texas Southern football players left their barracks and proceeded to travel twenty-six miles downtown, where they stayed until the next morning. The rules violation led Rod Paige, the Tigers' coach, to suspend the six.[54]

The Prairie View homecoming festivities attracted ten thousand fans, despite the poor record of the football team in 1973. The festivities included the annual parade, the coronation of "Miss Prairie View," and several dances. The football game, in which the Panthers defeated Texas Lutheran seventeen to six, received the least amount of attention from students and alumni, since it represented one of the few victories Prairie View registered that year.[55]

The Prairie View football season went so poorly that the school year-book, *Pantherland*, chose not to publish any individual game accounts or the team's final record. Instead, the yearbook published a team picture and individual pictures of a few players. Jesse and James Wolfe received recognition in the yearbook because professional football teams drafted the two defensive linemen. Jesse went to the Miami Dolphins while James went to the Pittsburgh Steelers.[56]

The Texas Southern University football season also proved a disap-pointment for its fans. The *Houston Informer* reported fan statements of "What is wrong with TSU?" and "Say man, when are you going to run Paige away from TSU?"[57] The fans changed their minds about the team and head coach Paige when Texas Southern upset Grambling thirty-five to twenty-one. The 53,859 spectators who watched the contest at the Astro-dome set an attendance record for a black college football game in Texas.[58]

As Texas Southern and Prairie View prepared to close out the season on November 17, the two schools announced the creation of the Texas Trophy. Prairie View and Texas Southern hoped to build excitement for the rivalry. Starting in 1973, the trophy went annually to the game's winner.[59] The Texas Trophy marked the second attempt at an annual award presented to the winner of the Texas Southern–Prairie View game. The first trophy appeared in the early 1950s but disappeared after just one game.

The addition of the Texas Trophy worked to create fan excitement. The football game between the two largest black colleges in Texas proved popular among their students and alumni. In his weekly article for the *Houston Informer*, Alex Durley, former head coach of Texas Southern, dubbed the Texas Southern–Prairie View contest the "black national championship of Texas."[60]

In the same article, however, Durley discussed the poor play of both football teams that year. Texas Southern and Prairie View finished in sixth and seventh places, respectively, in the SWAC in 1973. Durley credited the next to last and last-place finishes to the lack of quality personnel at the two colleges caused by the best black athletes attending integrated colleges. Texas Southern's offensive line, for example, possessed an average weight of less than 218 pounds. Durley exclaimed that sending the Tigers' players against other SWAC schools constituted the equivalent of "sending a slingshot army to knock off the Russians."[61]

When the two college football teams finally played each other, Texas Southern won easily, forty-one to fourteen. Despite the score, the game proved a sluggish affair with Prairie View's offense possessing "the punch of a glass of milk."[62] The highlight of the game for the twenty-two thousand fans on hand at the Astrodome came with the "super-fantastic" halftime performances of the Prairie View Marching Band and the Texas Southern University Ocean of Soul marching band.[63]

The success of African Americans on integrated college football teams in Texas became normalized in 1973 when the Texas Sportswriters Association named Roosevelt Leaks the Texas Amateur Athlete of the Year. Leaks dominated the Southwest Conference, setting a conference record for rushing in a single season with 1,415 yards. Leaks also set the Southwest Conference record for rushing yards in a single game with 342 yards against Southern Methodist University.[64]

Integrated Texas college football teams continued to dominate in signing the best black football players, as evident on national recruiting day in 1974. On February 12, 1974, the University of Texas signed more African American football players to scholarships than at any other time in the school's history—a total of six. Earl Campbell ranked as the top recruit of the class. A running back from Tyler's John Tyler High School, Campbell received scholarship offers from more than two hundred colleges around the country. At the University of Texas, he became one of the greatest college football players ever.[65]

More problems occurred for black college football in 1974 when the NCAA further limited football scholarships to 105 per team. To compensate for the decreased number of scholarships, the NCAA lessened academic requirements for high school athletes wanting to compete in college. Instead of maintaining a 1.6 grade point average as a freshman in college to remain eligible, athletes now only needed a 2.0 grade point average in high school. This granted students from high schools with fewer economic and academic resources, especially minority students, the opportunity to play at the collegiate level.[66]

The change in the NCAA eligibility requirements hurt black colleges. Black colleges traditionally required only a high school diploma for admittance and often attracted students with academic records that were not as strong. With the loosening of the NCAA requirements, more African American athletes found themselves able to attend integrated colleges, thus spurning black colleges that did not belong to the NCAA. Still, the black colleges in Texas continued to improve themselves academically. In 1974, Texas Southern University started a doctoral program. The move made Texas Southern the only African American college in the state to offer a PhD.[67]

On the football field, a game between a black college and an integrated college began the 1974 season. Playing at the Astrodome, Texas Southern barely defeated Sam Houston State, seventeen to fourteen.[68] The Tigers followed up their victory over Sam Houston State with a fourteen to six win over Southern University.[69]

For the 1974 Texas Southern–Southern contest, more than twenty thousand fans filled Jeppesen Stadium. The attendance at the game proved larger than the fifteen thousand fans who saw Rice University lose to the University of Cincinnati at Rice Stadium, and the eighteen thousand who watched the University of Houston lose to the University of Miami in the Astrodome. The Texas Southern–Southern University game was an anomaly, however, as integrated college football games regularly outdrew black college football games.[70]

The Prairie View football team continued its losing ways in 1974, finishing the season without a win. The school's yearbook summed up the season, saying that the team "did not experience the thrill of victory, but clearly understood the agony of defeat."[71] The yearbook staff added that if the Panthers' football team planned to build for tomorrow, then "let us hope tomorrow is today."[72]

The 1974 football season also marked other changes for Prairie View besides the school's first winless season. In the early 1970s, the State Fair Classic ceased to exist. Prairie View still faced another black college football team at the Cotton Bowl each year, but the contest no longer received any special promotion as the State Fair Classic. In 1974, Prairie View lost to Grambling in Dallas.[73]

Bishop received some attention from the black press in Texas during 1974. Ignored the previous few years, Bishop faced Prairie View at Cobb Stadium on Bishop's campus in Dallas. The game proved a lackluster affair as Bishop College, which entered the game with only one win, defeated winless Prairie View by a score of twenty-one to fourteen.[74]

The 1974 black college football season ended with Prairie View losing to Texas Southern thirty to twenty. A small crowd of fourteen thousand people attended the annual Texas Championship at the Astrodome. The low fan turnout stemmed from the poor records of both teams. Ar half-time when the Panthers led the Tigers twelve to ten, the score marked the first time all season that Prairie View led in a football game.[75]

The success of African American football players spread to other colleges throughout the state. In the 1974 Peach Bowl, tailback Larry Isaac of Texas Tech received recognition as the Most Valuable Player on offense. Isaac, an African American, gained 124 yards in a six to six tie with Vanderbilt University.[76]

Texas' three black college football teams achieved such little success during the mid-1970s that the *Houston Informer* chose not to publish any articles on their football games in 1975. For Bishop College, this consti-tuted a regular occurrence since the school rarely received any coverage. At Prairie View and Texas Southern, the move served as a tremendous slight since the two institutions were from the Houston area.

The *Informer* resumed covering black college football in 1976, but the season began with little happiness for Prairie View. As the Panthers practiced for their first game, Mark Brown, a freshman football player, died following a fainting spell. Harris Country medical examiners gave no cause of death as they waited for the results of an autopsy. Brown's family and the Prairie View football team were devastated.[77]

The Texas Southern season also began with disappointment for the Tigers' fans, but not to the level of anguish felt by Prairie View over the death of Brown. Texas Southern opened its football season with three losses, after falling to Texas A&I, Bethune-Cookman, and Southern University. The Texas A&I game continued the practice of annual competition against integrated teams.[78] The season continued to go poorly for Texas Southern as Tennessee State, ranked second nationally for black college football, defeated the Tigers twenty-one to three on September 25. The loss left Texas Southern winless.[79]

Despite the death of Brown at the start of the school year, the Prairie View football team experienced some unexpected success in 1976. The Panthers finished with a winning record for the first time in almost ten years. Prairie View lost its first three games, causing students and alumni to expect another dismal season.[80] They then defeated Southwest Texas State University. Prairie View scored twenty points in the second quarter on its way to a forty-eight to twenty-five victory.[81]

The Prairie View victory over integrated Southwest Texas State turned the Panthers' season around. Prairie View won five of its last seven games, including a four-game winning streak to close out the season. The Panthers' three wins and three losses in conference play placed Prairie View in the middle of the SWAC standings, a considerable improvement considering the recent string of last-place finishes.[82]

The Bishop College football team generated its one article in the Texas black press on October 23. Bishop rallied in the closing minutes of its game against Texas Southern to kick a thirty-two-yard field goal for a fifteen to fourteen victory. Bishop's win cost Texas Southern the opportunity for its first win of the season.[83]

As Texas' black colleges continued to lose games, the schools found it extremely difficult to build excitement among students and alumni. Texas Southern's lack of success led to an extremely low attendance of three thousand fans at the school's homecoming game against Mississippi Valley State College on October 23. The crowd was a dramatic decrease for the college's homecoming. The fans who chose to attend the game, however, experienced a victory as Texas Southern defeated Mississippi Valley State twenty-four to seven. The victory marked the Tigers' first of the year and assured the team would not finish last in the SWAC.[84]

As Prairie View put together a winning streak to close the 1977 football season, several significant events occurred. When the Panthers defeated Alcorn College on November 13, ABC broadcast the game on regional television.[85] Prairie View also recorded a win over Grambling when the Tigers forfeited their contest with the Panthers. Finally, Prairie View defeated Texas Southern by a score of twenty-two to fifteen before ten thousand fans in the Astrodome. The victory marked Prairie View's first against its rival college since 1966.[86]

At the start of the 1977 campaign, Texas Southern University's president G. M. Sawyer discussed the role of intercollegiate athletics at the African American colleges. Prairie View and Texas Southern remained the only members of the SWAC who received no state funds for athletics. This policy of the Texas legislature affected all public colleges, who were expected to make their athletic departments self-sufficient. To fund their football teams, Prairie View and Texas Southern had the ability to charge students an athletic fee. Since 80 to 85 percent of the students at the public African American colleges came from families whose incomes fell below the poverty level, the colleges chose not to impose the added cost. Instead, President Sawyer took the majority of the Texas Southern University athletic budget from gate receipts and fund-raising campaigns. As a result, the Prairie View and Texas Southern football teams operated with fewer funds than their conference foes and the integrated colleges in Texas, making it even more difficult to compete.[87]

President Sawyer defended intercollegiate athletics at the black colleges in Texas, even though the programs failed to generate profits. He stated: "I refuse to look at the value of inter-collegiate athletics in terms of money alone. I feel athletics is worth just as much to an individual as any other activity or course in the curriculum."[88] Sawyer supported his statement by saying that through athletics, students who might not have attended college received an opportunity to acquire a college education. With an education, African American athletes increased their jobs opportunities in business and industry.[89]

Through his statements, Sawyer expressed the role intercollegiate athletics came to play at Texas' black colleges. As the community in the state looked mainly to integrated colleges and professional football for cultural expression during the 1970s, black college football took on a new role. The colleges no longer held a dominant position among the African American community. Instead, black college football focused on offering athletes ignored by other institutions an opportunity to continue to play football and to receive an education.

Operating under these guidelines, the black colleges in Texas no longer dominated the SWAC. Neither Texas Southern nor Prairie View ever won the conference title again.[90] The colleges' football games attracted decent numbers of students and alumni. Curtis Goode, who attended Prairie View on a music scholarship in the mid-1970s, recalled that the college's football games attracted between five and ten thousand fans every week.[91]

The 1977 football season progressed with Texas' African American college football teams performing as they had throughout the 1970s. Prairie View defeated Bishop thirty-nine to seven on October 22. The win marked only the second for the Panthers that year. Bishop finished winless in 1977.[92]

Texas Southern performed slightly better than its counterparts, placing in the middle of the SWAC standings. With victories over Alcorn and Mississippi Valley State, the Tigers finished third place in the conference standing.[93] Grambling, however, defeated Texas Southern twenty-eight to fourteen on October 29, showing the talent difference between Texas' black colleges and the other conference members that received state funds for athletics.[94]

The Prairie View and Texas Southern football records failed to matter to their fans when the two schools met in the Texas Shootout. Texas Southern entered the 1977 contest on a hot streak after defeating Langston University by a score of eighty-five to thirteen. For the fans, though, the biggest attraction of the Texas Shootout involved the halftime ceremonies featuring the Panther Marching Band led by the school's drill team, the Black Foxes, and the Texas Southern band, the Ocean of Soul.[95]

Texas Southern defeated Prairie View in 1977 to win the Texas Trophy. The game was one of the most exciting in recent years. Prairie View led Texas Southern thirteen to zero before the Tigers came back. In the end, Texas Southern edged past Prairie View by a score of twenty-nine to twenty-eight.[96]

Two important events occurred in 1977 that drastically affected black college football history in Texas. First, following the 1977 football season, the NCAA created a new classification for college football, Division I-AA. The Prairie View and Texas Southern football teams, along with the rest of the SWAC and the majority of the country's black colleges, joined the new division. The inclusion of the schools brought official recognition by the NCAA, a recognition that black college football never possessed before. At the same time, the I-AA ranking placed black college football in a secondary position to the major integrated colleges around the country. Also, inclusion in the NCAA cost black colleges their autonomy in regard to athletics. While black college football no longer played an important cultural role in the African American community, throughout its history, the existence of black college football outside the control of whites proved the most important reason for why the sport served as a major cultural institution for African Americans.[97]

The second event occurred at the University of Texas. Earl Campbell, the Longhorn's star running back, won the Heisman Trophy in 1977. Campbell became the first African American from the state to win the award for being the best college football player in the country. As a result, the top black high school football players only looked to the state's major integrated colleges for the opportunity to play football.

With these two events, the independent history of black college football in Texas came to an end. Campbell's award solidified integrated college football as the ultimate recognition of African American athletes' ability. In the minds of the black community in Texas, to play football at one of Texas' black colleges meant the athlete probably lacked the talent to receive a scholarship from a top program.

The Division I-AA status of the Prairie View and Texas Southern football teams also solidified the secondary position of the programs in the black community. The importance of black college football in Texas continued to diminish throughout the 1970s. With only three African American colleges still playing football, the sport received little attention from the black press and the African American community. As integration increased throughout the decade at the predominantly white colleges in the state, the black college football teams in Texas watched as the most talented athletes chose to attend other schools. While Prairie View, Bishop, and Texas Southern all continued to field football teams and attract decent-sized crowds for individual games, such as the annual Prairie View–Texas Southern game at the Astrodome, black college football in Texas found its existence questioned by fans, students, and the black press. The success experienced by professional football in Texas, including the Super Bowl victory by the Dallas Cowboys in 1972, further diminished black college football as a cultural institution and a source of racial pride and black masculinity. As a result, by 1977 the history of black college football in Texas as an independent African American institution had come to an end.

Life Goes On

The 1977 football season marked the end of black college football's existence as an independent institution in the African American community. As a result, the sport experienced an even more rapid decline during the 1980s and 1990s. The African American community in Texas also underwent changes in the late twentieth century. Integration became the norm, while at the same time, the struggle for civil rights as a movement virtually disappeared. As African Americans distinguished themselves at integrated colleges throughout Texas, both blacks and whites in the state pointed to the accomplishments of black athletes as proof of successful integration in the higher educational system. Unfortunately, the claims of increased racial equity, at Texas' formerly white colleges and at the black state colleges, proved a myth.

In April 1978, the Office of Civil Rights (OCR) in the United States Department of Education informed Governor Dolph Briscoe that it was beginning an investigation into Texas' higher education system. The Office of Civil Rights planned to look at how Texas' colleges complied with Title VI of the Civil Rights Act of 1964 that outlawed discrimination in education. Specifically, the OCR looked to see if Texas increased the participation of minority students in the state's universities.[1]

Much to the dismay of the state's government and its public universities, in 1980 the OCR released its findings that Texas historically segregated its higher education system based on race. As a result, African Americans in Texas who wished to attend a state institution found themselves limited to Prairie View A&M and Texas Southern. Yet the two public black colleges received minimal resources from the state. Furthermore, the OCR declared that African Americans traditionally received little access to graduate and professional training, and that black students entered public higher education at a rate 20 percent lower than whites.[2]

The OCR study presented specific examples to illustrate the problems in the Texas higher education system, including the fact that African

American faculty and staff were overrepresented at black colleges and underrepresented at white colleges. The unequal funding Prairie View and Texas Southern received from the state government equaled one thousand dollars less per student than the funding for white colleges in Texas. The inequitable distribution of resources caused fewer class options, lower salaries, and unequal facilities for the African American colleges.[3]

The OCR report caused Cynthia Brown, the Assistant Secretary for Civil Rights of the US Department of Education, to find the State of Texas in violation of federal civil rights law in January 1981. Texas governor Bill Clements immediately responded by initiating actions to alleviate the violation. Clements hoped to comply with civil rights law without involving the federal courts, thus protecting federal funds for the Texas higher education system.[4]

Clements called his program the "Texas Plan." The Texas Plan professed several goals that sought to bring about compliance. The program promised to increase the percentage of African American and Hispanic high school graduates that entered public universities over a five-year period until the number equaled the percentage of white students entering the same universities. The Texas Plan also sought to enlarge minority graduate pools, promote racial balance on university campuses, and increase the hiring of minority faculty and staff.[5]

When the five-year deadline arrived for the Texas Plan, no visible progress had made for increasing the number of minorities in higher education. Some state-supported colleges, including the University of Houston at University Park, the University of Texas at Arlington, and East Texas State University, even reported lower minority enrollments than before the program began. The number of African American students who entered public, four-year colleges decreased over 4 percent from 1978 to 1988. During the same time period, the African American students who entered public universities dropped out at a rate of 36 percent. While the state government proclaimed that the Texas Plan had worked to increase minority enrollment in college, the number of African Americans enrolled in public universities in Texas decreased during the ten years from 1978 to 1988. Furthermore, no increase in the employment of minorities occurred in the Texas higher education system. As a result, Texas still appeared to violate federal laws pertaining to discrimination in higher education throughout the 1980s and 1990s.[6]

The restrictive racial climate at the white colleges in Texas during the 1980s and 1990s, which also included the exclusion of black students from fraternities and sororities, caused a movement by African Americans toward black colleges. The state legislature attempted in the 1980s to close Prairie View and Texas Southern, arguing that the state could save money with the closings since the two universities duplicated programs at other Texas colleges. Black Texans, though, resisted the action, and were even able to procure more funding for Prairie View and Texas Southern.[7]

These events showed that black colleges in Texas still played a role in the education of African Americans. With limited enrollments of minorities at predominately white colleges in Texas, institutions such as Prairie View and Wiley offered a viable alternative. Even with the virtual disappearance of black college football in Texas, the colleges themselves continued to serve the community.

While African American colleges adapted to their new roles in the US higher educational system in the late twentieth century, black college football also evolved. Many schools continued to conduct their programs as if they were still dominant social and cultural institutions. For example, from 1984 to 1986, the SWAC faced off in four all-star games against the Mid-Eastern Athletic Conference. The first three games took place in Atlanta's Fulton County Stadium. The final game occurred at RFK Stadium in Washington, DC. While the contest proved moderately popular, it failed to make a profit and was cancelled in 1986.[8]

In Texas, black college football continued to struggle. Bishop College ran into financial problems in the late 1980s despite its Dallas location. Because of mismanagement of funds, the college cancelled its football team in 1987. Then in 1988, Bishop closed its doors permanently.[9]

The failure of Bishop College marked a low point in the history of African American higher education in Texas, since Bishop had been one of the first black colleges in the state, as well as a founding member of the SWAC. Paul Quinn College quickly sought to capitalize on the availability of the Dallas campus. After years of struggling financially in Waco, Paul Quinn bought the Bishop campus in Dallas and moved there in 1990.[10]

Academically, the other black colleges in Texas performed well during the 1980s and 1990s. Prairie View's enrollment reached 5,640 students by 1988. Texas Southern, at the same time, enrolled more than eight thousand students. The urban colleges of Texas Southern and

Huston-Tillotson also saw their student populations change as they included one-third white students, representing a more diverse urban community in Texas' cities. Meanwhile, the black colleges in smaller, rural communities, like Jarvis Christian of Hawkins, remained almost entirely African American and possessed enrollments of between three hundred and eight hundred students.[11]

At the same time, African Americans continued to achieve success in integrated football in Texas. For the top black athletes in the state, integrated colleges offered greater national exposure and a better stepping-stone to professional football. In 1989, Andre Ware, the University of Houston's black quarterback, became the second African American from Texas to win the Heisman Trophy.[12]

Meanwhile, black college football continued to decline in the quality of play and in the amount of support fans gave to the teams. Prairie View set the national record for consecutive losses. From November 4, 1989, until September 26, 1998, the Panthers failed to win a football game, a streak that lasted eighty games.[13]

The losing streak for Prairie View stemmed from the fact that the historically black college sought to regain the prominence it held in college football under Billy Nicks, and to compete with integrated teams. While working to achieve these goals, the Prairie View athletic department undertook bad financial and management practices. According to Lt. Gen. Julius Becton, "The losing streak started because I cancelled football for a year."[14] Becton, who directed Prairie View's ROTC program in the late 1950s, returned to the school as president in 1989. Upon arriving on campus, Becton found the athletic department compensating for its annual budget deficits by taking funds from other programs, such as housing and dinning. Prairie View faced the option of finding a way for its athletic teams to pay for themselves, or having the state take over control of the university. As a result, Becton closed all sports in the spring of 1989 except for cross country and track. By the end of the school year, every sport but football presented plans to balance their budgets and make themselves self-sufficient. Since football presented no plan, Becton cancelled the sport for the 1990 season. When Prairie View returned to football in 1991, the team had no scholarships.[15]

Without scholarships, Prairie View found itself unable to recruit quality athletes. As a result, the Panthers attracted only football players passed over by other colleges, including some with serious injuries such as reconstructed knees and metal pins in their ankles. As the only college in the SWAC that failed to give scholarships, competing with its fellow conference members proved difficult. For example, in 1991, the Prairie View football team scored a total of forty-eight points in its entire season, while giving up an average of fifty-six points per game to its opponents.[16]

The move to the NCAA did not prove entirely detrimental to black college football nationally, though. In 1991, the Heritage Bowl took place at Miami's Joe Robbie Stadium. Featuring Alabama State, the champion of the SWAC, and North Carolina A&T, the champion of the MEAC, the bowl game represented the first postseason contest between two black colleges that the NCAA sanctioned. Alabama State won the game thirty-six to thirteen.[17]

Other positive events for Texans and the alumni of black colleges continued to occur. At Texas Southern, defensive end Michael Strahan received national acclaim during the early 1990s. He was the SWAC player of the year in 1991 and 1992, as well as the Black College Defensive Player of the Year and an AP All-American. Drafted by the New York Giants, Strahan went on to a fourteen-year career that included a Super Bowl victory and setting the NFL single season record for sacks with twenty-two and a half in 2001. He was inducted into the Pro Football Hall of Fame in 2014.

Another positive event took place at the end of the twentieth century. Prairie View finally ended its football drought in 1998 by defeating Langston University fourteen to twelve. The Panthers stopped Langston on a two-point conversion that would have tied the game with less than three minutes to play.[18]

Then, in 1999 at the age of ninety-four, Billy Nicks, former head coach at Prairie View A&M, was inducted into the National College Football Hall of Fame in South Bend, Indiana.[19] Nicks's selection brought national recognition to the accomplishments of African American college football programs during the period of segregation in the United States. Nicks joined twenty-one other inductees, all from major integrated colleges, including Auburn University running back Bo Jackson, Brigham Young University quarterback Jim McMahon, and University of Nebraska head coach Tom Osborne.[20]

Two months after his induction into the College Football Hall of Fame, Coach Nicks passed away. The *Houston Chronicle*, which had ignored black college football in Texas throughout the majority of the twentieth century, published an article praising Nicks as a coach and an innovator. The *Chronicle* stressed how Nicks became the first coach to script a series of offensive plays, decades before Bill Walsh received praise for doing the same thing with the San Francisco 49ers of the NFL.[21]

As black college football entered the twenty-first century, the teams recognized the problems they faced in the current world of college sports, and as a result shifted their efforts away from trying to regain past glories and competing with integrated college teams. Instead, black college football worked on maintaining financial stability, promoting African American higher education, and maintaining a solid fan base of alumni and students. The African American college teams focused their attention on individual contests and classics as a means of meeting athletic budgets. Prairie View received the bulk of its football budget from revenues generated by the annual State Fair Classic. The money received from this event, along with corporate sponsorships from companies such as State Farm Bank, provided Prairie View with enough resources to give out football scholarships again in the late 1990s, a number which reached sixty-three student-athletes receiving aid in 2003.[22] Black college football in the United States also received limited national television exposure. Black Entertainment Television (BET) began broadcasting one game each week featuring African American colleges. Also, NBC annually showed the Bayou Classic between Grambling and Southern. Both of these efforts brought national exposure to black college football around the country.

During the first decade of the twenty-first century, some of the smaller black colleges in Texas revived football at their campuses. Paul Quinn's squad played as a club team in 2001, before entering NAIA competition in 2004.[23] The school dropped football again in 2008 when faced with the economic challenges of the national recession, before turning their football field into an organic farm. Meanwhile, Texas College brought back football in 2004, competing in the Sooner Athletic Conference of the NAIA.[24] Prairie View A&M and Texas Southern also occasionally fielded successful teams, with the Panthers winning the SWAC in 2009 and the Tigers winning in 2010. While the league later voided the Texas Southern championship because of rules violations, the wins brought excitement during the season.[25]

Within the new framework, the black college football teams in Texas continued to field squads. The Prairie View Panthers and Texas Southern

Tigers began facing each other every year at NRG Stadium in Houston, the home of the NFL's Houston Texans. Furthermore, Prairie View and Grambling received a sponsorship for the State Fair Classic from State Farm Insurance, and later Southwest Airlines, continuing the contest in the Cotton Bowl. The continuous history of the State Fair Classic encouraged the State Fair of Texas to start a second classic between two HBCUs. Starting in 2018, Texas Southern University and Southern University faced off in the State Fair Showdown.

As the first hundred years of black college football in Texas came to a close, so did the vibrant history of the sport as a dominant feature of the African American community. This history served as a source of pride, cultural power, and community expression during a period of dramatic change in Texas and US history. In response to the change, the Texas African American colleges changed their approach to football. Instead of trying to compete with integrated colleges, Prairie View and Texas Southern used the revenue from specific games, such as the State Fair Classic, to maintain a balanced athletic budget. As a result, black college football in Texas survived, keeping alive the important legacy established by earlier generations.

Appendix A

Southwestern Athletic Conference Champions, 1921-2017[1]

1921	Wiley
1922	Paul Quinn
1923	Wiley
1924	Paul Quinn
1925	Bishop
1926	Samuel Huston
1927	Wiley
1928	Wiley
1929	Wiley
1930	Wiley
1931	Prairie View A&M
1932	Wiley
1933	Langston, Prairie View A&M, Wiley
1934	Texas College
1935	Texas College
1936	Texas College, Langston
1937	Southern, Langston
1938	Southern, Langston
1939	Langston
1940	Southern, Langston
1941	No Champion
1942	Texas College
1943	No Champion
1944	Texas College, Wiley, Langston, Wiley
1945	Southern
1946	Southern

1947   Southern
1948   Southern, Langston
1949   Southern
1950   Prairie View A&M
1951   Prairie View A&M
1952   Prairie View A&M
1953   Prairie View A&M
1955   Southern
1956   Texas Southern, Wiley
1957   Wiley
1958   Prairie View A&M
1959   Southern
1960   Southern, Prairie View A&M, Grambling State
1961   Jackson State
1962   Jackson State
1963   Prairie View A&M
1964   Prairie View A&M
1965   Grambling State
1966   Southern, Grambling State, Texas Southern, Arkansas AM&N
1967   Grambling State
1968   Alcorn State, Grambling State, Texas Southern
1969   Alcorn State
1970   Alcorn State
1971   Grambling State
1972   Grambling State, Jackson State
1973   Grambling State, Jackson State
1974   Grambling State, Alcorn State
1975   Grambling State, Alcorn State, Southern
1976   Alcorn State
1977   Alcorn State
1978   Grambling State
1979   Alcorn State, Grambling State
1980   Grambling State, Jackson State
1981   Jackson State
1982   Jackson State
1983   Grambling State
1984   Alcorn State
1985   Grambling State, Jackson State

1986	Jackson State
1987	Jackson State
1988	Jackson State
1989	Grambling State
1990	Jackson State
1991	Alabama State
1992	Alcorn
1993	Southern
1994	Grambling, Alcorn
1995	Jackson State
1996	Jackson State
1997	Southern
1998	Southern
1999	Southern
2000	Grambling
2001	Grambling
2002	Grambling
2003	Southern
2004	Alabama State
2005	Grambling
2006	Alabama A&M
2007	Jackson State
2008	Grambling
2009	Prairie View A&M
2010	Texas Southern
2011	Grambling
2012	Arkansas-Pine Buff
2013	Southern
2014	Alcorn State
2015	Alcorn State
2016	Grambling
2017	Gramblin

Appendix B

Texas Black College National Champions[1]

1921	Wiley, Talladega
1924	Wiley, Tuskegee
1928	Wiley, Bluefield State
1932	Wiley
1935	Texas College
1945	Wiley
1952	Texas Southern, Florida A&M, Lincoln, Virginia State
1953	Prairie View A&M
1954	Prairie View A&M, Tennessee State, Florida A&M, Southern
1958	Prairie View A&M
1963	Prairie View A&M
1964	Prairie View A&M

Notes

Introduction
1. *Houston Informer*, 7 January 1950.
2. Michael Hurd, *Black College Football, 1892–1992: One Hundred Years of Education, History, and Pride* (Virginia Beach: The Donning Company, 1992).
3. Ramachandra Guha, "Cricket and Politics in Colonial India," *Past and Present*, no. 161, (November 1998): 157.

Chapter 1
1. Gwendolyn Captain, "Enter Ladies and Gentlemen of Color: Gender, Sport, and the Ideal of African American Manhood and Womanhood During the Late Nineteenth and Early Twentieth Centuries," *Journal of Sport History* 18, no. 1 (Spring 1991): 81–82.
2. Michael R. Heintze, *Private Black Colleges in Texas, 1865–1954* (College Station: Texas A&M University Press, 1985), 16.
3. Ocania Chalk, *Black College Sports* (New York: Dodd, Mead and Company, 1976), 104.
4. Raymond Wolters, *The New Negro on Campus: Black College Rebellions of the 1920s* (Princeton: Princeton University Press, 1975), 3.
5. Olive D. Brown, "Mary Branch: Private College Educator," in *Black Leaders: Texans for their Times*, ed. Alwyn Barr and Robert A. Calvert (Austin: Texas State Historical Association, 1981), 113.
6. Heintze, *Private Black Colleges*, 17.
7. Graham Blackstone, *Staff Monograph: Higher Education for Negroes in Texas* (Austin: Staff of the Texas Legislative Council, 1950), 2.
8. Philip Harvey McClennon, *A Brief History of Paul Quinn* (Waco: Paul Quinn, 1965), 25.
9. Heintze, *Private Black Colleges*, 23.
10. Heintze, 25.
11. Heintze, 28.
12. Heintze, 34–38.
13. Heintze, 26–36.
14. Heintze, 39–40.
15. Heintze, 44.
16. George R. Woolfolk, *Prairie View: A Study in Public Conscience 1878–1946*

(New York: Pageant Press, 1962), 34.

17. George R. Woolfolk, "W. R. Banks: Public College Educator," in *Black Leaders: Texans for their Times*, ed. Alwyn Barr and Robert A. Calvert (Austin: Texas State Historical Association, 1981), 130.

18. Blackstone, *Staff Monograph: Higher Education for Negroes in Texas*, 3–4.

19. Arthur Ashe, *A Hard Road to Glory: A History of the African American Athlete, 1619–1918*, vol. 1 (New York: Amistad, 1988), 90.

20. Ronald A. Smith, *Sport and Freedom: The Rise of Big-Time College Athletics* (Oxford: Oxford University Press, 1988), 83.

21. Steven Riess, "Sport and the Redefinition of Middle Class Masculinity in Victorian America," North American Society for Sport History, Proceedings and Newsletter (1990), 41.

22. Andrew Doyle, "Foolish and Useless Sport: The Southern Evangelical Crusade against Intercollegiate Football," *Journal of Sport History* 24, no. 3 (Fall 1997): 317, 322.

23. Patrick B. Miller, "The Manly, the Moral, and the Proficient: College Sport in the New South," *Journal of Sport History* 24, no. 3 (Fall 1997): 287; Andrew Doyle, "George Denny, Intercollegiate Football, and the Institutional Modernization of the University of Alabama, 1912–1934," North American Society for Sport History, Proceedings and Newsletter (2002): 26–28.

24. Captain, "Enter Ladies and Gentlemen," 83–84.

25. Andrew Doyle, "College Football and the Culture of Segregation in the American South, 1890–1930," North American Society for Sport History, Proceedings and Newsletter (2001), 46.

26. Chalk, *Black College Sports*, 140.

27. Ashe, *A Hard Road to Glory*, 91.

28. Ashe, 92.

29. Ashe, 91.

30. Ashe, 92.

31. John Sayle Watterson, *College Football* (Baltimore: The Johns Hopkins University Press, 2000), 1.

32. Ashe, *A Hard Road to Glory*, 94.

33. Captain, "Enter Ladies and Gentlemen," 81, 91.

34. Captain, 81, 91.

35. Chalk, *Black College Sports*, 197.

36. Ashe, *A Hard Road to Glory*, 94.

37. Ashe, 94.

38. Chalk, *Black College Sports*, 198.

39. Ashe, *A Hard Road to Glory*, 94.

40. Chalk, *Black College Sports*, 199.

41. J. W. Williams, *Sizzling Southwest Football: For Sixty Years* (n.p.: J. W. Williams, 1956), 49.

42. Roger B. Saylor, "Black College Football," *College Football Historical Society Newsletter* (May 2000), 4–74.

43. Ashe, *A Hard Road to Glory*, 96.

44. Watterson, *College Football*, 17.

45. Smith, *Sport and Freedom*, 95–96.

46. Smith, 95–96.

47. Chalk, *Black College Sports*, 203.

48. Chalk, 203.

49. Ashe, *A Hard Road to Glory*, 92.

50. Chalk, *Black College Sports*, 203.

51. Chalk, 204.

52. Barr, *Black Texans*, 160.

53. Ashe, *A Hard Road to Glory*, 97.

54. Ashe, 97.

55. Williams, *Sizzling Southwest Football*, 49.

56. Ashe, *A Hard Road to Glory*, 97.

57. Chalk, *Black College Sports*, 207.

58. Benjamin G. Rader, *American Sports: From the Age of Folk Games to the Age of Televised Sports* (Upper Saddle River: Prentice Hall, 1999), 181–82.

59. Barr, *Black Texans*, 144.

60. Ashe, *A Hard Road to Glory*, 97.

61. Darleene Clark Hine, William C. Hine, and Stanley Harrold, *The African-American Odyssey* (Upper Saddle River, NJ: Prentice Hall, 2000), 373.

62. Heintze, *Private Black Colleges*, 169.

63. Woolfolk, *Prairie View*, 139–40.

64. Heintze, *Private Black Colleges*, 155–57.

65. Woolfolk, *Prairie View*, 139–40.

66. Woolfolk, 142.

67. Heintze, *Private Black Colleges*, 171.

68. Heintze, 171.

69. Woolfork, *Prairie View*, 143.

70. Woolfork, 143–44.

71. Saylor, "Black College Football," 4.

72. Chalk, *Black College Sports*, 222.

73. Arthur Ashe, *A Hard Road to Glory: A History of the African American Athlete, 1919–1945*, vol. 2 (New York: Amistad, 1988), 99.

74. David Williams, "A History of Higher Education for African American Texans, 1872–1977," in *Bricks without Straw: A Comprehensive History of African Americans in Texas*, ed. David Williams (Austin: Eakins Press, 1997), 229.

75. Harold V. Ratliff, *The Power and the Glory: The Story of Southwest Conference Football* (Lubbock: Texas Tech University Press, 1957), 1–2.

76. Ashe, *A Hard Road to Glory*, 100.

77. Ashe, 100.

78. Ashe, 100–101.

79. John Carroll, "Fritz Pollard," *College Football Historical Society Newsletter* 5, no. 1 (November 1991): 1.

80. John Carroll, *Fritz Pollard: Pioneer in Racial Advancement* (Urbana: University of Illinois Press, 1992), 88.

81. Carroll, "Fritz Pollard," 2.

82. David M. Kennedy, *Over Here: The First World War and American Society* (Oxford: Oxford University Press, 1980), 280.

83. Kennedy, *Over Here*, 158–62.

84. Barr, *Black Texans*, 114.

85. Barr, 114.

86. Chalk, *Black College Sports*, 225–26.

87. Barr, *Black Texans*, 115.

88. Barr, 144.

Chapter 2

1. Watterson, *College Football*, 143.

2. Watterson, 143.

3. Hine, Hine, and Harrold, *African-American Odyssey*, 395.

4. Patrick B. Miller, "The Anatomy of Scientific Racism: Racialist Responses to Black Athlete Achievement," *Journal of Sports History* 25, no. 1 (Spring 1998): 121.

5. Hine, Hine, and Harrold, *African-American Odyssey*, 397.

6. Hine, Hine, and Harrold, 399.

7. Ray Schmidt, "Changing Tides: College Football, 1919–1930, Part 3 of 3," *College Football Historical Society Newsletter* (November 2000): 18.

8. Ashe, *A Hard Road to Glory*, 100.

9. Alain Locke, ed., *The New Negro: Voices of the Harlem Renaissance* (New York: Atheneum, 1992), xxvii.

10. Albert C. Barnes, "Negro Art and America," in *The New Negro: Voices of the Harlem Renaissance*, 19.

11. J. A. Rogers, "Jazz at Home," in *The New Negro: Voices of the Harlem Renaissance*, 217.

12. James Sorelle, "The Emergence of Black Business in Houston, Texas: A Study of Race and Ideology, 1919–1945," in *Black Dixie: Afro-Texan History and Culture in Houston* (College Station: Texas A&M University Press, 1992), 103–4.

13. Sorelle, "The Emergence of Black Business," 104.

14. Rob Ruck, *Sandlot Seasons: Sport in Black Pittsburgh* (Urbana: University of Illinois Press, 1993), 3.

15. Gary Ross Mormino, "The Playing Fields of St. Louis: Italian Immigrants and Sports, 1925–1941," *Journal of Sport History* 9, no. 2 (Summer 1982): 5.

16. Susan G. Zieff, "From Badminton to the Bolero: Sport and Recreation in San Francisco's Chinatown, 1895–1950," *Journal of Sport History* 27, no. 1 (Spring 2000): 3, 5.

17. Raymond Schmidt, "Lords of the Prairie: Haskell Indian School Football, 1919–1930," *Journal of Sport History* 28, no. 3 (Fall 2001): 405.

18. Hurd, *Black College Football*, 146.

19. *Dallas Express*, 22 October 1921.

20. Vernon McDaniel, *History of the Teachers State Association of Texas* (Washington, DC: National Education Association, 1977), 21.

21. McDaniel, *History of the Teachers State Association of Texas*, 21.

22. *NCAA Football Records* (Indianapolis: The National Collegiate Athletic Association, 2001), 157.

23. Michael Oriard, *Reading Football: How the Popular Press Created an American Spectacle* (Chapel Hill: University of North Carolina Press, 2003), 59–61; Gerald R. Gems, "Blocked Shot: The Development of Basketball in the African-American Community in Chicago," *Journal of Sport History* 22, no. 2 (Summer 1995): 139.

24. *Dallas Express*, 22 October 1921.

25. *Houston Informer*, 28 October 1922.

26. *Houston Informer*, 28 October 1922.

27. *Houston Informer*, 28 October 1922.

28. *Houston Informer*, 11 November 1922.

29. *Dallas Express*, 11 November 1922.

30. *Dallas Express*, 11 November 1922.

31. *Houston Informer*, 11 November 1922.

32. *Houston Informer*, 23 December 1922.

33. *Houston Informer*, 6 January 1923.

34. *Houston Informer*, 6 January 1923.

35. *Houston Informer*, 8 September 1923.

36. *Houston Informer*, 20 October 1923.

37. *Houston Informer*, 10 November 1923.

38. *Dallas Express*, 11 October 1923.

39. *Houston Informer*, 17 November 1923.

40. *Houston Informer*, 1 December 1923.

41. *Houston Informer*, 1 December 1923.

42. *Houston Informer*, 1 December 1923.

43. *Houston Informer*, 1 December 1923.

44. *Houston Informer*, 8 December 1923.

45. *Houston Informer*, 15 December 1923, 5 January 1924.

46. *Houston Informer*, 30 May 1925.

47. Gerald R. Gems, "The Construction, Negotiation, and Transformation of Racial Identity in American Football," North American Society for Sport History, Proceedings and Newsletter (1998), 79.

48. *NCAA Football Records*, 157.

49. *Houston Informer*, 17 October 1925.

50. *Dallas Express*, 24 October 1925.

51. *Dallas Express*, 24 October 1925.

52. Robert Prince, *A History of Dallas from a Different Perspective* (n.p.: Nortex Press, 1993), 70.

53. *Houston Informer*, 24 October 1925.
54. *Dallas Express*, 31 October 1925.
55. *Houston Informer*, 7 November 1925.
56. *Houston Informer*, 7 November 1925.
57. *Houston Informer*, 5 December 1925.
58. *Houston Informer*, 5 December 1925.
59. *Houston Informer*, 12 December 1925.
60. *Houston Informer*, 19 December 1925.
61. *Houston Informer*, 25 September 1926.
62. *Houston Informer*, 2 October 1926.
63. *Houston Informer*, 2 October 1926.
64. *Dallas Express*, 23 October 1926.
65. *Houston Informer*, 9 October 1926.
66. *Houston Informer*, 16 October 1926.
67. *Dallas Express*, 23 October 1926.
68. *Houston Informer*, 6 November 1926.
69. *Houston Informer*, 13 November 1926.
70. *Houston Informer*, 13 November 1926.
71. *Houston Informer*, 13 November 1926.
72. *Dallas Express*, 13 November 1926.
73. *Dallas Express*, 20 November 1926.
74. *Houston Informer*, 27 November 1926.
75. *Houston Informer*, 27 November 1926.
76. *Houston Informer*, 4 December 1926.
77. *Houston Informer*, 15 January 1927.
78. *Houston Informer*, 15 January 1927.
79. *Houston Informer*, 15 January 1927.
80. *Houston Informer*, 10 September 1927.
81. *Dallas Express*, 10 September 1927.
82. *Houston Informer*, 10 September 1927.
83. *Dallas Express*, 24 September 1927.
84. John Carroll, "Red Storms East," *College Football Historical Society Newsletter* (February 1999): 7.
85. *Houston Informer*, 17 September 1927.
86. *Houston Informer*, 17 September 1927.
87. *Houston Informer*, 17 September 1927.
88. *Dallas Express*, 8 October 1927.
89. *Houston Informer*, 17 September 1927.
90. Hurd, *Black College Football*, 27.
91. *Houston Informer*, 8 October 1927.
92. *Houston Informer*, 8 October 1927.
93. *Houston Informer*, 8 October 1927.
94. *Dallas Express*, 22 October 1927.
95. *Houston Informer*, 22 October 1927.

96. *Houston Informer*, 22 October 1927.

97. *Houston Informer*, 22 October 1927.

98. *Houston Informer*, 29 October 1927.

99. *Houston Informer*, 29 October 1927.

100. *Houston Informer*, 29 October 1927.

101. *Houston Informer*, 29 October 1927.

102. *Houston Informer*, 9 November 1927.

103. *Houston Informer*, 12 November 1927.

104. *Houston Informer*, 12 November 1927.

105. *Houston Informer*, 12 November 1927.

106. *Houston Informer*, 12 November 1927.

107. *Houston Informer*, 26 November 1927.

108. *Houston Informer*, 26 November 1927.

109. *Houston Informer*, 26 November 1927.

110. *Houston Informer*, 3 December 1927.

111. *Houston Informer*, 17 December 1927.

112. *Houston Informer*, 24 December 1927.

113. *Houston Informer*, 21 January 1928.

114. Beeth and Wintz, *Black Dixie*, 161.

115. James M. SoRelle, "Race Relations in 'Heavenly Houston' 1917–1945," in *Black Dixie: Essays in Afro-Texas History in Houston*, ed. Howard Beeth and Cary Wintz (College Station: Texas A&M University Press, 1992), 178.

116. *Houston Informer*, 6 October 1928.

117. *Houston Informer*, 6 October 1928.

118. *Dallas Express*, 22 September 1928.

119. *Dallas Express*, 6 October 1928.

120. *Dallas Express*, 13 October 1928.

121. *Dallas Express*, 20 October 1928.

122. *Houston Informer*, 20 October 1928.

123. *Dallas Express*, 20 October 1928.

124. *Houston Informer*, 20 October 1928.

125. *Houston Informer*, 20 October 1928.

126. *Houston Informer*, 27 October 1928.

127. *Houston Informer*, 27 October 1928.

128. *Houston Informer*, 10 November 1928.

129. *Dallas Express*, 24 November 1928.

130. *Dallas Express*, 28 December 1928.

131. *Houston Informer*, 8 December 1928.

132. *NCAA Football Records*, 157.

133. *Houston Informer*, 15 December 1928.

134. *Houston Informer*, 29 December 1928.

135. *Houston Informer*, 29 December 1928.

136. *Houston Informer*, 5 January 1929.

137. *Houston Informer*, 5 January 1929.

138. *Houston Informer*, 12 January 1929.

139. *Dallas Express*, 17 November 1928.

140. *Dallas Express*, 17 November 1928.

141. *Houston Informer*, 12 January 1929.

142. Gerald Gems, "The Prep Bowl: Football and Religious Acculturation in Chicago, 1927–1963," *Journal of Sports History* 23, no. 3 (Fall 1996), 284, 289.

143. *Houston Informer*, 5 October 1929.

144. *Houston Informer*, 12 October 1929

145. *Houston Informer*, 19 October 1929.

146. *Houston Informer*, 19 October 1929.

147. *Houston Informer*, 19 October 1929.

148. *Houston Informer*, 19 October 1929.

149. *Houston Informer*, 19 October 1929.

150. *Houston Informer*, 19 October 1929.

151. *Houston Informer*, 19 October 1929.

152. Robert Heard, *Oklahoma vs. Texas: When Football Becomes War, 1900–1980* (Austin: Honey Hill Publishing, 1980), 75, 115.

153. *Houston Informer*, 2 November 1929.

154. *Houston Informer*, 16 November 1929.

155. *Houston Informer*, 7 December 1929.

156. *Houston Informer*, 21 December 1929.

Chapter 3

1. Hine, Hine, and Harrold, *African-American Odyssey*, 420.

2. Watterson, *College Football*, 177.

3. Hine, Hine, and Harrold, *African-American Odyssey*, 420

4. Barr, *Black Texans*, 153.

5. Barr, 154.

6. Robin D. G. Kelly, "'We Are Not What We Seem': Rethinking Black Working-Class Opposition in the Jim Crow South," *Journal of American History* 80 (1 June 1993): 76.

7. Hine, Hine, and Harrold, *African-American Odyssey*, 446.

8. Thomas Hietala, *The Fight of The Century: Jack Johnson, Joe Louis, and the Struggle for Racial Equality* (Armonk: M. E. Sharpe, 2002), 6.

9. Samuel Regaldo, "Sport and Community in California's Japanese American 'Yamato Colony,' 1930–1945," *Journal of Sport History* 19, no. 2 (Summer 1992): 135.

10. *Houston Informer*, 20 September 1930.

11. Ashe, *A Hard Road to Glory*, 102.

12. Hurd, *Black College Football*, 146.

13. *Houston Informer*, 4 January 1930.

14. *Houston Informer*, 4 January 1930.

15. *Houston Informer*, 30 August 1930.

16. *Houston Informer*, 30 August 1930.

17. *Houston Informer*, 13 September 1930.

18. *Houston Informer*, 27 September 1930.

19. *Houston Informer*, 4 October 1930.

20. *Houston Informer*, 25 October 1930.

21. *Houston Informer*, 25 October 1930.

22. *Houston Informer*, 25 October 1930.

23. *Houston Informer*, 8 November 1930.

24. *Houston Informer*, 22 November 1930.

25. *Houston Informer*, 6 December 1930.

26. *Houston Informer*, 20 December 1930.

27. *Houston Informer*, 20 December 1930.

28. *Houston Informer*, 3 January 1930.

29. Watterson, *College Football*, 182.

30. *Houston Informer*, 8 August 1931.

31. *Houston Informer*, 22 August 1931.

32. *Houston Informer*, 10 October 1931.

33. *Houston Informer*, 10 October 1931.

34. *Houston Informer*, 10 October 1931.

35. *Houston Informer*, 17 October 1931.

36. *Houston Informer*, 17 October 1931.

37. *Houston Informer*, 24 October 1931.

38. *Houston Informer*, 24 October 1931.

39. *Houston Informer*, 7 November 1931.

40. *Houston Informer*, 7 November 1931.

41. *Houston Informer*, 5 December 1931.

42. *Houston Informer*, 12 December 1931.

43. *Houston Informer*, 2 January 1932.

44. *Houston Informer*, 9 January 1932.

45. *Houston Informer*, 24 September 1932.

46. *Houston Informer*, 24 September 1932.

47. *Houston Informer*, 8 October 1932.

48. *Houston Informer*, 15 October 1932.

49. *Houston Informer*, 15 October 1932.

50. *Houston Informer*, 15 October 1932.

51. *Houston Informer*, 15 October 1932.

52. *Houston Informer*, 15 October 1932.

53. *Houston Informer*, 22 October 1932.

54. *Houston Informer*, 29 October 1932.

55. *Houston Informer*, 5 November 1932.

56. *Houston Informer*, 19 November 1932.

57. *Houston Informer*, 19 November 1932.

58. *Houston Informer*, 19 November 1932.

59. *Houston Informer*, 7 January 1933.

60. *Houston Informer*, 14 January 1933.

61. *NCAA Football Records*, 154.

62. John Hope Franklin, *From Slavery to Freedom: A History of Negro Americans*, 3rd ed. (New York: Vintage Books, 1967), 527, 530–33.

63. Hine, Hine, and Harrold, *African-American Odyssey*, 427.

64. *Houston Informer*, 26 November 1932.

65. *Houston Informer*, 9 September 1933.

66. *Houston Informer*, 16 September 1933.

67. Sara Caroline Moseley Junkin, "The Independent Negro College in Texas: Change and Challenge," MA thesis, University of Texas, 1969, 21.

68. *Houston Informer*, 30 September 1933.

69. Joy Flasch, *Melvin B. Tolson* (New York: Twayne Publishers, 1972), 25.

70. *Houston Informer*, 7 October 1933.

71. Joel Franks, "Crossing Sidelines, Crossing Borders: Basketball in the San Francisco Bay Area, 1930–1950," North American Society for Sport History, Proceedings and Newsletter (1997), 50

72. *Houston Informer*, 14 October 1933.

73. *Houston Informer*, 21 October 1933.

74. *Houston Informer*, 4 November 1933.

75. *Houston Informer*, 11 November 1933.

76. Christie L. Bourgeois, "Stepping Over Lines: Lyndon Johnson, Black Texans, and the National Youth Administration, 1935–1937," *Southwestern Historical Quarterly* 91, no. 2, (October 1987): 153–54.

77. *Houston Informer*, 18 November 1933.

78. *Houston Informer*, 9 December 1933.

79. *Houston Informer*, 16 December 1933.

80. *Houston Informer*, 6 January 1934.

81. *Houston Informer*, 30 December 1933.

82. *Houston Informer*, 27 January 1934.

83. Heintze, *Private Black Colleges*, 65.

84. Barr, *Black Texans*, 162.

85. *Houston Informer*, 13 October 1934.

86. *Houston Informer*, 13 October 1934.

87. *Houston Informer*, 13 October 1934.

88. Patrick B. Miller, "Slouching Toward a New Expediency: College Football and the Color Line During the 1930s," North American Society for Sport History, Proceedings and Newsletter (1996), 93.

89. Thomas G. Smith, "Outside the Pale: The Exclusion of Blacks from the National Football League, 1934–1946," *Journal of Sport History* 15, no. 3 (Winter 1988): 255.

90. *Dallas Express*, 13 October 1934.

91. *Dallas Express*, 13 October 1934.

92. *Dallas Express*, 20 October 1934.

93. *Houston Informer*, 27 October 1934.

94. *Houston Informer*, 3 November 1934.

95. John R. "Pete" Hendrick, "Mary Allen Junior College," *The New Handbook of Texas*, vol. 4 (Austin: The Texas State historical Association, 1996), 540.

96. *Houston Informer*, 17 November 1934.

97. *Houston Informer*, 15 December 1934.

98. *Houston Informer*, 10 August 1935.

99. *Houston Informer*, 24 August 1935.

100. *Dallas Express*, 7 September 1935.

101. *Houston Informer*, 5 October 1935.

102. *Houston Informer*, 5 October 1935.

103. *Houston Informer*, 12 October 1935.

104. *Dallas Express*, 26 October 1935.

105. *Dallas Express*, 26 October 1935.

106. *Dallas Express*, 23 November 1935.

107. *Houston Informer*, 7 December 1935.

108. *Houston Informer*, 28 December 1935.

109. *Houston Informer*, 4 January 1936.

110. *Houston Informer*, 29 August 1936.

111. Barr, *Black Texans*, 171–72.

112. *Dallas Express*, 12 September 1936.

113. *Houston Informer*, 3 October 1936.

114. *Houston Informer*, 24 October 1936.

115. *Dallas Express*, 24 October 1936.

116. *Houston Informer*, 24 October 1936.

117. *Houston Informer*, 31 October 1936.

118. *Houston Informer*, 10 October 1936.

119. *Houston Informer*, 7 November 1936.

120. *Dallas Express*, 7 November 1936.

121. *Houston Informer*, 21 November 1936.

122. *Dallas Express*, 5 December 1936.

123. *Houston Informer*, 5 December 1936.

124. *Houston Informer*, 5 December 1936.

125. *Houston Informer*, 12 December 1936.

126. *Dallas Express*, 9 January 1937.

127. David K. Wiggins, *Glory Bound: Black Athletes in White America* (Syracuse: Syracuse University Press, 1997), 62–63; Mark Dyreson, "American Ideals about Race and Olympic Races from the 1890s to the 1950s: Shattering Myths or Reinforcing Scientific Racism?" *Journal of Sport History* 28, no. 2 (Summer 2001): 173–74.

128. *Houston Informer*, 8 September 1937.

129. *Houston Informer*, 13 October 1937.

130. *Dallas Express*, 16 October 1937.

131. *Houston Informer*, 20 October 1937.

132. *Houston Informer*, 23 October 1937.

133. *Houston Informer*, 27 October 1937.

134. *Houston Informer*, 3 November 1937.
135. *Houston Informer*, 3 November 1937.
136. *Houston Informer*, 3 November 1937.
137. *Houston Informer*, 1 December 1937.
138. *Houston Informer*, 1 December 1937.
139. *Houston Informer*, 22 December 1937.
140. *Dallas Express*, 8 October 1938.
141. *Houston Informer*, 15 October 1938.
142. *Dallas Express*, 22 October 1938.
143. *Houston Informer*, 22 October 1938.
144. *Houston Informer*, 5 November 1938.
145. *Dallas Express*, 5 November 1938.
146. *Houston Informer*, 12 November 1938.
147. *Houston Informer*, 7 January 1939.
148. Watterson, *College Football*, 182.
149. *Houston Informer*, 2 September 1939.
150. *Houston Informer*, 23 September 1939.
151. *Houston Informer*, 12 August 1939.
152. *Houston Informer*, 26 August 1939.
153. *Houston Informer*, 30 September 1939.
154. *Dallas Express*, 7 October 1939.
155. *Dallas Express*, 21 October 1939.
156. *Dallas Express*, 21 October 1939.
157. *Dallas Express*, 18 November 1939.
158. *Dallas Express*, 2 December 1939.
159. *Dallas Express*, 9 December 1939.
160. *Dallas Express*, 6 January 1940.
161. Hurd, *Black College Football*, 166.

Chapter 4

1. *Houston Informer*, 7 September 1940.
2. *Houston Informer*, 7 September 1940.
3. *Houston Informer*, 7 September 1940.
4. *Houston Informer*, 16 September 1939.
5. *Houston Informer*, 16 September 1939.
6. Walter Day, *Remembering the Past with Pride: State Championship Football for Blacks in Texas, 1940–1969* (Fort Worth: Walter Day, 1994), 11.
7. *Dallas Express*, 6 January 1940.
8. *Dallas Express*, 6 January 1940.
9. Donald Spivey, "'End Jim Crow in Sports': The Protest at New York University, 1940–1941," *Journal of Sport History* 15, no. 3 (Winter 1998), 285–86, 298.
10. *Houston Informer*, 28 September 1940.
11. *Houston Informer*, 5 October 1940.

12. *Houston Informer*, 12 October 1940.
13. *Houston Informer*, 10 October 1940.
14. *Houston Informer*, 10 October 1940.
15. *Houston Informer*, 10 October 1940.
16. *Houston Informer*, 10 October 1940.
17. *Houston Informer*, 5 October 1940.
18. *Houston Informer*, 19 October 1940.
19. *Houston Informer*, 26 October 1940.
20. *Houston Informer*, 2 November 1940.
21. *Houston Informer*, 23 November 1940.
22. *Houston Informer*, 30 November 1940.
23. *Houston Informer*, 30 November 1940.
24. *Houston Informer*, 7 December 1940.
25. *Houston Informer*, 13 September 1941.
26. *Houston Informer*, 27 September 1941.
27. *Dallas Express*, 4 October 1941.
28. *Dallas Express*, 4 October 1941.
29. *Houston Informer*, 11 October 1941.
30. *Dallas Express*, 18 October 1941.
31. *Houston Informer*, 18 October 1941.
32. *Houston Informer*, 18 October 1941.
33. *Houston Informer*, 25 October 1941.
34. *Dallas Express*, 1 November 1941.
35. *Houston Informer*, 1 November 1941.
36. *Houston Informer*, 8 November 1941.
37. *Houston Informer*, 22 November 1941.
38. *Houston Informer*, 29 November 1941.
39. *Dallas Express*, 6 December 1941.
40. Watterson, *College Football*, 201.
41. *Houston Informer*, 13 December 1941.
42. *Dallas Express*, 13 December 1941.
43. *Houston Informer*, 20 December 1941.
44. *Dallas Express*, 10 January 1942.
45. Hurd, Black College Football, 147.
46. Watterson, *College Football*, 201.
47. Kern Tips, *Football, Texas Style: An Illustrated History of the Southwest Conference* (Garden City: Doubleday, 1964), 102.
48. Hine, Hine, and Harrold, *The African-American Odyssey*, 476.
49. Ashe, *A Hard Road to Glory*, 98.
50. *Houston Informer*, 29 August 1942.
51. *Dallas Express*, 12 September 1942.
52. Ashe, *A Hard Road to Glory*, 105.
53. *Houston Informer*, 19 September 1942.
54. *Houston Informer*, 26 September 1942.

55. *Dallas Express*, 26 September 1942.

56. Chalk, *Black College Sports*, 279.

57. *Houston Informer*, 26 September 1942.

58. *Houston Informer*, 10 October 1942.

59. *Houston Informer*, 17 October 1942.

60. Prairie View A&M University, *The Panther*, 1943.

61. *Dallas Express*, 24 October 1942.

62. *Dallas Express*, 7 November 1942.

63. *Houston Informer*, 7 November 1942.

64. *Houston Informer*, 7 November 1942.

65. *Houston Informer*, 19 December 1942.

66. *Houston Informer*, 9 January 1943.

67. *Houston Informer*, 9 January 1943.

68. Barr, *Black Texans*, 213.

69. *Houston Informer*, 2 October 1943.

70. *Houston Informer*, 9 October 1943.

71. *Houston Informer*, 23 October 1943.

72. *Houston Informer*, 20 November 1943.

73. *Houston Informer*, 16 October 1943.

74. Hurd, *Black College Football*, 147

75. *Dallas Express*, 8 January 1944.

76. *Houston Informer*, 14 October 1944.

77. *Houston Informer*, 14 October 1944.

78. *Houston Informer*, 21 October 1944.

79. *Dallas Express*, 14 October 1944.

80. *Houston Informer*, 28 October 1944.

81. *Houston Informer*, 18 November 1944.

82. *Houston Informer*, 16 December 1944.

83. *Dallas Express*, 6 January 1945.

84. *Houston Informer*, 27 January 1945.

85. Watterson, *College Football*, 202–3.

86. Heintze, *Private Black Colleges*, 77.

87. Prairie View A&M University, *The Purple and Gold*, 1946.

88. Prairie View A&M University, *The Panther*, 1949.

89. Williams, "A History of Higher Education," 231–32.

90. Charles Estus, interview by the author, 24 July 2003.

91. Williams, "A History of Higher Education," 235.

92. *Houston Informer*, 29 September 1945.

93. *Houston Informer*, 13 October 1945.

94. *Houston Informer*, 20 October 1945.

95. *Dallas Express*, 20 October 1945.

96. *Houston Informer*, 27 October 1945.

97. *Houston Informer*, 3 November 1945.

98. *Houston Informer*, 10 November 1945.

99. *Dallas Express*, 17 November 1945.

100. *Houston Informer*, 24 November 1945.

101. *Houston Informer*, 8 December 1945.

102. *Dallas Express*, 15 December 1945.

103. *Houston Informer*, 5 January 1946.

104. Jules Tygel, *Baseball's Great Experiment: Jackie Robinson and His Legacy* (New York: Vintage Books, 1983), 178.

105. Graham Blackstone, *Staff Monograph: Higher Education for Negroes in Texas*, by the Staff of the Texas Legislative Council, Austin, Texas, November 1950, 33.

106. *Houston Informer*, 24 August 1946.

107. *Houston Informer*, 31 August 1946.

108. *Houston Informer*, 7 September 1946.

109. *Dallas Express*, 12 October 1946.

110. *Houston Informer*, 19 October 1946.

111. *Dallas Express*, 12 October 1946.

112. *Dallas Express*, 12 October 1946.

113. Watterson, *College Football*, 205.

114. *Houston Informer*, 2 November 1946.

115. *Houston Informer*, 2 November 1946.

116. *Dallas Express*, 9 November 1946.

117. *Dallas Express*, 16 November 1946.

118. *Houston Informer*, 28 December 1946.

119. *Houston Informer*, 11 January 1947.

120. Ira M. Bryant, *Texas Southern University: Its Antecedents, Political Origin and Future* (Houston: Ira Bryant, 1975), 35.

121. Bryant, *Texas Southern University*, 35–36.

122. Bryant, 41.

123. *Houston Informer*, 6 September 1947.

124. *Houston Informer*, 6 September 1947.

125. *Houston Informer*, 20 September 1947.

126. *Houston Informer*, 20 September 1947.

127. Arthur Ashe, *A Hard Road to Glory: Since 1946*, vol. 3 (New York: Amistad, 1988), 103.

128. *Houston Informer*, 27 September 1947.

129. *Houston Informer*, 27 September 1947.

130. *Houston Informer*, 4 October 1947.

131. *Houston Informer*, 18 October 1947.

132. *Dallas Express*, 11 October 1947.

133. *Dallas Express*, 18 October 1947.

134. Earvin Garnett, interview by the author, 4 May 2018.

135. *Dallas Express*, 25 October 1947.

136. Texas Southern University, *The Tiger*, 1948.

137. *Houston Informer*, 8 November 1947.

138. *Dallas Express*, 8 November 1947.

139. *Houston Informer*, 29 November 1947.

140. *Dallas Express*, 6 December 1947.

141. *Houston Informer*, 29 November 1947.

142. Earvin Garnett, interview by the author, 4 May 2018; Prairie View A&M University, *The Panther*, 1949.

143. Charles H. Martin, *Benching Jim Crow: The Rise and Fall of the Color Line in Southern College Sports, 1890–1980* (Urbana: University of Illinois Press, 2010), 63–64.

144. *Dallas Express*, 9 October 1948.

145. *Houston Informer*, 16 October 1948.

146. *Dallas Express*, 23 October 1948.

147. *Houston Informer*, 30 October 1948.

148. *Dallas Express*, 6 November 1948.

149. *Houston Informer*, 13 November 1948.

150. *Houston Informer*, 13 November 1948.

151. *Dallas Express*, 13 November 1948.

152. *Houston Informer*, 4 December 1948.

153. *Houston Informer*, 11 December 1948.

154. *Houston Informer*, 1 January 1949.

155. Charles H. Martin, "Integrating New Year's Day: The Racial Politics of College Bowl Games in the American South," *Journal of Sport History* 24, no. 3 (Fall 1997): 358–59.

156. Ashe, *A Hard Road to Glory*, 104.

157. *Houston Informer*, 20 August 1949.

158. *Houston Informer*, 24 September 1949.

159. Texas Southern University, *The Tiger*, 1949.

160. *Dallas Express*, 1 October 1949.

161. *Houston Informer*, 8 October 1949.

162. *Dallas Express*, 8 October 1949.

163. *Dallas Express*, 15 October 1949.

164. *Dallas Express*, 22 October 1949.

165. *Dallas Express*, 5 November 1949.

166. *Houston Informer*, 26 November 1949.

167. *Dallas Express*, 26 November 1949.

168. *Dallas Express*, 10 December 1949.

169. Hurd, *Black College Football*, 112.

170. *Houston Informer*, 27 August 1949.

171. Barr, *Black Texans*, 215.

Chapter 5

1. Blackstone, *Staff Monograph*, 17.

2. Blackstone, 73.

3. Blackstone, 77.

4. *Houston Informer*, 30 September 1950.

5. Bryant, *Texas Southern University*, 97.

6. Barr, *Black Texans*, 185.

7. Barr, 185.

8. *Houston Informer*, 12 August 1950.

9. *Houston Informer*, 16 September 1950.

10. *Houston Informer*, 16 September 1950.

11. *Dallas Express*, 30 September 1950.

12. *Dallas Express*, 7 October 1950.

13. *Dallas Express*, 21 October 1950.

14. *Houston Informer*, 28 October 1950.

15. *Houston Informer*, 28 October 1950.

16. *Dallas Express*, 21 October 1950.

17. *Dallas Express*, 28 October 1950.

18. *Houston Informer*, 28 October 1950.

19. *Houston Informer*, 28 October 1950.

20. Willie Dunn, interview by the author, 24 July 2003.

21. *Houston Informer*, 25 November 1950.

22. *Dallas Express*, 2 December 1950.

23. *Houston Informer*, 30 December 1950.

24. *Dallas Express*, 6 January 1951.

25. Bryant, *Texas Southern University*, 86.

26. Bryant, 87.

27. *Houston Informer*, 1 September 1951.

28. *Houston Informer*, 22 September 1951.

29. *Dallas Express*, 22 September 1951.

30. *Houston Informer*, 13 October 1951.

31. Julius Becton Jr., interview by the author, 24 July 2003.

32. *Dallas Express*, 29 September 1951.

33. *Houston Informer*, 13 October 1951.

34. *Dallas Express*, 20 October 1951.

35. *Dallas Express*, 27 October 1951.

36. *Dallas Express*, 27 October 1951.

37. *Houston Informer*, 27 October 1951.

38. Texas Southern University, *The Tiger*, 1952.

39. *Dallas Express*, 1 December 1951.

40. *Houston Informer*, 1 December 1951.

41. *Houston Informer*, 1 December 1951.

42. *Houston Informer*, 1 December 1951.

43. Prairie View A&M University, *The Panther*, 1952.

44. *Houston Informer*, 29 December 1951.

45. *Houston Informer*, 29 December 1951.

46. Prairie View A&M University, *The Panther*, 1952.

47. *Houston Informer*, 5 January 1952.

48. *Houston Informer*, 5 January 1952.
49. James William Kitchen, "A Master Site Plan for Prairie View Agricultural and Mechanical College of Texas," MS thesis, Texas Tech University, 1952, 5.
50. Becton, interview, 24 July 2003.
51. Peter Golenbeck, *Cowboys Have Always Been My Heroes: The Definitive Oral History of America's Team* (New York: Warner Books, 1997), 15.
52. Golenbeck, *Cowboys Have Always Been My Heroes*, 17–18.
53. Barr, *Black Texans*, 226.
54. *Houston Informer*, 20 September 1952.
55. *Dallas Express*, 20 September 1952.
56. Becton, interview, 24 July 2003.
57. Becton, interview, 24 July 2003.
58. Heintze, *Private Black Colleges* in Texas, 149.
59. Heintze, 149.
60. *Houston Informer*, 27 September 1952.
61. *Houston Informer*, 27 September 1952.
62. *Dallas Express*, 4 October 1952.
63. *Houston Informer*, 11 October 1952.
64. *Dallas Express*, 11 October 1952.
65. *Houston Informer*, 11 October 1952.
66. *Dallas Express*, 11 October 1952.
67. *Houston Informer*, 11 October 1952.
68. *Houston Informer*, 18 October 1952.
69. *Dallas Express*, 18 October 1952.
70. *Houston Informer*, 18 October 1952.
71. Texas Southern University, *The Tiger*, 1953.
72. *Dallas Express*, 25 October 1952.
73. *Houston Informer*, 25 October 1952.
74. *Houston Informer*, 25 October 1952.
75. *Houston Informer*, 1 November 1952.
76. *Dallas Express*, 28 December 1952.
77. Texas Southern University, *The Tiger*, 1953.
78. Texas Southern University, *The Tiger*, 1953.
79. *Houston Informer*, 10 January 1953.
80. *Houston Informer*, 10 January 1953.
81. *Houston Informer*, 5 September 1953.
82. Barr, *Black Texans*, 215–16.
83. *Dallas Express*, 19 September 1953.
84. *Dallas Express*, 3 October 1953.
85. *Houston Informer*, 17 October 1953.
86. *Houston Informer*, 17 October 1953.
87. *Houston Informer*, 24 October 1953.
88. *Dallas Express*, 24 October 1953.
89. *Houston Informer*, 24 October 1953.

90. Becton, interview by the author, 24 July 2003.

91. *Houston Informer*, 31 October 1953.

92. Texas Southern University, *The Tiger*, 1954.

93. *Dallas Express*, 14 November 1953.

94. *Houston Informer*, 28 November 1953.

95. *Dallas Express*, 5 December 1953.

96. *Dallas Express*, 12 December 1953.

97. *Houston Informer*, 19 December 1953.

98. *Houston Informer*, 9 January 1954.

99. *Houston Informer*, 9 January 1954.

100. Hine, Hine, and Harrold, *African-American Odyssey*, 492–93.

101. *Houston Informer*, 11 September 1954.

102. *Houston Informer*, 18 September 1954.

103. *Houston Informer*, 25 September 1954.

104. *Houston Informer*, 2 October 1954.

105. *Houston Informer*, 9 October 1954.

106. *Houston Informer*, 9 October 1954.

107. *Houston Informer*, 16 October 1954.

108. *Houston Informer*, 23 October 1954.

109. *Dallas Express*, 3 November 1954.

110. *Houston Informer*, 13 November 1954.

111. *Dallas Express*, 4 December 1954.

112. Hurd, *Black College Football*, 164.

113. *Houston Informer*, 1 January 1955.

114. *Dallas Express*, 8 January 1955.

115. "Charlie 'Choo Choo' Brackins," Black College Football Hall of Fame, http://www.blackcollegefootballhof.org/inductees/charles-choo-choo-brackin, retrieved 9 May 2018.

116. *Dallas Express*, 20 August 1955.

117. George Forkerway, interview by the author, 29 August 1999.

118. Tommy Williams, interview by the author, 24 July 2003.

119. Barr, *Black Texans*, 216.

120. *Dallas Express*, 15 October 1955.

121. *Houston Informer*, 22 October 1955.

122. *Houston Informer*, 22 October 1955.

123. *Houston Informer*, 22 October 1955.

124. *Dallas Express*, 12 November 1955.

125. Tommy Wyatt, interview by the author, 8 May 2018.

126. *Dallas Express*, 12 November 1955.

127. *Houston Informer*, 26 November 1955.

128. *Dallas Express*, 3 December 1955.

129. *Houston Informer*, 31 December 1955.

130. *Dallas Express*, 7 January 1956.

131. Martin, *Benching Jim Crow*, 80–81.

132. Martin, 80–81.

133. Ronald Marcello, "The Integration of Intercollegiate Athletics in Texas: North Texas State College as a Test Case, 1956," *Journal of Sport History* 14, no. 3 (Winter 1987): 287, 315.

134. *Dallas Express*, 29 September 1956.

135. *Dallas Express*, 29 September 1956.

136. *Houston Informer*, 6 October 1956.

137. *Dallas Express*, 13 October 1956.

138. *Dallas Express*, 13 October 1956.

139. *Houston Informer*, 20 October 1956.

140. *Dallas Express*, 27 October 1956.

141. *Dallas Express*, 3 November 1956.

142. *Dallas Express*, 10 November 1956.

143. *Houston Informer*, 10 November 1956.

144. *Houston Informer*, 10 November 1956.

145. *Dallas Express*, 17 November 1956.

146. *Houston Informer*, 29 December 1956.

147. *Houston Informer*, 5 January 1957.

148. Will Grimsley. *Football: The Greatest Moments in the Southwest Conference* (Boston: Little, Brown and Company, 1968), 95.

149. *Houston Informer*, 5 January 1957.

150. *Dallas Express*, 5 January 1957.

151. *Dallas Express*, 5 January 1957.

152. Pennington, *Breaking the Ice*, 9.

153. Pennington, 11.

154. *Dallas Express*, 5 January 1957.

155. Branch, *Parting the Waters*, 220–22.

156. *Houston Informer*, 24 August 1957.

157. *Houston Informer*, 5 October 1957.

158. *Dallas Express*, 5 October 1957.

159. *Dallas Express*, 14 September 1957.

160. *Dallas Express*, 12 October 1957.

161. *Houston Informer*, 26 October 1957.

162. *Dallas Express*, 19 October 1957.

163. *Houston Informer*, 26 October 1957.

164. *Houston Informer*, 9 November 1957.

165. *Dallas Express*, 7 December 1957.

166. *Dallas Express*, 14 December 1957.

167. *Dallas Express*, 7 December 1957.

168. *Houston Informer*, 4 January 1958.

169. Hurd, Black College Football, 147.

170. *Houston Informer*, 20 September 1958.

171. *Houston Informer*, 30 August 1958.

172. *Dallas Express*, 4 October 1958.

173. Tommy Wyatt, interview by the author, 8 May 2018.

174. Wyatt, interview, 8 May 2018.

175. *Dallas Express*, 4 October 1958.

176. *Houston Informer*, 18 October 1958.

177. Prairie View A&M, *The Panther*, 1959.

178. *Dallas Express*, 18 November 1958.

179. *Houston Informer*, 1 November 1958.

180. *Dallas Express*, 1 November 1958.

181. *Houston Informer*, 8 November 1958.

182. *Dallas Express*, 29 November 1958.

183. Prairie View A&M, *The Panther*, 1959.

184. *Houston Informer*, 20 December 1958.

185. *Dallas Express*, 10 January 1959.

186. *Houston Informer*, 27 December 1958.

187. Martin, *Benching Jim Crow*, 77.

188. *Houston Informer*, 5 September 1959.

189. *Houston Informer*, 5 September 1959.

190. *Houston Informer*, 10 October 1959.

191. *Houston Informer*, 17 October 1959.

192. *Dallas Express*, 17 October 1959.

193. *Houston Informer*, 24 October 1959.

194. *Houston Informer*, 31 October 1959.

195. *Houston Informer*, 14 November 1959.

196. *Dallas Express*, 14 November 1959.

197. *Houston Informer*, 28 November 1959.

198. *Houston Informer*, 12 December 1959.

199. *Houston Informer*, 26 December 1959.

Chapter 6

1. John Pirkle, *Oiler Blues: The Story of Pro Football's Most Frustrating Team* (Houston: Sports Line Publishing, 2000), 12.

2. Pirkle, *Oiler Blues*, 27.

3. "At North Texas, Famine No Threat with Odus Around," *Texas Football* (1960): 63.

4. Carlton Stowers, *Dallas Cowboys: The First Twenty-Five Years* (Dallas: Taylor Publishing Company, 1984), 10–15.

5. Hine, Hine, and Harrold, *African-American Odyssey*, 510.

6. Barr, *Black Texans*, 187.

7. Williams, interview, 27 July 2003.

8. Becton, interview, 27 July 2003.

9. Becton, interview, 27 July 2003.

10. F. Kenneth Jensen, "The Houston Sit-In Movement of 1960–1961," in *Black Dixie*, 214.

11. Jensen, "The Houston Sit-In," 215–16.

12. Thomas, R. Cole, *No Color Is My Kind: The Life of Eldrewey Stearns and the Integration of Houston* (Austin: University of Texas Press, 1997), 51.
13. Grimsley, *Football*, 102.
14. Barr, *Black Texans*, 216.
15. *Houston Informer*, 27 August 1960.
16. *Houston Informer*, 10 September 1960.
17. *Houston Informer*, 17 September 1960.
18. *Houston Informer*, 24 September 1960.
19. Texas Southern University, *The Herald*, 30 September 1960.
20. *Dallas Express*, 8 October 1960.
21. *Houston Informer*, 15 October 1960.
22. *Houston Informer*, 22 October 1960.
23. *Dallas Express*, 22 October 1960.
24. Prairie View A&M University, *The Panther*, 1961.
25. *Houston Informer*, 29 October 1960.
26. Prairie View A&M University, *The Panther*, 1961.
27. "Texas Independents Take on a Bigger and Better Look," *Texas Football*, 1962, 55.
28. Pirkle, *Oiler Blues*, 25.
29. Kurt Edward Kemper, "The Smell of Roses and the Color of the Players: College Football and the Expansion of the Civil Rights Movement in the West," *Journal of Sport History* 31, no. 3 (Fall 2004): 318.
30. *Houston Informer*, 16 September 1961.
31. *Dallas Express*, 14 October 1961.
32. *Dallas Express*, 21 October 1961.
33. *Houston Informer*, 18 November 1961.
34. *Dallas Express*, 18 November 1961.
35. *Houston Informer*, 2 December 1961.
36. Hurd, *Black College Football*, 159.
37. *Houston Informer*, 16 December 1961.
38. Thomas G. Smith, "Civil Rights on the Gridiron: The Kennedy Administration and the Desegregation of the Washington Redskins," *Journal of Sport History* 14, no. 2 (Summer 1987): 189.
39. Jack E. Davis, "Baseball's Reluctant Challenge: Desegregating Major League Spring Training Sites, 1961–1964," *Journal of Sport History* 19, no. 2 (Summer 1992): 144, 155, 157.
40. Pirkle, *Oiler Blues*, 32.
41. Barr, *Black Texans*, 185.
42. Barr, 186.
43. Barr, 186.
44. *Houston Informer*, 8 September 1962.
45. *Houston Informer*, 15 September 1962.
46. *Houston Informer*, 22 September 1962.
47. *Houston Informer*, 6 October 1962.

48. *Dallas Express*, 6 October 1962.

49. *Dallas Express*, 13 October 1962.

50. *Houston Informer*, 20 October 1962.

51. *Houston Informer*, 10 November 1962.

52. *Houston Informer*, 17 November 1962.

53. *Dallas Express*, 24 November 1962.

54. *Houston Informer*, 1 December 1962.

55. *Houston Informer*, 15 December 1962.

56. Pirkle, *Oiler Blues*, 37–39.

57. *Houston Informer*, 29 December 1962.

58. *Houston Informer*, 12 January 1963.

59. Pirkle, *Oiler Blues*, 42.

60. *Houston Informer*, 5 October 1963.

61. *Dallas Express*, 12 October 1963.

62. *Houston Informer*, 19 October 1963.

63. *Houston Informer*, 2 November 1963.

64. *Houston Informer*, 9 November 1963.

65. *Dallas Express*, 16 November 1963.

66. *Houston Informer*, 23 November 1963.

67. *Houston Informer*, 30 November 1963.

68. *Sacramento Union*, 12 December 1963.

69. *Sacramento Union*, 13 December 1963.

70. *Sacramento Union*, 15 December 1963.

71. *Sacramento Union*, 15 December 1963.

72. *Houston Informer*, 4 January 1963.

73. Watterson, *College Football*, 319.

74. *Sacramento Union*, 12 December 1963.

75. Pirkle, *Oiler Blues*, 47.

76. Hine, Hine, and Harrold, *African-American Odyssey*, 519–20.

77. *Houston Informer*, 16 May 1964.

78. *Houston Informer*, 19 September 1964.

79. *Houston Informer*, 17 October 1964.

80. *Houston Informer*, 24 October 1964.

81. *Houston Informer*, 31 October 1964.

82. *Houston Informer*, 31 October 1964.

83. *Houston Informer*, 14 November 1964.

84. *Houston Informer*, 21 November 1964.

85. *Houston Informer*, 28 November 1964.

86. *Houston Informer*, 5 December 1964.

87. Hurd, *Black College Football*, 147.

88. Hine, Hine, and Harrold, *African-American Odyssey*, 532.

89. Stokely Carmichael, "What We Want," in *The Negro in the Twentieth Century: A Reader on the Struggle for Civil Rights*, ed. John Hope Franklin and Isidore Starr (New York: Vintage Books, 1967), 176–77.

90. Quintard Taylor, *In Search of the Racial Frontier: African Americans in the American West, 1528-1990* (New York: W. W. Norton and Company, 1998), 304–7.

91. Bryant, Texas Southern University, 98.

92. Richard Pennington, *Breaking the Ice: The Racial Integration of Southwest Conference Football* (Jefferson: McFarland, 1987), 25.

93. Pennington, 25–26.

94. Pennington, 25–26.

95. San Antonio Friends of Houston University, advertisement, *Texas Football*, 1965, 71.

96. San Antonio Friends of Houston University, advertisement, *Texas Football*, 1965, 71.

97. Pennington, *Breaking the Ice*, 45–47.

98. *Houston Informer*, 11 September 1965.

99. Prairie View A&M University, *Pantherland*, 1966.

100. *Houston Informer*, 9 October 1965.

101. *Dallas Express*, 9 October 1965.

102. *Dallas Express*, 16 October 1965.

103. *Dallas Express*, 23 October 1965.

104. *Houston Informer*, 23 October 1965.

105. Prairie View A&M University, *Pantherland*, 1966.

106. *Dallas Express*, 13 November 1965.

107. *Houston Informer*, 11 December 1965.

108. Barr, *Black Texans*, 210.

109. Frank Fitzpatrick, *And the Walls Came Tumbling Down: The Basketball Game That Changed American Sports* (Lincoln: University of Nebraska Press, 1999), 214–16

110. Pennington, *Breaking the Ice*, 63.

111. Jack Gallagher, "New Faces, 1966: Super Is the Word for the Sophomores," *Texas Football* (1966): 21.

112. Pennington, *Breaking the Ice*, 83–84.

113. Pennington, 87, 97–98.

114. Pennington, 100–101.

115. *Houston Informer*, 3 September 1966.

116. *Houston Informer*, 24 September 1966.

117. *Houston Informer*, 24 September 1966.

118. *Houston Informer*, 1 October 1966.

119. *Houston Informer*, 1 October 1966.

120. *Houston Informer*, 8 October 1966.

121. *Dallas Express*, 8 October 1966.

122. *Dallas Express*, 29 October 1966.

123. Prairie View A&M University, *Pantherland*, 1967.

124. *Houston Informer*, 29 October 1966.

125. *Houston Informer*, 26 November 1966.

126. Bishop College, *The Tiger*, 1967.

127. *Dallas Express*, 3 December 1966.

128. Williams, interview, 27 July 2003.

129. Wiggins, *Glory Bound*, 111–12.

130. *Houston Informer*, 2 September 1967.

131. Barr, *Black Texans*, 192.

132. Barr, 192–93.

133. Barr, 193.

134. *Dallas Express*, 16 September 1967.

135. *Houston Informer*, 14 October 1967.

136. *Houston Informer*, 21 October 1967.

137. Prairie View A&M University, *Pantherland*, 1968.

138. *Houston Informer*, 14 October 1967.

139. *Houston Informer*, 28 October 1967.

140. Hurd, *Black College Football*, 158.

141. Day, *Remembering the Past with Pride*, 11.

142. *Houston Informer*, 28 October 1967.

143. *Dallas Express*, 4 November 1967.

144. *Dallas Express*, 4 November 1967.

145. Tommy Williams, interview, 24 July 2003.

146. Gregory J. Kaliss, "Un-Civil Discourse: Charlie Scott, the Integration of College Basketball, and the 'Progressive Mystique,'" *Journal of Sport History* 35, no. 1 (Spring 2008): 99, 104–5.

147. Pirkle, *Oiler Blues*, 76.

148. Barr, *Black Texans*, 218.

149. Blair Justice, *Violence in the City* (Fort Worth: Texas Christian University Press, 1969), 50.

150. Hine, Hine, and Harrold, *African-American Odyssey*, 545.

151. *Houston Informer*, 14 September 1968.

152. *Houston Informer*, 14 September 1968.

153. Pennington, *Breaking the Ice*, 124, 137, 142, 145.

154. *Dallas Express*, 14 September 1968.

155. *Houston Informer*, 14 September 1968.

156. *Houston Informer*, 21 September 1968.

157. *Houston Informer*, 28 September 1968.

158. *Houston Informer*, 5 October 1968.

159. *Houston Informer*, 12 October 1968.

160. *Houston Informer*, 19 October 1968.

161. Harry Edwards, *The Revolt of the Black Athlete* (New York: Free Press, 1970), 58–59.

162. John Matthew Smith, "'It's Not Really My Country': Lew Alcindor and the Revolt of the Black Athlete," *Journal of Sport History* 36, no. 2 (Summer 2009): 236.

163. Edwards, *Revolt of the Black Athlete*, 102.

164. Edwards, 103–4.

165. David K. Wiggins, "'The Future of College Athletics Is at Stake': Black Athletes and Racial Turmoil on Three Predominantly White University Campuses, 1968–1972," *Journal of Sport History* 15, no. 3 (Winter 1988): 305.

166. Prairie View A&M University, *Pantherland*, 1969.

167. *Houston Informer*, 9 November 1968.

168. *Houston Informer*, 16 November 1968.

169. *Houston Informer*, 23 November 1968.

170. Prairie View A&M University, *Pantherland*, 1969

171. *Dallas Express*, 30 November 1968.

172. *Houston Informer*, 7 December 1968.

173. *Dallas Express*, 7 December 1968.

174. *Houston Informer*, 6 September 1969.

175. *Houston Informer*, 6 September 1969.

176. A. J. Jaffe, Walter Adams, and Sandra G. Meyers, *Negro Higher Education in the 1960s* (New York: Frederick A. Praeger, 1968), 3–10.

177. *Houston Informer*, 13 September 1969.

178. Hurd, *Black College Football*, 147, 169.

179. *Houston Informer*, 27 September 1969.

180. Prairie View A&M University, *Pantherland*, 1970.

181. *Houston Informer*, 4 October 1969.

182. *Houston Informer*, 4 October 1969.

183. *Houston Informer*, 11 October 1969.

184. *Houston Informer*, 18 October 1969.

185. Prairie View A&M University, *Pantherland*, 1970.

186. *Houston Informer*, 1 November 1969.

187. *Houston Informer*, 8 November 1969.

188. Prairie View A&M University, *Pantherland*, 1970.

189. Prairie View A&M University, *Pantherland*, 1970.

190. *Houston Informer*, 22 November 1969.

191. Terry Frei, *Horns, Hogs, and Nixon Coming: Texas vs. Arkansas in Dixie's Last Stand* (New York: Simon and Schuster, 2002), 63, 84, 259, 286.

192. Prairie View A&M University, *Pantherland*, 1970.

193. *Houston Informer*, 13 December 1969.

Chapter 7

1. Freeman, *Hook'em Horns*, 150.

2. Bryant, *Texas Southern University*, 117–18.

3. *Dallas Morning News*, 1 November 1970.

4. Barr, *Black Texans*, 231.

5. Texas Southern University, *The Tiger*, 1970.

6. Texas Southern University, *The Tiger*, 1970.

7. *Houston Informer*, 22 August 1970.

8. *Houston Informer*, 22 August 1970.

9. *Houston Informer,* 12 September 1970.

10. *Houston Informer,* 26 September 1970.

11. Prairie View A&M University, *Pantherland,* 1971.

12. *Houston Informer,* 3 October 1970.

13. Prairie View A&M University, *Pantherland,* 1971.

14. *Houston Informer,* 10 October 1970.

15. *Houston Informer,* 17 October 1970.

16. Prairie View A&M University, *Pantherland,* 1971.

17. *Houston Informer,* 12 December 1970.

18. Prairie View A&M University, *Pantherland,* 1971.

19. *Houston Informer,* 12 December 1970.

20. Martin Kane, "An Assessment of 'Black Is Best,'" *Sports Illustrated* 34, no. 3 (18 January 1971): 73–75.

21. Watterson, *College Football,* 303.

22. Watterson, 304.

23. *Houston Informer,* 25 September 1971.

24. *Houston Informer,* 2 October 1971.

25. *Houston Informer,* 9 October 1971.

26. *Houston Informer,* 16 October 1971.

27. *Houston Informer,* 16 October 1971.

28. *Houston Informer,* 6 November 1971.

29. *Houston Informer,* 13 November 1971.

30. *Houston Informer,* 13 November 1971.

31. *Houston Informer,* 4 December 1971.

32. *Houston Informer,* 13 November 1971.

33. Stowers, *Dallas Cowboys,* 33.

34. Hine, Hine, and Harrold, *African-American Odyssey,* 546.

35. Curtis Goode, interview by the author, 24 July 2003.

36. *Houston Informer,* 23 September 1972.

37. *Houston Informer,* 23 September 1972.

38. Texas Southern University, *The Herald,* 27 October 1972.

39. Texas Southern University, *The Herald,* 27 October 1972.

40. Texas Southern University, *The Tiger,* 1973.

41. *Houston Informer,* 28 October 1972.

42. Prairie View A&M University, *Pantherland,* 1973.

43. Stowers, *Dallas Cowboys,* 38.

44. Stowers, *Dallas Cowboys,* 38.

45. Bryant, Texas Southern University, 99.

46. *Houston Informer,* 1 September 1973.

47. *Houston Informer,* 18 August 1973.

48. *Houston Informer,* 18 August 1973.

49. *Houston Informer,* 8 September 1973.

50. *Houston Informer,* 15 September 1973.

51. *Houston Informer,* 22 September 1973.

52. *Houston Informer,* 29 September 1973.

53. Texas Southern University, *The Herald,* 5 October 1973.

54. *Houston Informer,* 6 October 1973.

55. *Houston Informer,* 20 October 1973.

56. Prairie View A&M University, *Pantherland,* 1974.

57. *Houston Informer,* 3 November 1973.

58. *Houston Informer,* 3 November 1973.

59. *Houston Informer,* 10 November 1973.

60. *Houston Informer,* 17 November 1973.

61. *Houston Informer,* 17 November 1973.

62. *Houston Informer,* 24 November 1973.

63. *Houston Informer,* 24 November 1973.

64. Freeman, *Hook'em Horns,* 160.

65. Freeman, *Hook'em Horns,* 160.

66. Watterson, *College Football,* 305.

67. Bryant, Texas Southern University, 121.

68. Texas Southern University, *The Tiger,* 1975.

69. *Houston Informer,* 24 September 1974.

70. *Houston Informer,* 24 September 1974.

71. Prairie View A&M University, *Pantherland,* 1975.

72. Prairie View A&M University, *Pantherland,* 1975.

73. *Houston Informer,* 1 October 1974.

74. *Houston Informer,* 22 October 1974.

75. *Houston Informer,* 30 November 1974.

76. Gina Augustini, Kent Best, Darrel Tomas, ed. *Raiding the SWC: The Collective History of Red Raiders Sports in the Southwest Conference* (Lubbock: Texas Tech University Press, 1996), 51.

77. *Houston Informer,* 28 August 1976.

78. *Houston Informer,* 25 September 1976.

79. *Houston Informer,* 2 October 1976.

80. Prairie View A&M University, *Pantherland,* 1977.

81. *Houston Informer,* 16 October 1976.

82. Prairie View A&M University, *Pantherland,* 1977.

83. *Houston Informer,* 23 October 1976.

84. *Houston Informer,* 30 October 1976.

85. *Houston Informer,* 20 November 1976.

86. *Houston Informer,* 27 November 1976.

87. *Houston Informer,* 17 September 1977.

88. *Houston Informer,* 17 September 1977.

89. *Houston Informer,* 17 September 1977.

90. Hurd, *Black College Football,* 148.

91. Goode, interview, 24 July 2003.

92. *Houston Informer,* 29 October 1977.

93. *Houston Informer,* 29 October 1977.

94. *Houston Informer*, 5 November 1977.

95. *Houston Informer*, 21 November 1977.

96. *Houston Informer*, 26 November 1977.

97. *NCAA Football Records*, 148.

Chapter 8

1. Ronald T. Vera, "Texas Responds to the Office of Civil Rights: Progress Made under the Texas Equal Education Opportunity Plan for Higher Education," Barbosa and Vera Law Firm, Los Angeles, Tomas Rivera Center Working Paper, 1989, 1.

2. Vera, "Texas Responds to the Office of Civil Rights," 4.

3. Vera, 4–5.

4. Vera, 1.

5. Vera, 7–8.

6. Vera, 10, 12, 16, 17, 18, 20, 34.

7. Barr, *Black Texans*, 242–43.

8. Hurd. *Black College Football*, 148.

9. Barr, *Black Texans*, 243.

10. Barr, 243.

11. Barr, 243.

12. Barr, 246.

13. *NCAA Football Records*, 120.

14. Becton, interview, 24 July 2003.

15. Becton, interview, 24 July 2003.

16. John Ed Bradley, "Once Upon a Time . . .," *Sports Illustrated*, 28 August 1995, 129–30.

17. Hurd, *Black College Football*, 163.

18. "Prairie View's Agony Finally Over," Billy Nicks Papers, Prairie View University Archives, William Rutherford Banks Library, Prairie View University, Prairie View, Texas, http://www.msnbc.com/news/200046.asp.

19. Letter from Jon F. Hanson, Chair of the Board for the National Football Foundation and College Football Hall of Fame Inc., in South Bend, Indiana, to Billy Nicks, Houston, Texas, April 12, 1999, in the Billy Nicks Papers, Prairie View A&M University Archives, William Rutherford Banks Library, Prairie View, Texas.

20. "Enshrinement Festival, NFF & CFHOF Inductees," handout, National Football Foundation and College Football Hall of Fame Inc., Billy Nicks Papers, Prairie View University Archives, William Rutherford Banks Library, Prairie View, Texas.

21. *Houston Chronicle*, 14 November 1999.

22. *Dallas Morning News*, 3 October 2003.

23. *Dallas Morning News*, 25 September 2004.

24. "Sooner Athletic Conference," http://www.soonerathletic.org/sport/0/1, retrieved 24 November 2018.

25. Bill Connelly, "How Prairie View A&M Emerged from the Worst Losing Streak Ever," SBNATION, 8 September 2016, http://www.sbnation.com/2016/9/8/12803480/prairie-view-am-football-losing-streak-sturdy-program, retrieved 1 June 2017.

Appendix A

1. NCAA, *Football Conference Standings and Championships*, http://fs.ncaa.org/Docs/stats/football_records/2017/Conference.pdf; *2017 SWAC Football Conference Championship*, http://www.swac.org/sports/2018/7/6/2130818.html.aspx.

Appendix B

1. Hurd, *Black College Football*, 164.

Bibliography

Primary Sources
Government Documents
Blackstone, Graham. *Staff Monograph: Higher Education for Negroes in Texas.* Austin: Staff of the Texas Legislative Council, 1950.

Vera, Ronald T. *Texas Responds to the Office of Civil Rights: Progress Made under the Texas Equal Educational Opportunity Plan for Higher Education.* Claremont: Tomas Rivera Center, 1989.

Archival Material
"Enshrinement Festival, NFF & CFHOF Inductees, 1999." Handout, National Football Foundation and College Football Hall of Fame, Inc. Billy Nicks Papers. Prairie View University Archives. William Rutherford Banks Library. Prairie View, Texas.

"Prairie View's Agony Finally Over." Billy Nicks Papers. Prairie View A&M University Archives. William Rutherford Banks Library. Prairie View, Texas. http://www.msnbc.com/news/200046.asp.

Interviews
Becton, Julius. Interview by the author, 24 July 2003.

Dunn, Willie. Interview by the author. 24 July 2003.

Dyer, Frank. Interview by the author. 24 July 2003.

Estus, Charles. Interview by the author. 24 July 2003.

Forkerway, George. Interview by the author. 29 August 1999.

Garnett, Earvin. Interview by the author. 4 May 2018.

Goode, Curtis. Interview by the author. 24 July 2003.

Reliford, Tommie. Interview by the author. 24 July 2003.

Williams, Tommy. Interview by the author. 24 July 2003.

Wyatt, Tommy. Interview by the author, 8 May 2018.

Letters
Letter from Hanson, Jon F. Chair of the Board for the National Football Foundation and College Football Hall of Fame Inc., in South Bend, Indiana, to Billy Nicks, in Houston, Texas. 12 April 1999. Billy Nicks Papers. Prairie View A&M University Archives. William Rutherford Banks Library. Prairie View, Texas.

Articles

Carmichael, Stokely. "What We Want." In *The Negro in the Twentieth Century: A Reader on the Struggle for Civil Rights*, edited by John Hope Franklin and Isidore Starr, 175–81. New York: Vintage Books, 1967.

Newspapers

Dallas Express 22 October 1921; 11 November 1922; 11 October 1923; 24, 31 October 1925; 23, 30 October; 13, 20 November 1926; 10, 24 September; 8, 22 October 1927; 22 September; 6, 20 October; 17, 24 November; 28 December 1928; 13, 20 October 1934; 7 September; 9, 23 November 1935; 2, 5, 12 September; 10, 24, 26 October; 7 November; 5 December 1936; 9 January; 2, 16 October; 13, 20 November 1937; 8, 22 October; 5, 26 November 1938; 7, 21, 28 October 1939; 6 January 1940; 4, 18 October; 1, 15, 22 November; 6, 13 December 1941; 10 January; 12, 26 September; 24 October; 7 November 1942; 8 January; 14 October 1944; 2 December 1944; 6 January; 6, 20 October; 17 November; 15 December 1945; 12 October; 9, 16 November 1946; 11, 18, 25 October; 8 November; 6 December 1947; 3 January; 2, 9, 23 October; 6, 13 November 1948; 1, 8, 15, 22 October; 5, 26 November; 10 December 1949; 30 September; 7, 21 October; 18 November; 2 December 1950; 6 January; 22, 29 September; 20, 27 October; 1 December 1951; 20 September; 4, 11, 18, 25 October; 22 November; 6, 28 December 1952; 19 September; 3, 10, 24 October; 14 November; 5, 12 December 1953; 2 October; 3 November; 4, 25 December 1954; 8 January; 20 August; 8, 15 October; 12 November; 3 December 1955; 7 January; 29 September; 13, 27 October; 3, 10, 17 November 1956; 5 January; 14 September; 5, 12, 19 October; 7, 14 December 1957; 4 October; 1, 18, 29 November 1958; 10 January; 3, 17 October; 14 November 1959; 8, 22 October; 12, 23 November 1960; 7 January; 14, 21 October; 18 November 1961; 6, 13, 27 October; 3, 24 November 1962; 12, 19 October; 16 November 1963; 9, 16, 23 October; 13 November 1965; 8, 29 October; 3 December 1966; 16 September 1967; 4 November 1967; 14 September; 5, 12 October; 2, 30 November; 7 December 1968.

Dallas Morning News, 1 November 1970; 3 October 2003; 25 September 2004.

The Herald. Texas Southern University, 30 September; 18 November 1960; 27 October 1972; 5 October 1973.

Houston Chronicle 14 November 1999.

Houston Informer 28 October; 11 November; 23 December 1922; 6 January; 8 September; 20 October; 10, 17 November; 1, 8, 15 December 1923; 5 January 1924; 30 May; 17, 24 October; 7, 21 November; 5, 12, 19 December 1925; 25 September; 2, 9, 16, 23, 30 October; 6, 13, 27 November; 4 December 1926; 15 January; 10, 17 September; 8, 22, 29 October; 9, 12, 19, 26 November; 3, 17, 24 December 1927; 21 January; 6, 13, 20, 27 October; 3, 10, 17 November; 1, 8, 15, 29 December 1928; 5, 12 January; 5, 12, 19, 26 October; 2, 16 November; 7, 21 December 1929; 4 January; 30 August; 13, 20 27 September;

4, 11, 18, 25 October; 1, 8, 22 November; 6, 20 December 1930; 3 January;
8, 22 August; 12, 17 September; 3, 10, 17, 24, 31 October; 7, 14, 21 November;
5, 12 December 1931; 2, 9 January; 24 September; 8, 15, 22, 29 October;
5, 12, 19, 26 November 1932; 7, 14 January; 9, 16, 30 September; 7, 14, 21
October; 4, 11, 18, 25 November; 9, 16, 30 December 1933; 6, 13, 27 January;
15 September; 13, 20, 27 October; 3, 17 November; 5, 8 December 1934;
10, 24 August; 5, 12, 19, 26 October; 9, 16 November; 7, 28 December 1935;
4 January; 29 August; 12 September; 3, 10, 24, 31 October; 7, 14, 21, 28
November; 5, 12 December 1936; 1, 8 September; 6, 13, 16, 20, 23, 27, 30
October; 3, 17 November; 1, 22 December 1937; 27 August; 3 September; 1,
15, 22, 29 October; 5, 12, 19 November 1938; 7 January; 12, 26 August; 2, 23,
30 September; 14, 21, 28 October; 18 November; 2, 9, 16 December 1939; 6
January 1940. 7, 16, 21, 28 September; 5, 10, 12, 19, 26 October; 2, 9, 16, 23,
30 November; 7, 21, 28 December 1940; 4, 11 January; 13, 27 September; 4,
11, 18, 25 October; 1, 8, 22, 29 November; 13, 20 December 1941; 29 August;
12, 19, 26 September; 10, 17 October; 7 November; 19 December 1942; 9
January; 2, 9, 16, 23 October; 20 November 1943; 14, 21, 28 October; 18
November; 9, 16 December 1944; 27 January; 29 September; 13, 20, 27
October; 3, 10, 24 November; 8 December 1945; 5 January; 24, 31 August; 7
September; 19 October; 2 November; 28 December 1946; 11 January; 6, 20,
27 September; 4, 18 October; 8, 29 November 1947; 3 January; 2, 9, 16, 30
October; 13 November; 4, 11 December 1948; 1 January; 20, 24 September;
1, 8, 15, 22, 29 October; 26 November 1949; 27 August; 30 September; 12
August; 16 September; 28 October; 25 November; 30 December 1950; 1, 22
September; 13, 20, 27 October; 1, 29 December 1951; 5 January; 24 May;
20, 27 September; 11, 18, 25 October; 1 November 1952; 10 January; 27
June; 29 August; 5 September; 17, 24, 31 October; 7, 14, 28 November; 19
December 1953; 9 January; 11, 18, 25 September; 2, 9, 16, 23 October; 13
November 1954; 1 January; 1, 8, 22 October; 26 November; 31 December
1955; August; 8, 15 September; 6, 20 October; 10 November; 29 December
1956; 5 January; 24 August; 5, 26 October; 9 November 1957; 4 January;
30 August; 20 September; 4, 18 October; 1, 8 November; 20, 27 December
1958; 5; 26 September; 3, 10, 17, 24, 31 October; 14, 28 November; 12, 26
December 1959; 3 September; 27 August; 10, 17, 24 September; 1, 15, 22, 29
October; 10 December 1960; 7 January; 16 September; 18 November; 2, 16
December 1961; 8, 15, 22 September; 6, 20 October; 10; 17 November; 1, 15,
29 December 1962; 12 January; 5, 19 October; 2, 9, 23, 30 November 1963;
4 January 1964; 16 May; 12, 19 September; 17, 24, 31 October; 7, 14, 21, 28
November; 5 December 1964; 11 September; 9, 23 October; 11 December
1965; 3, 24 September; 1, 8, 15, 22, 29 October; 26 November; 3 December
1966; 2, 30 September; 7, 14, 21, 28 October; 4, 25 November 1967; 14, 21, 28
September; 5, 12, 19, 26 October; 9, 16, 23 November; 7 December 1968; 6,
13, 27 September; 4, 11, 18 October; 1, 8 , 22 November; 13 December 1969;
22 August; 12, 26 September; 3, 10, 17 October; 7 November; 12 December

1970; 25 September; 2, 9, 16 October; 6, 13 November; 4 December 1971;
23 September; 28 October 1972; 18 August; 1, 8, 15, 22, 29 September; 6,
20 October; 3, 10, 17, 24 November 1973; 24 September; 1, 22 October; 30
November 1974; 28 August; 25 September; 2, 16, 23, 30 October; 20, 27
November 1976; 17 September; 29 October; 5, 21, 26 November 1977.
Sacramento Union, 12, 13, 15 December 1963.

Yearbooks

Bishop College. *The Tiger*. 1967, 1969.
Prairie View A&M University. *The Panther*. 1943, 1949, 1952, 1959, 1961.
———. *Pantherland*. 1966, 1967, 1968, 1969, 1970, 1971, 1973, 1974, 1975, 1977, 1978.
———. *The Purple and Gold*. 1946.
Texas Southern University, *The Tiger*, 1948, 1949, 1952, 1953, 1954, 1970, 1973, 1975.

Secondary Sources
Books

Ashe, Arthur. *A Hard Road to Glory: A History of the African American Athlete, 1619–1918*, vol. 1. New York: Amistad, 1988.
———. *A Hard Road to Glory: A History of the African American Athlete, 1919–1945*, vol. 2. New York: Amistad, 1988.
———. *A Hard Road to Glory: A History of the African American Athlete, since 1945*, vol. 3. New York: Amistad, 1988.
Augustini, Gina, Kent Best, and Darrel Tomas, eds. *Raiding the SWC: The Collective History of Red Raiders Sports in the Southwest Conference*. Lubbock: Texas Tech University Press, 1996.
Bak, Richard. *Joe Louis: The Great Black Hope*. Dallas: Taylor Publishing Company, 1996.
Barr, Alwyn. *Black Texans: A History of African Americans in Texas, 1528–1995*. Norman: University of Oklahoma Press, 1996.
Barr, Alwyn, and Robert Calvert, eds. *Black Leaders: Texans for Their Times*. Austin: Texas State Historical Association, 1981
Barr, Robert Cooper. *Pre-College Football*. New York: Frederick A. Stokes, 1939.
Beeth, Howard, and Cary D. Wintz, eds. *Black Dixie: Afro-Texan History and Culture in Houston*. College Station: Texas A&M University Press, 1992.
Benderman, Gail. *Manliness and Civilization: A Cultural History of Race and Gender in the United States, 1880–1917*. Chicago: University of Chicago Press, 1995.
Bible, Dana. *Championship Football*. New York: Prentice Hall, 1947.
Bierman, Bernard. *Winning Football*. New York: McGraw-Hill, 1937.

Bonder, Jim. *Fundamental Line Drills for Line Skills in the "T" Formation.* Dubuque: W. C. Brown Co., 1952.

Branch, Taylor. *Parting the Waters: America in the King Years, 1954–1963.* New York: Simon and Schuster, 1988.

———. *Pillar of Fire: America in the King Years, 1963–1965.* New York: Simon and Schuster, 1998.

Brooks, Dana D., and Ronald C. Althouse, eds. *Racism in College Athletics: The African-American Athlete's Experience.* Morgantown, WV: Fitness Information Technology, 1993.

Bryant, Ira Babington. *Texas Southern University: Its Antecedents, Political Origins, and Future.* Houston: Bryant, 1975.

Bynum, E. B. *These Carried the Torch: Pioneers of Christian Education in Texas.* Dallas: Walter F. Clark Co., 1946.

Caldwell, C. W. *Modern Football for the Spectator.* Philadelphia: Lippincott, 1953.

Camp, Walter. *American Football.* New York: Arno Press, 1974.

Carroll, Bob. *The Hidden Game of Football.* New York: Warner Bros., 1988.

Carroll, John. *Fritz Pollard: Pioneer in Racial Advancement.* Urbana: University of Illinois Press, 1992.

Chalk, Ocania. *Black College Sports.* New York: Dodd, Mead Press, 1976.

Cole, Thomas, R. *No Color Is My Kind: The Life of Eldrewey Stearns and the Integration of Houston.* Austin: University of Texas Press, 1997.

Crisler, Herbert. *Modern Football, Fundamentals and Strategy.* New York: Whittlesey House, 1949.

DaGrosa, John. *Functional Football.* Philadelphia: W. B. Saunders Company, 1936.

Day, Walter. *State Championship Football for Blacks in Texas, 1940–1969.* Fort Worth: Walter Day, 1994.

England, Forrest William. *The T Formation from A to Z.* Danville: School-Aid Co., 1952.

Edwards, Harry. *The Revolt of the Black Athlete.* New York: Free Press, 1970.

Evans, Wilbur, and H. B. McElroy. *The Twelfth Man.* Huntsville: Strode Publishers, 1974.

Fitzpatrick, Frank. *And the Walls Came Tumbling Down: Kentucky, Texas Western, and the Game That Changed American Sports.* New York: Simon & Schuster, 1999.

Flasch, Joy. *Melvin B. Tolson.* New York: Twayne Publishers Inc., 1972.

Franklin, John Hope. *From Slavery to Freedom: A History of Negro Americans,* 3rd ed. New York: Vintage Books, 1967.

Freeman, Denne. *Hook'em Horns.* Huntsville: Strode Publishers, 1974.

Frei, Terry. *Horns, Hogs, and Nixon Coming: Texas vs. Arkansas in Dixie's Last Stand.* New York: Simon and Schuster, 2002.

Golenbeck, Peter. *Cowboys Have Always Been My Heroes: The Definitive Oral History of America's Team.* New York: Warner Books, 1997.

Graham, Otto. *Otto Graham—"T" Quarterback*. New York: Prentice Hall, 1953.

Grange, Harold. *Zuppke of Illinois*. Chicago: A. L. Glaser, 1937.

Grimsley, Will. *Football: The Greatest Moments in the Southwest Conference*. Boston: Little, Brown and Company, 1968.

Harris, Reed. *King Football: The Vulgarization of the American College*. New York: Vanguard Press, 1932.

Heard, Robert. *Oklahoma vs. Texas: When Football Becomes War, 1900–1980*. Austin: Honey Hill, 1980.

Heintze, Michael R. *Private Black Colleges in Texas, 1865–1954*. College Station: Texas A&M University Press, 1985.

Henderson, Edwin Bancroft. *The Black Athlete: Emergence and Arrival*. New York: Publisher's Co., 1968.

Hietala, Thomas R. *The Fight of the Century: Jack Johnson, Joe Louis, and the Struggle for Racial Equality*. Armonk: M. E. Sharpe, 2002.

Hine, Darleene Clark, William C. Hine, and Stanley Harrold. *The African-American Odyssey*, combined volume. Upper Saddle River: Prentice Hall, 2000.

Hine, Darleene Clark, and Earnestine Jenkins, eds. *A Question of Manhood, Vol 2: A Reader in U.S. Black Men's History and Masculinity*. Bloomington: Indiana University Press, 2001.

Hurd, Michael. *Black College Football, 1892–1992: One Hundred Years of History, Education, and Pride*. Virginia Beach: Donning, 1993.

Jaffe, Abram, Walter Adams, and Sandra G. Meyers. *Negro Higher Education in the 1960s*. New York: Praeger, 1968.

Jones, Gomer. *Modern Defensive Football*. Englewood Cliffs: Prentice Hall, 1958.

Justice, Blair. *Violence in the City*. Fort Worth: Texas Christian University Press, 1969.

Kennedy, David M. *Over Here: The First World War and American Society*. New York: Oxford University Press, 1980.

Leahy, Frank. *Defensive Football*. New York: Prentice Hall, 1951.

Little, Louis. *How to Watch Football: The Spectator's Guide*. New York: McGraw-Hill, 1935.

Locke, Alain ed. *The New Negro: Voices of the Harlem Renaissance*. New York: Atheneum, 1992.

Martin, Charles H. *Benching Jim Crow: The Rise and Fall of the Color Line in Southern College Sports, 1890–1980*. Urbana: University of Illinois Press, 2010.

McClennon, Phillip Harvey. *A Brief History of Paul Quinn*. Waco: Paul Quinn, 1965.

McDaniel, Vernon. *History of the Teachers State Association of Texas*. Washington, DC: National Education Association, 1977.

Miller, Giles. *The Dallas Texans' Saga*. Dallas: Giles E. Miller, 1972

Miller, Richard. *The Truth about Big-Time Football with Cartoons by John Massey*. New York: Sloane, 1953.

Mumford, Kevin J. *Interzones: Black/White Sex Districts in Chicago and New York in the Early Twentieth Century*. New York: Columbia University Press, 1997.

NCAA Football Records. Indianapolis: National Collegiate Athletic Association, 2001.

Nugent, Tom. *Football for Boys*. New York: Ronald Press, 1962.

Oriard, Michael. *Reading Football: How the Popular Press Created an American Spectacle*. Chapel Hill: University of North Carolina Press, 1993.

Pennington, Richard. *Breaking the Ice: The Racial Integration of Southwest Conference Football*. Jefferson: McFarland, 1987.

Prairie View Agricultural and Mechanical College. *The First Seventy-Five Years, 1876–1951*. Prairie View, Texas: Prairie View A&M College, 1951.

Prince, Robert. *A History of Dallas from a Different Perspective*. n.p.: Nortex Press, 1993.

Pirkle, John. *Oiler Blues: The Story of Pro Football's Most Frustrating Team*. Houston: Sports Line Publishing, 2000.

Rader, Benjamin G. *American Sports: From the Age of Folk Games to the Age of Televised Sports*. Upper Saddle River: Prentice Hall, 1999.

Ratliff, Harold V. *The Power and the Glory: The Story of Southwest Conference Football*. Lubbock: Texas Tech University Press, 1957.

Robinson, Jackie. *I Never Had It Made: An Autobiography*. Hopewell: Echo Press, 1995.

Rotundo, Anthony. *American Manhood: Transformations in Masculinity from the Revolution to the Modern Era*. New York: Basic Books, 1993.

Royal, Darrell. *Darrell Royal Talks Football*. Englewood Cliffs: Prentice Hall, 1963.

Ruck, Rob. *Sandlot Seasons: Sport in Black Pittsburgh*. Urbana: University of Illinois Press, 1993.

Sellmeyer, Ralph, and James E. Dickson. *The Red Raiders: Texas Tech Football*. Huntsville: Strode Publishers, 1978.

Sloan, Steve. *A Whole New Ball Game*. Nashville: Broadman Press, 1975.

Smith, Ronald A. *Sport and Freedom: The Rise of Big-Time College Athletics*. New York: Oxford University Press, 1988.

Stagg, Amos Alonzo. *Touchdown!* New York: Longmans, and Green and Co., 1927.

Stockdale, Ken. *Southwest Conference Football: The Classic 60s*. Shippensburg, PA: Companion Press, 1992.

Stowers, Carlton. *Dallas Cowboys: The First Twenty-Five Years*. Dallas: Taylor Publishing Company, 1984.

Tabarlet, John. *Half the Distance to the Goal: 1975–1998: Observations on Reforming What High School Football Has Become*. Carencro: Forty Two Forty Publishing, 1998.

Taylor, Quintard. *In Search of the Racial Frontier: African Americans in the American West, 1528–1990*. New York: W. W. Norton and Company, 1998.

Tippette, Giles. *Saturday's Children*. New York: MacMillan, 1973.

Tips, Kern. *Football, Texas Style: An Illustrated History of the Southwest Conference*. Garden City, NY: Doubleday, 1964.

Tygel, Jules. *Baseball's Great Experiment: Jackie Robinson and His Legacy*. New York: Vintage Books, 1983.

Underwood, John. *The Death of an American Game: The Crisis in Football*. Boston: Little, Brown and Co., 1979.

Wallace, J. W. *Sizzling Southwest Football for 60 Years*. Wichita Falls, TX: J. W. Williams, 1956.

Watterson, John Sayle. *College Football*. Baltimore: The Johns Hopkins University Press, 2000.

Wiggins, David K. *Glory Bound: Black Athletes in a White America*. Syracuse: Syracuse University Press, 1997.

Williams, David A. *Bricks without Straw: A History of Higher Education for Black Texans, 1872–1977*. Austin: D. A. Williams, 1980.

Williams, J. W. *Sizzling Southwest Football: For Sixty Years*. n.p.: J. W. Williams, 1956.

Wolters, Raymond. *The New Negro on Campus: Black College Rebellions of the 1920s*. Princeton: Princeton University Press, 1975.

Woolfolk, George R. *Prairie View: A Study in Public Conscience 1878–1946*. New York Pageant Press, 1962.

Theses and Dissertations

Evans, Virden. "A Factor and Discriminant Analysis of Football Playing Ability among *Black High School Athletes*." EdD thesis, Northwestern State University, 1972.

Junkin, Sara Caroline Moseley. *The Independent Negro College in Texas: Change and Challenge*. Austin: University of Texas, 1969.

Kitchen, James. "A Master Site Plan for Prairie View Agricultural and Mechanical College of Texas." MA thesis, Texas Technical College, 1952.

MacDonald, James Douglas. *A Comparative Study of Opinions toward Athletics Held by Students of Samuel Huston College and the University of Texas*. MEd thesis, University of Texas, 1949.

Prult, Sherman. *The Relationship between Personality Factors and Football Ability*. MEd thesis, Texas Technical College, 1969.

White, Annie Mae Vaught. *The Development of the Program of Studies of the Prairie View State Normal and Industrial College*. MA thesis, University of Texas, 1938.

Wilhelm, Arnold. *The Relationship of Certain Measurable Traits to Success in Football*. DPhysEd, dissertation, Indiana University, 1951.

Articles

"At North Texas, Famine No Threat with Odus Around," *Texas Football* (1960): 62–63.

Benson, Mark. "T. R. and Football Reform." *College Football Historical Society Newsletter* 16, no. 3 (May 2003): 1–5.

Bourgeois, Christie L. "Stepping over Lines: Lyndon Johnson, Black Texans, and the National Youth Administration, 1935–1937." *Southwestern Historical Quarterly* 91 (2, October 1987): 149–72.

Bradley, John Ed. "Once Upon a Time . . ." *Sports Illustrated*, 28 August 1995, 126–39.

Bullock, Steve. "Playing for their Nation: the American Military and Baseball During World War II." *Journal of Sport History* 27, no. 1 (Spring 2000): 67–89.

Captain, Gwendolyn. "Enter Ladies and Gentlemen of Color: Gender, Sport, and the Ideal of African American Manhood and Womanhood During the Late Nineteenth and Early Twentieth Centuries." *Journal of Sport History* 18, no. 1 (Spring 1991): 81–102.

Carroll, John M. "Fritz Pollard." *College Football Historical Society Newsletter* 5, no. 1 (November 1991): 1–3.

———. "Red Storms East." *College Football Historical Society Newsletter* (February 1999): 7–9.

"Charlie 'Choo Choo' Brackins." Black College Football Hall of Fame. http://www.blackcollegefootballhof.org/inductees/charles-choo-choo-brackin, retrieved 9 May 2018.

Connelly, Bill. "How Prairie View A&M Emerged from the Worst Losing Streak Ever." SBNATION. 8 September 2016, http://www.sbnation.com/2016/9/8/12803480/prairie-view-am-football-losing-streak-sturdy-program, retrieved 1 June 2017.

Davis, Jack E. "Baseball's Reluctant Challenge: Desegregating Major League Spring Training Sites, 1961–1964." *Journal of Sport History* 19, no. 2 (Summer 1992): 144–62.

Doyle, Andrew. "College Football and the Culture of Segregation in the American South, 1890–1930." North American Society for Sport History, Proceedings and Newsletter (2001): 46–48.

———. "George Denny, Intercollegiate Football, and the Institutional Modernization of the University of Alabama, 1912–1934." North American Society for Sport History, Proceedings and Newsletter (2002): 26–28.

———. "Foolish and Useless Sport: The Southern Evangelical Crusade against Intercollegiate Football." *Journal of Sport History* 24, no. 3 (Fall 1997): 317–40.

Dyreson, Mark. "American Ideals about Race and Olympic Races from the 1890s to the 1950s: Shattering Myths or Reinforcing Scientific Racism?" *Journal of Sport History* 28, no. 2 (Summer 2001): 173–215.

Franks, Joel. "Crossing Sidelines, Crossing Borders: Basketball in the San Francisco Bay Area, 1930–1950. North American Society for Sport History, Proceedings and Newsletter (1997): 50.

Gallagher, Jack. "New Faces, 1966: Super Is the Word for These Sophomores." *Texas Football* (1966): 21–24.

Gems, Gerald R. "Blocked Shot: The Development of Basketball in the African-

American Community in Chicago." *Journal of Sport History* 22, no. 2 (Summer 1995): 135–48.

———. "Football and Cultural Values." *College Football Historical Society Newsletter* 10, no. 4 (August 1997): 1–4.

———. "The Construction, Negotiation, and Transformation of Racial Identity in American Football." North American Society for Sport History, Proceedings and Newsletter (1998): 79–80.

———. "The Prep Bowl: Football and Religious Acculturation in Chicago, 1927–1963." *Journal of Sports History* 23, no. 3 (Fall 1996): 284–302.

Guha, Ramachandra. "Cricket and Politics in Colonial India." *Past and Present* (161, November 1998): 155–90.

Hendrick, John R. "Pete." "Mary Allen Junior College." In *The New Handbook of Texas*, vol. 4, 540. Austin: Texas State Historical Association, 1996.

Kaliss, Gregory J. "Un-Civil Discourse: Charlie Scott, the Integration of College Basketball, and the 'Progressive Mystique.'" *Journal of Sport History* 35, no. 1 (Spring 2008): 98–117.

Kane, Martin. "An Assessment of 'Black Is Best.'" *Sports Illustrated* 34, no. 3 (18 January 1971): 72–83.

Kelly, Robin D. G. "'We Are Not What We Seem': Rethinking Black Working-Class Opposition in the Jim Crow South." *Journal of American History* 80 (1 June 1993): 75–112.

Kemper, Kurt Edward. "The Smell of Roses and the Color of the Players: College Football and the Expansion of the Civil Rights Movement in the West." *Journal of Sport History* 31, no. 3 (Fall 2004): 317–39.

Marcello, Ronald E. "The Integration of Intercollegiate Athletics in Texas: North Texas State College as a Test Case, 1956." *Journal of Sport History* 14, no. 3 (Winter 1987): 286–316.

Martin, Charles H. "Integrating New Year's Day: The Racial Politics of College Bowl Games in the American South." *Journal of Sport History* 24, no. 3 (Fall 1997): 358–77.

Miller, Patrick B. "Slouching toward a New Expediency: College Football and the Color Line During the 1930s." North American Society for Sport History, Proceedings and Newsletter (1996): 93–94.

———. "The Anatomy of Scientific Racism: Racist Responses to Black Athletic Achievement." *Journal of Sport History* 25, no. 1 (Spring 1998): 119–51.

———. "The Manly, the Moral, and the Proficient: College Sport in the New South." *Journal of Sport History* 24, no. 3 (Fall 1997): 285–316.

Mormino, Gary Ross. "The Playing Fields of St. Louis: Italian Immigrants and Sports, 1925–1941." *Journal of Sport History* 9, no. 2 (Summer 1982): 5–19.

Nathan, Daniel A. "Sugar Ray Robinson, the Sweet Science, and the Politics of Meaning." *Journal of Sport History* 26, no. 1 (Spring 1999): 163–74.

"New Faces Could Leave Texans Class of League." *Texas Football* (1961): 63.

Regaldo, Samuel. "Sport and Community in California's Japanese American

'Yamato Colony,' 1930–1945." *Journal of Sport History* 19, no. 2 (Summer 1992): 130–43.

Riess, Steven A. "Sport and the Redefinition of Middle Class Masculinity in Victorian America." North American Society for Sport History, Proceedings and Newsletter (1990): 41.

San Antonio Friends of Houston University, advertisement, *Texas Football* (1965): 71.

Saylor, Roger B. "Black College Football." *College Football Historical Society Newsletter*. May 2000, 4–7.

Schmidt, Ray. "Changing Tides: College Football, 1919–1930, Part 3 of 3." *College Football Historical Society Newsletter*, November 2000, 15–18.

Schmidt, Raymond. "Lords of the Prairie: Haskell Indian School Football, 1919–1930." *Journal of Sport History* 28, no. 3 (Fall 2001): 403–26.

Smith, John Matthew. "'It's Not Really My Country': Lew Alcindor and the Revolt of the Black Athlete." *Journal of Sport History* 36, no. 2 (Summer 2009): 223–44.

Smith, Thomas G. "Civil Rights on the Gridiron: The Kennedy Administration and the Desegregation of the Washington Redskins." *Journal of Sport History* 14, no. 2 (Summer 1987): 189–208.

———. "Outside the Pale: The Exclusion of Blacks from the National Football League, 1934–1946." *Journal of Sport History* 15, no. 3 (Winter 1988): 255–81.

Spivey, Donald. "'End Jim Crow in Sports': The Protest at New York University, 1940–1941." *Journal of Sport History* 15, no. 3 (Winter 1988): 282–303.

"Texas Independents Take on a Bigger and Better Look." *Texas Football* (1962): 55–57.

Watterson, John S. "The Football Crisis of 1909–1910: The Response of the 'Big Three.'" *Journal of Sport History* 8, no. 1 (Spring 1981): 33–49.

———. "The Gridiron Crisis of 1905: Was It Really a Crisis?" *Journal of Sport History* 27, no. 2 (Summer 2000): 291–98.

Wiggins, David K. "Great Speed but Little Stamina: The Historical Debate over Black Athletic Superiority." *Journal of Sport History* 16, no. 2 (Summer 1989): 158–85.

———. "'The Future of College Athletics Is at Stake': Black Athletes and Racial Turmoil on Three Predominantly White University Campuses, 1968–1972." *Journal of Sport History* 15, no. 3 (Winter 1988): 304–33.

Zieff, Susan G. "From Badminton to the Bolero: Sport and Recreation in San Francisco's Chinatown, 1895–1950." *Journal of Sport History* 27, no. 1 (Spring 2000): 1–29.

Index

Holland, Buford, 120

homecoming, 32, 38, 40, 51, 55–56, 59, 62, 66, 68, 69, 75, 77, 81, 83, 85, 86, 89, 97, 121, 133, 135, 141, 150, 158, 167, 170, 174, 180, 182, 193, 195–96, 198, 202

Hopkins, "Hippo," 76, 80

Hornsby, Betty June, 61

Hoskins, Dave, 126

Houston Baptist College, 15

Houston Chronicle, 211, 212

Houston College for Negroes, 88, 90

Houston Informer, 1, 26, 27, 28, 30, 31, 32, 33, 34, 36, 37, 38, 39, 40, 41, 43, 49, 50, 51, 53, 54, 55, 56, 57, 58, 59, 60, 63, 65, 66, 67, 70, 74, 75, 76, 77, 78, 80, 81, 83, 86, 87, 92, 93, 118, 119, 121, 122, 123, 125, 127, 128, 129, 132–33, 137, 145, 146, 149, 155, 156, 160, 163, 167, 169, 170, 171, 173, 174, 177, 179, 180, 184, 185, 186, 187, 192, 194, 196, 197, 198, 199, 201

Houston, Ken, 183

Houston Negro Junior College, 40, 50, 52, 54

Houston Oilers, 152, 155, 156, 158, 159, 162, 163, 170, 175, 176, 179, 183, 190, 193

Houston Race Riot of 1917, 21

Houston Texans, 213

Howard University, 11, 13, 14, 15, 17, 21, 23, 33, 35, 79–80

HT Taxi Company, 24

Hunt, Lamar, 152, 153, 162

Hurd, Michael, 1

Hutchison, Ralph, 95

Huston-Tillotson College, 127, 151, 210

Iglehart, Ike, 144

Indianapolis Freeman, 12

Ingram, "Black Beauty," 76

Institute Politecnico National, Mexico City, 122

integration, 3

College football in Texas, 139–140; Del Mar Junior College, Corpus Christi 131; Houston Airport, 119; Houston City Facilities, 160; Municipal golf course in Houston, 118–119; Rice University football, 180; San Angelo Junior College, 131; Southwest Conference football, 172; Southwest Conference Universities, 137; Southwestern Theological Seminary, 131; State Fair of Texas and Fair Park, 157–58; Sylvan Beach, La Porte, 160; Texas A&M football, 180; Texas League (baseball), 126; Texas schools, 171–172; United States military, 120; University of Texas football, 180; University of Texas Law School, 89–90, 117; Walgreen's Drug Store, 154; Wayland Baptist University, 131; Woolworth's Drug Store, 154

Intercollegiate Athletic Association (IAA), 16

Intercollegiate Conference of Faculty Representatives. *See* Big Ten Conference

International Classic, 145

Isaac, Larry, 201

Italian invasion of Ethiopia, 72

Jack Yates High School, 122, 136, 183

Jackson, Bo, 211

Jackson State University, 140, 145, 162, 164, 171, 177, 184, 185, 195, 197

Jackson, William Tecumseh Sherman, 10

Jacque and his Merry Makers, 60

James, Arthur, 180

Jarvis Christian College Bulldogs, 8, 9, 18, 25–26, 27, 48, 49, 50–51, 52, 54, 57, 63, 65, 68, 74, 76, 77, 80, 88, 92, 124, 141, 143, 149, 150, 151, 160, 161, 163, 167, 171, 177, 210

Jarvis, Mr. and Mrs. J. J., 9

jazz, 23–24

Jewett, George, 11

Johnson, Edgar, 140

Johnson, Lee Otis, 179, 180

Johnson, Lyndon Baines, 166

Johnson, Mitchell, 132

Johnson, Rex, 131

Johnson, "Runt," 43

Johnson, William, 11

Jones, "Red," 42

Jordan, Barbara, 189, 194
Jordan, M. W., 36
Juneteenth, 30, 63

Kane, Martin, 192
Kansas City Chiefs, 140, 179
Kansas City Monarchs, 48
Katy Lines, 55
Kearney, Jim, 165, 167
Kearny State University, 165
Kemp, Ray, 61
Kennedy, John Fitzgerald, 159
Kentucky State University, 58, 69, 70, 78,
    84, 86, 124
King, Leon, 139
King, Martin Luther Jr., 162, 163, 179
Kowalski, "Killer," 130
Ku Klux Klan, 22–23
Kuba, Louis, 176

Ladd, Ernie, 152–153, 159
Lafayette College, 95
Lang, Ernest, 122, 140
Langston University, 29, 32, 34, 36, 39,
    40, 42, 43, 54, 55, 60, 62, 68, 70, 75, 93,
    95, 92, 97, 120, 128, 129, 132, 145, 180
Latex Classic, 124
Law, James "Jimmie," 31, 33, 34, 41
Leaks, Roosevelt, 188, 199
Lee, Bivian, 185, 191
Lee, Howard J., 11
Lee, Ralph, 145
Levias, Jerry, 172, 173, 175, 183, 187, 188
Lewis, William, 10, 15
Lillard, Joe, 61
Lincoln High School, Port Arthur, 136
Lincoln Theater, 42
Lincoln University, 13, 23, 79–80, 82, 89,
    129, 130, 141
Livingston College, 12, 13
Lone Star Conference, 180
Long, Fred, 39, 45, 51, 82, 84, 87, 93, 95,
    127, 170
Long, Harry, 87
Los Angeles Rams, 97, 175

Louis, Joe, 48
Louisiana Normal School, 77
Louisiana State Fair, 71
Love, Howard, 56

Manpower Resource Project, 169, 196
Marks, "Jeru," 36
Marshall, George Preston, 159
Mary Allen College, 8, 62, 124
Maryland, Warren, 140
Masculinity, Ideals of, 9–10, 14, 15–16, 85,
    87, 151, 187, 188, 196, 206
Mason, E. A., 145
Mason, H. J., 36, 42
Massachusetts Institute of Technology
    (MIT), 11
Mays, David, 177, 190
McDill Field, Florida, 79
McElroy, Hugh, 180
McMurry College, 190
McMahon, Jim, 211
McNutt, Paul V., 79
McVea, Warren, 169–170, 173, 178
Meharry Medical College, 16
Merchant, George, 175
Mid-Eastern Athletic Conference
    (MEAC), 209, 211
Midwestern Athletic Association
    Conference (MWAC), 78, 119
Migration experience for African
    Americans, 24–25
Military Academy of Mexico, 145
Miller, Dorie, 79
Miller, Giles, 126
"Miss Wiley's Homecoming Prom," 75
Mississippi State University, 143
Mississippi Valley State University, 177,
    185, 186, 193, 196, 202, 203, 204
Mitchell, "Thunderbolt," 37
Mohr, Dean, 38
Molett, Rosetta, 43
Montgomery, Lou, 73
Moody, "Big Train," 80
Morehouse College, 14, 15
Morgan College, 14, 15

Morgan State University, 185, 186, 187
Morgan, Edward, 97
Morrill Land Grant Act: of 1862, 9; of
    1891, 9, 18–19
Morris Brown University, 59
Mosquito Bowl, 149
Muhammad Ali, 181
Mumford, Arnett W., 37, 39, 52, 62, 64, 161
Mumford, Ted, 80

National Association for the Advancement
    of Colored People (NAACP), 16–17, 21,
    23, 89, 119
National Association of Intercollegiate
    Athletics (NAIA), 165, 192, 194, 212, 212
National College Football Hall of Fame, 211
National Collegiate Athletic Association
    (NCAA), 4, 16, 165, 192, 200, 205
National Football League (NFL), 61, 136,
    149, 151, 152, 153, 159, 166, 178, 190
National Youth Administration (NYA), 62
Nazi racist ideology, 67
Negro Associated Press, 90
Negro Coaches' Association Coach of the
    Year Award, 130
Negro Day at the State Fair of Texas, 2,
    29–30, 34, 36, 39–40, 50, 55, 67, 70, 74,
    76, 80, 81, 82, 85, 86, 91, 93, 96, 120, 123,
    128, 132–133, 135, 137, 146, 151, 158, 166
Negro leagues, 3
Nellum, J. N., 51
Nellum, W. A., 51
New Deal, 56–57, 59
"New Negro" movement, 2, 23, 24, 25
New Orleans University, 30, 31, 40
New York Giants, 211
New York Titans, 159
New York University, 61, 73
New York Yankees (NFL team), 126
Nicks, Billy, 134, 135, 148, 150, 165, 168,
    173, 210, 211, 212
Nixon, Richard, 186, 189
Norris, Lenora, 133
North Carolina A&T, 211

North Carolina Mutual Life Insurance
    Company, 72
North Dallas Club, 63
North-South All-Star Football Game, 191
North Texas State University, 139, 142,
    143, 153, 183
Northwestern University, 11
NRG Stadium, Houston, 213

Oakland Raiders, 155, 178
Ocean of Soul, 199, 204
Office of Civil Rights, 207
Oklahoma City University, 58
Oklahoma State Fair, 34
Oliphant, John, 135
Olympic Project for Human Rights
    (OPHR), 181, 182
O'Neal, Leon Jr., 180
Orange Blossom Classic, 66, 71, 81, 87, 124,
    133, 148, 150, 162
Original Wiley Collegians, 63
Osborne, Tom, 211
Oves, Ralph, 80
Owens, Jesse, 48, 67

Paige, Rod, 198
Panther Marching Band, 58, 199, 204
Patterson, Pat, 55, 60
Paul Quinn College Tigers, 8, 15, 18, 25, 26,
    27, 29, 31, 35, 36, 37, 39, 40, 59, 50–51,
    53, 54, 58, 60, 61, 77, 81, 91, 92, 96, 120,
    124, 127, 129, 131, 134, 135, 138, 141, 145,
    146, 148, 149, 150, 151, 158, 209, 212
Payton, John, 135
Payton, Walter, 197
Peach Bowl, 201
Pearl Harbor attack, 78, 79
Pedro, "Pistol Pete," 56
Penn State University, 92, 93, 96
Perry, Ervin, 166
Phi Beta Sigma, 17
Philander Smith College, 51, 77, 88, 124,
    138, 150
Phillips, "Buzzing Bill," 93